© Jonny Donovan

BEN RAWLENCE is a former researcher for Human
Rights Watch in the horn of Africa. He is the author
of *Radio Congo* and has written for a wide range of
publications, including *The Guardian*, the *London
Review of Books*, and *The New York Times*. He lives in
Wales with his family.

Additional Praise for *City of Thorns*

"*City of Thorns* . . . brilliantly details the intimate histories of residents of Dadaab: a massive, United Nations–maintained camp in Kenya for people stuck in legal limbo after escaping from sectarian violence in Somalia." —*Chicago Tribune*

"In light of the contemporary crisis, *City of Thorns* serves as a cautionary tale. Rawlence's portrait of nine Dadaab residents offers a stark counterpoint to the rhetoric that too often speaks for refugees. . . . This is a vital book at a critical moment in global history." —*Minneapolis Star Tribune*

"The most absorbing book in recent memory about life in refugee camps . . . Mr. Rawlence's major feat is stripping away the anonymity that so often is attached to the word 'refugee' by delving deeply into the lives of nine people in the camp. By doing so, he transforms its denizens from faceless victims into three-dimensional human beings. Along the way, Dadaab emerges from the ever-present heat and dust to become much more than a refugee camp. It is a real, if very peculiar, city." —*The Wall Street Journal*

"[A] remarkable book . . . Like Dadaab itself, the story has no conclusion. It is a portrait, beautifully and movingly painted. And it is more than that. At a time when newspapers are filled with daily images of refugees arriving in boats on Europe's shores, when politicians and governments grapple with solutions to migration and erect ever-larger walls and fences, it is an important reminder that a vast majority of the world's refugees never get as far as a boat or a border of the developed world. They remain, like the inhabitants of Dadaab, in an indefinite limbo of penury and fear, unwanted and largely forgotten." —*The New York Times Book Review*

City of Thorns

Nine Lives in the World's Largest Refugee Camp

BEN RAWLENCE

PICADOR   NEW YORK

picadorusa.com • picadorbookroom.tumblr.com
twitter.com/picadorusa • facebook.com/picadorusa

Picador® is a U.S. registered trademark and is used by Macmillan Publishing Group, LLC, under license from Pan Books Limited.

For book club information, please visit facebook.com/picadorbookclub or e-mail marketing@picadorusa.com.

The Library of Congress has cataloged the hardcover edition as follows:

Rawlence, Ben, author.
    City of thorns : nine lives in the world's largest refugee camp / Ben Rawlence.—First U.S. edition.
        p. cm.
    ISBN 978-1-250-06763-0 (hardcover)
    ISBN 978-1-250-06764-7 (e-book)
    1. Refugee camps—Kenya. 2. Refugees—Kenya. 3. Refugees—Somalia.
4. Somali-Ethiopian Conflict, 1979–. I. Title.
    HV640.4.K4R39 2016
    967.7305'3—dc23   2015029505

Picador Paperback ISBN 978-1-250-11873-8

Our books may be purchased in bulk for promotional, educational, or business use. Please contact your local bookseller or the Macmillan Corporate and Premium Sales Department at 1-800-221-7945, extension 5442, or by e-mail at MacmillanSpecialMarkets@macmillan.com.

Originally published in Great Britain by Portobello Books

First published in the United States by Picador

First Picador Paperback Edition: January 2017

10 9 8 7 6 5

For the residents of Dadaab
And for Louise

'There is a crime here that goes beyond denunciation. There is a sorrow here that weeping cannot symbolize. There is a failure here that topples all our success.'

John Steinbeck, *The Grapes of Wrath*

Contents

I
The Horn of Africa

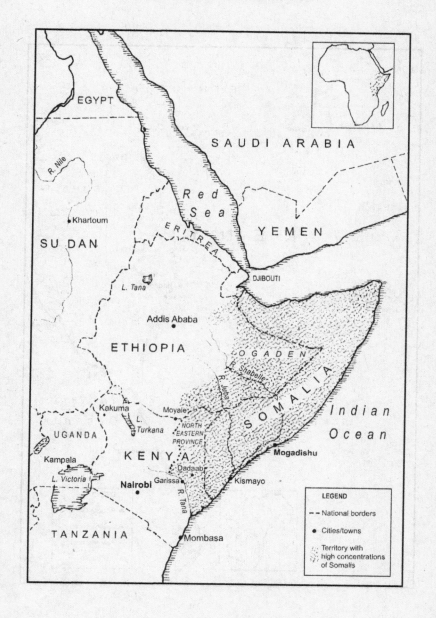

LEGEND

– – National borders

● Cities/towns

Territory with high concentrations of Somalis

II
Kenya-Somalia Border

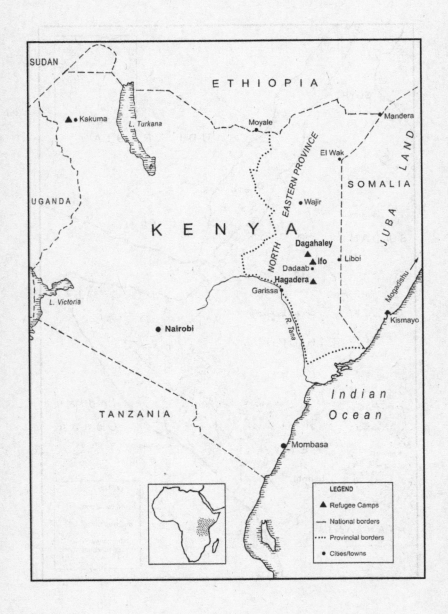

SUDAN

ETHIOPIA

▲ • Kakuma

L. Turkana

Moyale

• Mandera

UGANDA

El Wak

EASTERN PROVINCE

SOMALIA

• Wajir

K E N Y A

JUBA LAND

NORTH

Dagahaley ▲

▲ Ifo

Liboi

Dadaab •

Hagadera ▲

Garissa

Mogadishu

L. Victoria

• Nairobi

R. Tana

Kismayo

Indian
Ocean

TANZANIA

• Mombasa

LEGEND
▲ Refugee Camps
— National borders
⋯ Provincial borders
• Cities/towns

III
Dadaab Refugee Complex
[As of March 2012]

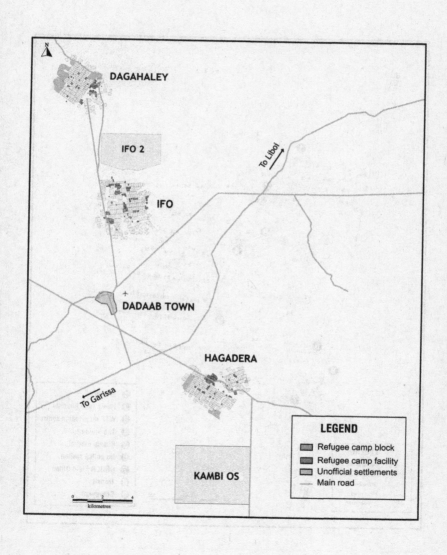

IV
Ifo Refugee Camp
[As of January 2012]

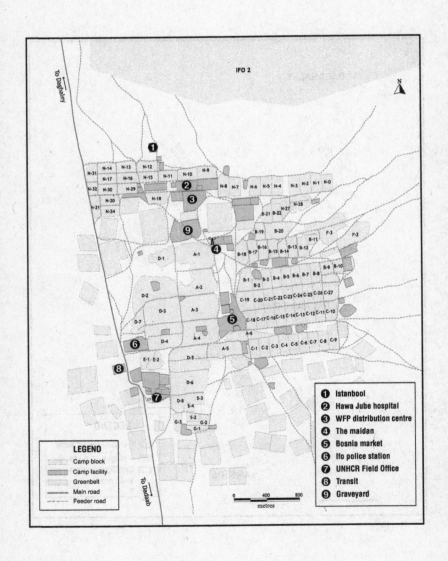

IFO 2

To Daghaley

To Dadaab

① Istanbool
② Hawa Jube hospital
③ WFP distribution centre
④ The maidan
⑤ Bosnia market
⑥ Ifo police station
⑦ UNHCR Field Office
⑧ Transit
⑨ Graveyard

LEGEND
Camp block
Camp facility
Greenbelt
Main road
Feeder road

0   400   800
metres

V

Ifo 2 Refugee Camp
[As of June 2013]

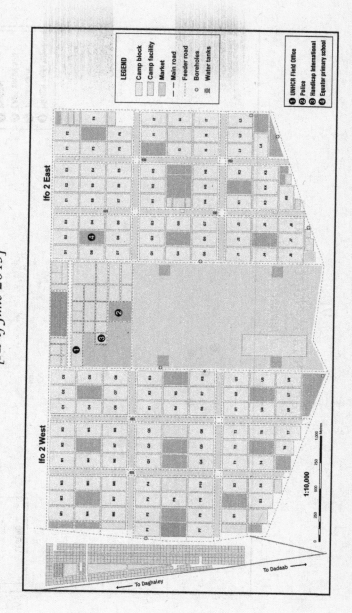

LEGEND

Camp block
Camp facility
Market
— — Main road
· · · · Feeder road
○ Boreholes
≋ Water tanks

① UNHCR Field Office
② Police
③ Handicap International
④ Equator primary school

Ifo 2 East

Ifo 2 West

1:10,000

0   250 500 750 1,000
Meters

To Daghaley ⟵

To Dadaab ⟶

VI

Hagadera Refugee Camp

[As of January 2012]

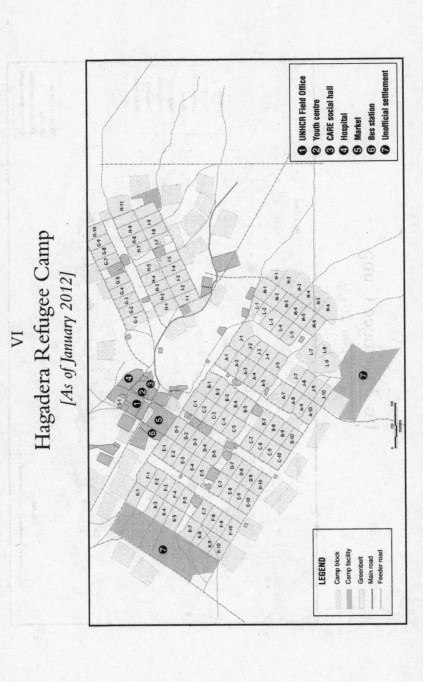

LEGEND

- Camp block
- Camp facility
- Greenbelt
- Main road
- Feeder road

1. UNHCR Field Office
2. Youth centre
3. CARE social hall
4. Hospital
5. Market
6. Bus station
7. Unofficial settlement

The Residents of Dadaab Who Appear in the City of Thorns

Ahmed (Gab) – *husband of Isha, born around 1970 and came to Dadaab following the death of their livestock during the drought of 2011.*

Apshira –*wife of Tawane, also his cousin, born in Kenya in 1985 and came to Dadaab voluntarily to live with Tawane in 2003.*

Billai – *wife of Nisho, born in 1995 in southern Somalia, came to Dadaab with her family fleeing the famine in 2011.*

Christine – *daughter of Muna and Monday, born in Dadaab in 2011.*

Fish – *friend of Tawane and sports chairman in Hagadera camp, born near Kismayo in 1984 and came to Dadaab with his mother fleeing the civil war in 1992.*

Guled – *husband of Maryam, born in Mogadishu in 1993, came to Dadaab fleeing al-Shabaab in 2010*

Idris – *father of Tawane, born around 1950, came to Dadaab after losing two sons in the civil war in 1991.*

Isha – *wife of Ahmed (Gab), born in Somalia around 1970, came to Dadaab with her five children escaping the famine of 2011.*

Kheyro – *a student in the camp and later a teacher, came to the camp aged two, with her mother, Rukia, fleeing civil war in 1992.*

Mahat – *casual labourer in the market and friend of Nisho, lost his father in the war and came to Dadaab with his mother in 2008, aged eight or nine.*

Maryam – *wife of Guled, born in 1992, she followed him from Mogadishu to Dadaab in 2011.*

Monday – *husband of Muna and former 'Lost Boy', born in Abyei, Sudan in 1981, arrived in Dadaab via several refugee camps in Ethiopia and Kenya in 2004.*

Muna – *wife of Monday, born in Somalia in 1990, came to Dadaab aged six months with her parents in 1991 after most of her extended family were killed.*

Nisho – *porter in Ifo market and husband of Billai, born en route to Dadaab in 1991 as his parents were fleeing the civil war in Baidoa, central Somalia.*

Professor Indha Dae (White Eyes) – *born blind but later recovered his sight, a trader and then journalist, came to Dadaab aged four or five with his grandmother, fleeing the fighting in 1991.*

Tawane – *husband of Apshira, businessman and youth leader, came to Dadaab aged seven with his family in 1991 after his brothers were killed in the civil war.*

Prologue

The White House, Washington DC, 31 October 2014

The members of the National Security Council (NSC) were arranged around a grey table in a grey room without windows. On the walls, photographs depicted a sporty-looking President Obama on a recent trip to Wales for a NATO summit. The officials attending from the Africa desk were a middle-aged white man leaning back slightly in his chair; a younger one in a tight new suit who hunched forward and stared at a notepad; a short blonde woman who sat perfectly still throughout the whole meeting with her hands in her lap so that her impassive face appeared to float above the surface of the table; and the chief, a well-dressed woman in tweed skirt and matching tan shoes, expensive, who smiled and nodded and said little, just like the rest of them.

I was there to brief the NSC about Dadaab, a refugee camp located in northern Kenya close to the border with Somalia. Since 2008, when al-Shabaab, an al-Qaida-linked militant group, assumed control of most of Somalia, the Horn of Africa has been at the fulcrum of what policymakers like to call the 'arc of instability' that reaches across Africa from Mali in the west, to Boko Haram in Nigeria, through Chad, Darfur, Sudan, southern Ethiopia, Somalia and on to Yemen, Saudi Arabia and Pakistan and Afghanistan in the east. Extremism in Africa has been rising up international agendas as terrorist attacks have mushroomed. Twelve months earlier, al-Shabaab had attacked Westgate shopping mall in the Kenyan capital Nairobi. And six months after our meeting, al-Shabaab would hit the headlines again with the slaughter of 148 students at Garissa

University College in the north of the country. After both attacks, the Kenyan government claimed the gunmen came from Dadaab and vowed to close the refugee camp, branding it 'a nursery for terrorists'. In essence, the NSC wanted to know, was this my experience? The US is the main funder of the camp.

I had spent the previous three years researching the lives of the inhabitants of the camp and five years before that reporting on human rights there. How to describe to people who have never visited, the many faces of that city? The term 'refugee camp' is misleading. Dadaab was established in 1992 to hold 90,000 refugees fleeing Somalia's civil war. At the beginning of 2016 it is twenty-five years old and nearly half a million strong, an urban area the size of New Orleans, Bristol or Zurich unmarked on any official map. I tried to explain to the NSC officials my own wonder at this teeming ramshackle metropolis with cinemas, football leagues, hotels and hospitals, and to emphasize that, contrary to what they might expect, a large portion of the refugees are extremely pro-American. I said that the Kenyan security forces, underwritten by US and British money, weapons and training, were going about things in the wrong way: rounding up refugees, raping and extorting them, encouraging them to return to war-racked Somalia. But I sensed that the officials were not really listening. I was asking them to undo a lifetime of stereotyping and to ignore everything that they were hearing in their briefings and in the media.

My friends, the refugees in the camp, had been so excited to hear that I was going to the White House! Here I was, at the pinnacle of the US policy-making machine, poised to exercise my influence, yet floundering. Raised on the meagre rations of the United Nations for their whole lives, schooled by NGOs and submitted to workshops on democracy, gender mainstreaming and campaigns against female genital mutilation, the refugees suffered from benign illusions about the largesse of the international community. They were forbidden from leaving and not allowed to work, but they believed that if only people came to know about their plight, then the world would be moved to help, to bring to an end the protracted situation that has seen them confined to camps for generations, their children and then grandchildren born in the open prison in the desert. But the officials in the grey room saw the world from only one angle.

'If what you are saying is true,' said the young man in the tight suit, 'what accounts for the resilience of Dadaab for so long?' He meant why had all the young men in the camp not joined al-Shabaab? I had once asked that question myself. I thought of Nisho, the young man who works as a porter in the market, his face clouding into a scowl as he stormed out of an interview when I asked why he had not joined the militants: they paid well and he was poor. The very question was an insult. To him, and to all the refugees he knew, al-Shabaab were crazy, murderous criminals. I thought of the former child soldier Guled and the many like him, who had fled to the camp to escape the extremists, not to join them.

But the young official persisted: 'The picture you describe: a loss of identity, no work, hostile political environment, deteriorating conditions – these sound like the conditions for radicalization ...' The terms of the conversation seemed to allow for only two kinds of young people: terrorists and those at risk of becoming one.

'Poverty does not necessarily lead to extremism,' I said. In my head, images of the proud Imams defending their traditions against the murderous corruptions; of the determined youth leader Tawane, risking his life to provide services for the refugees when the aid agencies withdrew for fear of being kidnapped; of Kheyro, working to educate the children of the camp for a pittance; of Professor White Eyes broadcasting his reports on the camp radio.

How could I convey their towering dignity, their courage and independence of spirit when they only featured in the official mind as potential terrorists?

'Right, right,' said the chief. There were no further questions and the meeting came to an early conclusion. I had fallen into the liberal lobbyist's trap: if the youth were not at risk of being radicalized, then perhaps the NSC didn't need to worry about Dadaab after all; the refugees could be safely forgotten. Such official attitudes have created a false debate: both those for and against the war on terror must make their arguments on the terrain of radicalization; as though young poor Muslims face only this choice.

Outside, it was bitterly cold. At the rear of the White House, the balustrades of the twin white staircases were draped with black cloth and a giant inflatable pumpkin bobbed above the gently curving lawn. The First Lady was preparing for a party. Overhead, a helicopter carrying her husband buzzed the rooftops. I had once been a student of his, had sat across the table and shared Christmas dinner and stories. Looking up at his helicopter from the sidewalk of Pennsylvania Avenue, he was as far from me now as were the sands of the refugee camp. The refugees seeking sanctuary in his ancestral country saw themselves in his story and yet the most powerful man on the planet was no more able to help the most vulnerable than anyone else. His country would not accept the exiled Somalis, at least not in any meaningful numbers, and nor would any other.

At a time when there are more refugees than ever, the rich world has turned its back on them. Our myths and religions are steeped in the lore of exile and yet we fail to treat the living examples of that condition as fully human. Instead, those fleeing the twenty-first century's wars in Syria, Iraq, Afghanistan, Somalia and elsewhere are seen as a potential fifth column, a threat. Each year far too few are officially referred by the UN and given asylum in other countries. Thousands instead resort to the illegal route, paying traffickers for a spot on the boats or scrambling through holes cut in fences. I sympathized with the young NSC official struggling to make sense of the refugee experience. It is a wonder that so many die in the sea, reaching for another life, and not for a martyr's ending. But they are the few. Millions more, the vast majority, remain in camps. And through our tax contributions to the UN, we all pay billions of dollars to keep them there. In Dadaab that means funding schools, hospitals and shipping 8,000 tonnes of food per month into the middle of the blistering desert to feed everyone.

This book is a glimpse into the strange limbo of camp life through the eyes of those who allowed me into their world and shared their stories. No one wants to admit that the temporary camp of Dadaab has become permanent: not the Kenyan government who must host it, not the UN who must pay for it, and not the refugees who must live there. This paradox makes the ground unsteady. Caught between the ongoing war in Somalia and a world unwilling to welcome them, the refugees can only survive in the camp by imagining a life elsewhere. It is unsettling: neither the past, nor the present, nor the future is a safe place for a mind to linger for long. To live in this city of thorns is to be trapped mentally, as well as physically, your thoughts constantly flickering between impossible dreams and a nightmarish reality. In short, to come here you must be completely desperate.

PART ONE

Ma'a Lul – Famine

1

The Horn of Africa

In the lands of the Somali, it had barely rained for two and a half years. From the dagger point of Cape Guardafui, the very Horn of Africa aimed at the belly of Yemen, to the hills of Ethiopia in the west and the plains of Kenya in the south, the year 2010 was dry. The nomads and the farmers saw the clouds scudding east from the Indian Ocean over the red plains and the yellow hills, but no rain fell. They saw their animals weaken and their crops struggle to stand with the weight of the dust, and they began to worry.

There are three seasons here: the *Hagar, Jiilaal* and *Gu*. The Hagar is the windy season, from May to September, when the Indian Ocean monsoon blows clockwise taking the cool water from the southern seas up the coast of East Africa, around the curve of Arabia, Iran and Pakistan to Bombay, the ancient trade route of the Swahilis. Since at least 1000 BC, the dhows have sailed east in March returning in September, riding the anti-clockwise currents that take the now warm water south again. With the monsoon, India is only three weeks from the coast of Somalia. Against it, the journey can take three months and is often fatal. Thousands of miles from the coastal ports of Bossaso, Mogadishu and Kismayo, trade in the interior of the Horn of Africa still keeps time with these natural rhythms.

Once upon a time, when the climate was predictable, the Hagar would come to an end with the short rains, *Deyr*, in October that would give way to the steady accumulation of heat and dust that

was the dry season, Jiilaal. If God willed it, the heat would build
and build and turn humid, eventually breaking into the blessed
rainy season from March to May: Gu. Then the thorn trees would
spring immediately into a luminous green. Overnight, the sand
would grow a light fuzz of grass. The camels and goats of the
nomads would turn fat.

Sometimes the Gu didn't come. Then the heat that built and
built had nowhere to go. When the Hagar arrived again, it swirled
the desiccated sand into little twisters that had a life of their own,
getting into everything. The skin on the animals shrank and the
nomads watched the sky, full of fear of the *abaar*, drought.
Sometimes the Gu failed for more than one year and that usually
spelled trouble. In a part of the world where man's struggle with
nature for survival is so finely balanced, famine and war have
always gone together. Now the Gu had failed for two years in a
row and the short rains were perilously late.

Under a hardening sky, the people grew uneasy. In the countryside, the land had nothing to give and so the inhabitants had
nothing to offer their rulers in tithes or taxes. Across most of
South-Central Somalia, the rulers were the Islamic extremist
group al-Shabaab. It needed all the taxes it could get to fund its
'massive war' to drive what it saw as an infidel government backed
by the United Nations out of Mogadishu and into the sea. Militias
press-ganged truckloads of men away from the farms and forced
them to the battlefield, and they took the meagre harvest as
'*Zakaht*' – a contribution to their holy war – and the people went
hungry.

To make matters worse, al-Shabaab had banned all food aid that
bore the US logo and ejected the World Food Programme (WFP)
from its territory. At the same time, the US Office of Foreign
Assets Control (OFAC) put sanctions on al-Shabaab: this meant
jail sentences for aid agencies that paid the militants for humani-

tarian access which, after twenty years of war, was the norm for delivering aid in Somalia. And the few aid ships that did sail risked the infamous pirates. So, in what agencies had been calling a 'perfect storm' since the drought began two years earlier, the people of Somalia would face one of the most telegraphed emergencies the world had ever seen largely without assistance.

In the city, the 'Battle of Mogadishu', as al-Shabaab's offensive was known, intensified street by street with trenches, snipers and indiscriminate shelling. The militants' war effort drew all the men, resources and even children into the fight just as the twisters of the eternal Jiilaal sucked the dust of the hard-baked plain into the air and lent everything a brown tinge. The coming tragedy would be played out in sepia.

After so much death, it was a wonder anyone remained in the country at all. No one really knows the population of Somalia but, during the past twenty years, somewhere between one third and one half of the six-to-eight million inhabitants had fled their homes. There were over one and a half million refugees abroad, many of them in the camps of Dadaab. The people who still lived in Somalia were the ones without the bus fare to flee, the ones with property to guard or money to make, or the ones who had simply lost their minds. Many were afraid to take the risk of running into the unknown and held to the adage, 'better the devil you know'. Many more were so inured to the roulette of war, it had simply become the landscape of life. Guled was one of these.

2

Guled

The last time the world had paid much attention to Somalia was in 1993 when two American military Black Hawk helicopters, part of Operation Restore Hope, were shot down among the tightly packed houses of Wardighley district of Mogadishu. Jubilant crowds had dragged the bodies of several US Special Forces Rangers through the streets. The US and UN withdrew and the world washed its hands of the country.

At about the time those black steel birds crashed out of the sky, the wife of a former military officer of the collapsed Somali government of the dictator Siad Barre gave birth. Guled was born in a modest house near the stadium, just a few blocks away from the crash site, and he grew up in the shattered city playing among the shells of those two ruined helicopters. During his childhood, Mogadishu's beautiful boulevards, its grand mosques and cathedrals, its ancient Omani, Portuguese and Italian waterfront and sparkling white villas had been reduced to rubble thrice over. Growing up in a country without a government, in a permanent state of civil war, Guled learned to go with the grain.

He was a slight boy with a narrow head that tapered to a pointed chin. His eyes were black and quick; they missed nothing and betrayed nothing. By adolescence, both his parents had died, the city had changed hands more times than he could count and he had perfected the art of looking nondescript. He still lived in the house by the stadium with his sister and a collection of other children whom, one by one, the war had methodically orphaned. They survived on the little money his elder sister made from selling biscuits, cakes and sweets and, when she could get it, petrol.

While over a million Somalis fled to the vast refugee camps in Kenya, across the sea to Yemen or on foot through the Sahara to Libya and then Italy, he and his sister stayed. The main effect was to inoculate Guled against ambition. 'I don't have dreams,' he would say, conscious that his life choices up until that point resembled more a series of lucky each-way bets. Guled's priorities were playing football and staying alive.

Unfortunately for a boy addicted to soccer, Guled's coming of age coincided with the rise of the Islamic Courts Union (ICU) and its most powerful faction, al-Shabaab, who placed a ban on what they saw as the decadent hobbies of soccer, smoking and watching movies. At the outset, in 2006, the ICU had been a hopeful thing. After fifteen years of conflict, the warlords seemed to have fought themselves to a standstill and, for a brief moment, it looked as though a harsh peace might break out in Somalia beneath the common flag of sharia law. But Ethiopia and America were nervous of an Islamic government and the US and other nations sponsored Ethiopia to invade Somalia and dispatch the ICU. This they did in 2006 with astonishing speed, force and cruelty, pounding Mogadishu to rubble and blazing a trail of looted homes, massacred civilians and raped women across the country, while those who had paid for the invasion looked away.

With UN backing, the Ethiopians reinforced the puppet administration called the Transitional Federal Government (TFG) and made a base at the stadium near Guled's house. When things were quiet, Guled played football after school nearby but games were often cut short by explosions. The ICU had been defeated but its radical rump, al-Shabaab, had been energized and now it sought revenge. Western governments, unwilling to risk their own forces again, paid for an African Union peacekeeping force called AMISOM to guard the TFG. But the Ugandan and Burundian soldiers charged with the difficult mission could not distinguish al-Shabaab among the ruins and they simply kept up a desperate, random stream of mortars. In turn, al-Shabaab would fire rockets at their bases with little regard for accuracy. During Guled's early teenage years, heavy bombardment was routine as the al-Shabaab counter-attack pushed AMISOM towards the sea and sent the Ethiopians home.

Guled experienced the Ethiopians' surrender on the soccer pitch: one day a militia arrived on the playing field and the game came to a halt. In their black uniforms and headscarves, the austere believers admonished the boys for wearing shorts and for playing football during prayer time. As al-Shabaab reclaimed the stadium it became the place where the militants paraded traitors, spies, unbelievers and others who had made mistakes. They cut off hands, stoned and beheaded people according to their interpretation of Islamic law. You could be punished for listening to music, for shaving your beard or for not wearing a dress of sufficient thickness and length. Sometimes they filmed the punishments and put them on the internet to burnish their image among the jihadist community abroad.

Harakat al-Shabaab al-Mujahidin – 'The Movement of Striving Youth', or 'the Youth' for short – were a shadowy presence; they ruled through a mixture of iconoclasm, charisma and fear. Militants would enter schools, take pupils hostage then try to convince them of their cause with ideological lectures. Some of the propaganda could seem quite persuasive. 'Jihad' was needed, they said, to cleanse Somalia of foreigners: Ethiopians, Americans, Christians. Their Swahili-language newsletter was called *Gaidi Mtaani* – Terrorist in the street. 'All over the world,' it proclaimed, 'people have heard about Somalia and they think that life is impossible here.' But we are here, the dispossessed youth would answer. And for a moment a different life might be glimpsed.

Al-Shabaab seemed right about many things. The newsletter said that international aid was brought to ruin Somali agriculture and to make people dependent on foreign food; both had indeed been side effects of the relief effort. They said that the West wanted Somalis to be held in 'camps, like animals', which could be an accurate description of Dadaab. Most of all though, it was the rhetorical question posed in the newsletter that had the biggest impact among Guled's traumatized generation: 'Why invade a country that has been fighting a civil war for a decade and a half the moment they have decided to live in peace?' The Islamic Courts Union had brought peace. It had been wildly popular and Somalis resented the US-sponsored Ethiopian invasion. 'The United States cannot abide a situation in which Islam is the solution,' the newsletter argued. And to many that seemed like the truth.

The message was preached by recruiters in playing fields and playgrounds by teachers who had been imposed on schools by al-Shabaab. But it wasn't only a question of ideology. 'A whole generation,' a teacher lamented, 'join the armed groups because of hunger.' He took to paying his students to come to school instead of joining the fight. But in a lawless city where money had little value and could be taken from you by any number of armed crooks, the boys even had a chant that summed up their stark choice: 'no gun, no life'. The recruiters' work was terrifyingly easy.

Guled was a normal kid with a strong sister and an affection for music and Manchester United football club: he wanted nothing to do with al-Shabaab. But it wasn't always a choice. Some children who refused to join had their hands cut off. One boy who lived nearby had said no when the recruiters came knocking. They took him anyway. The next day his thirteen-year-old sister opened the front door of their house to find his head on the step: a warning.

Al-Shabaab had even come to Guled's school, Shabelle primary, a modern concrete building near the old spaghetti factory in Yaqshid district. The previous year, the school had closed briefly after al-Shabaab held a parent-teacher meeting and forced parents to sign an agreement permitting their children to join the group. The bodies of two fathers who refused were later found in the central Bakaara market with notes pinned to their clothes explaining the consequences of refusing to allow children to join al-Shabaab. They had been shot.

When the fighting got too hot or came too close, when they ran from a mortar behind them only to meet another one in front, Guled and his sister and friends would go to Warshadeh, the former industrial area on the edge of town. When it went quiet, they would creep back to see if their house was still standing. Sometimes they could predict when the storm of ammunition would hit. At night, they watched the sky to see which way the fire was moving. The 'Katyusha' rockets people called *foriya* (the whistlers) made a signature sound so you had time to take cover. With the mortars – *hobiya* – death came silently. The flames burned so fierce they could melt a metal bed. The children ran and returned countless times. Once, people fled across the street using mattresses as shields. Then one day at the end of 2009, about the time al-Shabaab had come to Guled's school, a silent *hobiya* hit their block, littering the street with injured people and filling their home with shrapnel. In the neighbouring house, a mother and all her children were dead.

Guled and his sister weighed their chances and fled further, across the industrial road, out into the bush beyond to a place called Debideh, near the ruined hospital of Arafat. They found a tree, stretched a piece of fabric over the thorns to protect them from the harsh sunlight and slept on the sand along with a thousand others. No one looked at the situation of the war and considered their options rationally: you took decisions like a rock climber on a treacherous face making one move at a time to stay alive. The children had finally become part of the 870,000 who had been displaced from their homes in the capital since the Ethiopian invasion in 2006.

The year before the invasion, Mogadishu had had a bustling population of 1.2 million. But now the city was an advertisement for what Ethiopian Mi-24 helicopter gunships, T-55 tanks and AMISOM mortars could do. It was a ghost town. Many of those who remained, flitting among the ruins, roaming the eerie streets, fighting with the crows for scraps of food, were children: Mogadishu's orphans, abandoned by parents or separated from them in the chaos. Child-headed households ballooned, surviving however they could. This created certain opportunities for a sharp boy who knew how to drive.

Guled was lucky. Grown men were in short supply and he landed a job driving a minibus. In the morning he went to school from his perch beneath the tree, and in the evening he drove the route along the edge of the city through the zone controlled by al-Shabaab: Arafat–Warshadeh–Towfiq–Afgoye–El-Shabiye. Sometimes he went down into the city to Hodan and Tarbuunka and he saw the slums made of sticks, cloth and plastic of the people huddled among the ruins. He saw them camped in the stadium, in the roofless ruined nave of the cathedral, on waste ground near the parliament and the harbour and in the countless little campsites in between advertised on hand-painted tin signs. They had nice names like 'Saviour Camp' or 'Charity Camp', but everyone knew the words were a lie. The gatekeepers who controlled the camps used the presence of 'Internally Displaced Persons' as bait and then stole the aid that came.

Sometimes, when Guled drove his minibus across the front line into the coastal strip where the TFG was still clinging on with its fingernails, the Ugandan troops manning the checkpoints, sweating in their heavy flak jackets, demanded money, and, one time, his phone. They viewed all those crossing from al-Shabaab areas as terrorists and treated them as such. Everything here was sandbagged with bomb-proof walls encased in green mesh and the streets were filled with men in dark glasses and an array of uniforms: light blue, khaki, green. There were peacekeepers, military, police and even special traffic police who controlled the vehicles at the central K4 roundabout with gunshots. For barely a square mile of territory, there was a surfeit of internationally remunerated armed men.

On the way back into al-Shabaab territory, Guled would stop the bus some way from the checkpoint and ask all the female passengers to move to the rear; al-Shabaab doesn't permit men and women to sit together. But sometimes frail old women could not be safely squeezed into the back and Guled didn't like to force them. For such acts of kindness he would be told to park the bus and dismount to receive twenty strokes with a cane. He learned to take his punishment without argument or emotion. The same thing happened when he tried to overtake. There was no overtaking on al-Shabaab roads; God wanted you to wait in line.

After a while, in early 2010, Guled and his makeshift family moved to a larger settlement of displaced people on the outskirts of the city where agencies were operating with the consent of al-Shabaab, giving out food and tents. It was called El-Shabiye – the boreholes. Life acquired a pattern, which, in the war, was as much as one could hope for; Guled remembers those days almost fondly. There was enough food, he had money. He went to school in the morning, drove in the afternoon, and at night he watched the battle for the city light up the sky.

As the rains failed, in July 2010 al-Shabaab launched its 'massive war' called the 'Ramadan Offensive', a final push against

AMISOM. And, for a while, it seemed as though Mogadishu might be the first capital to fall into the hands of extremists since the Taliban took Kabul in 1996. But the US sent in private contractors to train AMISOM snipers, as well as weapons in violation of the UN arms embargo, and by October al-Shabaab was in a bad way, trucking in ever more reluctant and inexperienced conscripts from the drought-stricken countryside. In three months it had lost an estimated 1,300 fighters, and a further 2,300 civilians were dead. Despite all of this, Guled and his sister didn't think of leaving: they had food and an income; neither of which they could be sure of elsewhere.

'It's only the poor left in Mogadishu now,' said a man who had fled the fighting to the Dadaab camps in Kenya, but that wasn't the whole story. To flee one needed three things: money, courage and imagination. Money, because nothing in Somalia was free and transport was especially expensive when in demand. Courage, because the route south was booby-trapped with checkpoints, lawless militias and bandits that attacked one in three vehicles heading for the border. And imagination because, for a mind shaped by the confusion of war, the ability to imagine that life might be different or better elsewhere is an uncommon leap. It helped if you knew someone who lived there. Guled knew one boy, Noor, who had run away to Kenya, but Guled's sister, his only family, was in Mogadishu and solidarity was in many ways as important as survival.

That was why, despite the risks, he was still here. And why he went to school as normal that October morning in 2010. At seven o'clock, having swept his classroom, Guled lined up in the courtyard along with the other remaining pupils for the assembly they called 'energizing'. As usual that day, one boy read out the results of the sports competitions between the classes and another recited verses from the Koran. Two girls read poems, one in English and one in Somali. Another did a comedy sketch. Afterwards, Guled's class teacher, Abdirashid, made an announcement. In recent weeks al-Shabaab had started kidnapping children from some other schools in the city, so, he said, 'Go straight home after school and if you see al-Shabaab, avoid them.'

That there were still children in school at all seemed remarkable. That year, only a quarter of those left in the country were enrolled in primary schools. And in Mogadishu even half of those had dropped out. Still, some students carried on. Sweeping the class-rooms. Ringing the bell. Running the gauntlet and showing up for class. Like al-Shabaab, the teachers were committed to an idea, desperately tugging the soul of a generation from the clutches of cynicism and despair.

At break time, Guled bought samosas. In the school uniform of yellow shirt and blue trousers he and the other children stood out as one of the few slabs of colour amid the white rubble and jagged grey ruins of the city; the Indian Ocean shimmered blue on the horizon. The students threaded in and out of the school gates and bunched around the snack stall, habituated to the sound of gun-fire in the distance.

After break, Guled returned to his classroom and rearranged the desks while another boy cleaned the blackboard. Discipline was rarely necessary in Shabelle primary. What happened next, he remembers precisely.

The teacher Abdirashid wrote the date in the top left-hand corner of the blackboard, and the subject: 'Geography'. As he faced the class, his face appeared taut, stretched in alarm. Turning, Guled saw five men at the back of the classroom, swathed in black with only their eyes showing. They shouldered machine guns, and calmly surveyed the room. Two of them moved towards the teacher and, silently, took him by the arms and marched him out-side. Three other fighters strode among the desks and began

pointing at the bigger boys as the class watched, rigid. The pointing was accompanied by a voice, commanding in Somali, 'Stand
up . . . Stand up . . . Stand up.' A finger halted on Guled. His lips
trembled. His stomach loosened. The room was silent, brittle as
glass.

'Stand up!' said the man. Guled's immediate thought was that
he was going to die. Either in battle, or for a crime he could not
yet comprehend: for playing football, for wearing shorts, for listening to music, for going to a secular school; his offences were
several. His second thought was that he would never see home
again.

Six boys were on their feet now. The class held their breath. No
one moved. One of the fighters announced with foreboding: 'You
are going to fight the Christians and the infidel government. This
will be your last day at school.'

With that, the armed men hustled the chosen ones down the
corridor and out into a pick-up truck with canvas sides that was
waiting on the street outside. Two other trucks crammed with
gunmen were behind. Guled saw that the teacher Abdirashid was
already in the truck before he felt hands over his face and a blindfold cover his eyes. He could hear the other classes still blithely
chanting their lessons. It had taken less than a minute for Guled to
become one of the two thousand children kidnapped that year in
Somalia. His heart was hammering out of control. He was puzzled
that his hands were free, not tied, and he gripped the bench
beneath him as the truck zig-zagged at speed through Mogadishu's
gridded streets.

3

Maryam

When the blindfold was removed Guled found himself standing under a tree. Now they were only five. The teacher Abdirashid and one of the boys were gone. But there were others he didn't recognize, sitting on the ground. A light-skinned man dressed in black with a large beard and his face uncovered addressed them mechanically in Somali: 'You must work and you must die for Islam,' he said, and then left them, under the tree, to wait.

The tree was in a wide open space. Off to the side, armed men walked in and out of low buildings. The camp was surrounded with a fence made of feeble sticks, easily scaled, but it was fear, not the sticks, that made it a prison. The new conscripts chattered anxiously about being asked to put on suicide vests, about being sent to carry food to the front line or to retrieve the bodies of fallen mujahedin. They all knew what could happen to boys who refused to fight, and, worse still, what could happen to their families if they escaped. Guled had someone else to think of now too. Beneath the tree, he agitated a ring with a coloured stone on his middle finger. It was a wedding ring. Of all the fears racing through his mind, he was surprised at himself that the most pressing need was to tell his new wife that he was alive.

Maryam was a quiet, determined girl, with a round face and perfect skin. Like Guled, she had fled with her family to one of the settlements on the outskirts of Mogadishu in the Afgoye corridor. It was the first line removed from the fighting in the city and the first place people fleeing the drought in the countryside arrived. At the end of 2010, the corridor, heaving with over half a million of the displaced and the dispossessed, was a vast slum controlled by al-Shabaab. Maryam too had gone to school in the city and, like Guled, every day she caught the same bus in from El-Shabiye.

Talking to a boy in public is a risky endeavour for a young Somali girl. In a densely populated refugee settlement that was little more than a giant campsite, privacy was non-existent. Their best chance to be together was the bus, with plenty of time to chat and, as Guled put it, 'to allow the love to grow'. Guled didn't know what it was he liked about her, 'just a feeling', he said. But for Maryam, it was 'his slow-moving', he was not rash, hot-headed. Among the boys she knew, he was possessed of a rare calm.

According to the 1975 family code, enacted under the rule of the former dictator Siad Barre, the legal age of marriage in Somalia is eighteen. But whatever traction the law had had before the conflict, it had none now. Nearly half of girls in Somalia are married before the age of eighteen. In some parts of the country a girl is considered ready for marriage as soon as her breasts start to show. Forced marriage has become more common too – a way for the bride's family to get money and to offload the responsibility of feeding another mouth. The love of a poor man will not feed his in-laws, and so youngsters in love, without the money to compete for a formal betrothal, often pre-empt the process and deliberately devalue themselves by eloping.

Tradition has it that couples wishing to elope must travel at least ninety kilometres (sixty miles) from their home area before tying the knot. For this reason, the town of Woloweyne, at ninety-one kilometres from Mogadishu, has become the Las Vegas of Somalia, stuffed with rent-a-sheikhs. Four months before the kidnapping, certain that they'd never be able to raise the money for a formal engagement, Guled and Maryam had skipped school and taken the bus to Woloweyne. On the edge of the road, they joined a line of other couples waiting to see a ragged-looking Imam, his skin blackened from his outdoor business. The ceremony lasted ten minutes and cost 40,000 Somali shillings (about $2) during which the Imam raised a book and a handful of beads and muttered some words beneath a tree. And with that, they were married: he was sixteen, she seventeen.

The newlyweds managed to keep their secret for three months, until the rumours reached her mother. After a respectable amount of hysterics, Guled succeeded in calming his mother-in-law enough to receive a delegation of uncles in the family tent. The uncles formalized his taking of Maryam without asking permission and everyone was satisfied with a compensatory dowry of two million Somali shillings (around $50). Guled agreed to pay in instalments, when he could. In addition, he had furnished his own tent with the equipment of matrimony: cooking utensils and a bed. They were adults now: the war caused a whole generation to grow up fast. Married bliss, though, was brief.

At midday, more fighters came. The sun burned through the sparse shade of the trees from which the new recruits had not moved. The fighters lined the boys up and gave them soup and bread, and then uniforms – black trouser suits that the Somalis call *futushari*. Later, the light-skinned commander with the beard divided the volunteers from the conscripts and then divided them again according to age. The bigger ones were taken 'to the battlefield', the commander said, while the younger ones, like Guled, were given sticks and whips and ordered into a truck. The sun had gone over now and it was nearing the time for the *Asad*, afternoon, prayer. They were told to go to the market and make sure no shops were open during the prayer. Guled's fate was now clear: he was to be an officer of the *Hizbat* – the al-Shabaab police. With the men needed at the front, al-Shabaab was backfilling the *Hizbat* with stolen children.

For the willing recruits, being assigned to the *Hizbat* was a disappointment: they'd dreamed of joining the *Amniyat* – the feared al-Shabaab intelligence corps – or the *Istishahadyin* – the suicide bombing unit. To blow yourself up in the name of God, there was a waiting list of three years; only the best recruits were chosen. But for Guled, the assignment was a reprieve.

The duties of the *Hizbat* were, by comparison, mundane. Across al-Shabaab areas they had a broad remit concerning law and order as well as religious observance and cultural or nationalist purity. Somali ways of doing things were championed, such as wearing trousers above the ankle and favouring sandals over shoes, what al-Shabaab considered the indigenous style. For men, Guled recalled, there were to be 'no Balotelli haircuts' (the flamboyant striker of, at that time, Manchester City), no mohawks, no flattops, no fringe and no perms. Conversely, women were encouraged to adopt al-Shabaab's preferred sartorial choice of heavy dense polyester hijabs rather than the cooler colourful indigenous cotton that a century ago made the coast of Somalia rich and famous; the militants deemed it too transparent. Al-Shabaab had a troubled relationship with modernity that often resulted in hypocrisy. In 2014 it would ban the internet and force Somalia's main telecoms providers to switch off the 3G signal in Mogadishu, while the militia's media unit maintained an active Twitter account and al-Shabaab governors conducted press interviews on their iPads.

After a short drive, the truck dropped the *Hizbat* patrol in the market of El-Shabiye, and Guled's heart raced again. The al-Shabaab camp was ten minutes from his tent; ten minutes from Maryam. The patrol of fifteen boys fanned out down the street. As the businessmen of El-Shabiye saw the boy soldiers coming they started closing up their shops themselves; they knew the law, and the punishments for breaking it. Beating was routine. If you had music or inappropriate pictures on your phone you might be forced to swallow the SIM card. Smokers often had their faces burned with their own cigarettes. One man who had been beaten for smoking in El-Shabiye later broke down crying when he recounted the story – not for the physical pain he had suffered but for the heartbreak of being assaulted by children. Guled might well have been among them.

Every day for two weeks the routine was the same. The patrol would move down the edge of the market, checking the expiry dates on the packaged food and tins and pulling over vehicles that were moving during the prayer time. They walked through the cardboard city where the displaced people, including Guled, had pitched their tents and thatched their makeshift huts. And one day on a corner, they came across two girls and a young boy, their faces turned towards the counter of a shop that was still open. In her hands, one of the girls held a bag of vegetables.

'Stop!' the leader of the patrol yelled. The children turned and froze.

'Lie down!' The patrol knew what to do. The two boys assigned the whips moved forward. The others hung back, watching. From the dusty ground, the terrified eyes of the young girls looked up at the patrol of their fellow children clad in black. Guled stared at the elder girl, kept staring, even after the surge of recognition warned him to look away.

It was Maryam. Their eyes touched. He felt his black uniformed limbs burning with fear and shame. He saw her face detonate in silent shock before he turned away concentrating furiously on stemming his tears, hoping none of the others had noticed. Maryam knew that a single word could condemn them both so she kept mute as the slim boy, younger than her perhaps, brought the whip down across her back and those of her sister and her male relative. She had heard from friends that Guled had been among those taken. Now she knew what it meant.

As the days went on, the conscripts waited for some terrible order. The camp was a place of suspicion. A glance was a weighty thing and conversations had multiple meanings. Guled made friends with one boy but after he absconded during a patrol one day, there was nobody else he could confide in. He found the neutral small talk exhausting while his mind smouldered, plotted.

In the evenings after patrol, the *Hizbat* of Guled's group would eat together and then sit around and tell stories; carefully balanced to be interesting enough, carefully pitched not to reveal too much about their real thoughts: you didn't know which boy was reporting to the leaders but you could be sure one of them was. And at night, they slept together on mats under the trees.

After a month, the commander with the big beard made a speech. It was a Friday. 'Since we've trained you new recruits and since you've done well, today is a free day. After the prayer you may wear normal clothes and leave the base, but you must be back by the evening prayer.' He couldn't quite believe it, but al-Shabaab, full of its own hubris, was actually trusting the kidnapped boys to return. As Guled listened to the instructions, he knew he would try and escape.

After the prayer, Guled took off his al-Shabaab uniform, put on his school one and walked into town. He dared not go to Maryam. He went instead to the tent of his aunt who was overcome with shock at the sight of him.

'*Mashallah, Mashallah,*' God be praised, she repeated over and over. 'Why have you grown so thin?'

He told her the story. By the time he had finished, the sound of the muezzin calling the faithful to prayer was ringing out across the refugee city: he was late. How long would it be before they started looking for him? He didn't know.

'Shall I take you to your tent?' asked the aunt.

'No. They will come looking for me there.'

'Where do you want to go?'

'Kenya,' he said. 'To the refugee camps.' It was the only place Guled thought al-Shabaab would not find him. Knowledge about the camps in Mogadishu was, like most information in the war, patchy and replete with rumour. But with the keen instincts of someone who had spent sixteen years staying alive in an urban war zone, he knew in his bones that if he delayed he would be dead. The moment he had avoided for so long had arrived. Even saying goodbye to Maryam was a risk. His aunt gave him fifty dollars that she had been saving for an emergency and with the money gripped in his fist, he tried to walk calmly through the streets of El-Shabiye to the bus station.

Avoiding conversation, he located a vehicle going direct to Dhobley, the border town hundreds of miles south of Mogadishu. To get there the bus would have to cross a dozen checkpoints, all manned by different units of al-Shabaab which, he could only hope, were not adept at communicating with each other. Even without the charge of 'traitor' hanging above his head, simply being a military-age male at that time of drought and gathering war was sufficient to get one conscripted again. Guled desperately needed an alibi.

When the bus got a puncture just outside the city, it seemed like divine intervention. Guled helped the driver change the wheel and the man, keen to avoid the nightshift, gave him $20 back again and asked him to share the driving. The oil that was all over his yellow school shirt helped maintain Guled's story that he was the assistant driver of the vehicle and thus not escaping but returning. This fiction carried Guled sweating but unquestioned through all the checkpoints he had been fearing. In Dhobley, though, another test awaited him.

To get to the camps, you take a bus, if you have money. If you don't, you walk. The camps lie seventy miles inside Kenya across the barren scrub of the border country and the crossing is dangerous. The police in Kenya jokingly refer to undocumented Somalis as 'ATM machines'. Rape is routine. Bandits are the preferred attackers, for they simply take what you have and let you on your way. The police are evaluated on the number of people they arrest and so they fill the hot stinking concrete cells of the border towns with asylum seekers, charge them with being 'illegally outside a designated area', an offence under the Kenyan Refugee Act, and collect up to $250 in ransom before deporting the failed refugees back to Somalia with bruised legs and a warning: 'Think again before coming back to Kenya.' If you could make it to the camps and register with the UN without being stopped, then you were allowed to stay, but it didn't pay to be caught trying.

As Guled's bus arrived in Dhobley, the roads were lined with long-wheeler trucks, what the Kenyans call *miguu kumi* – ten feet – taking contraband into Kenya. Mostly, they carry sugar. The sugar trade has a long history in this region; ever since Kenyan politicians discovered that an inefficient domestic sugar industry was a useful thing. It justified keeping import tariffs ridiculously high. Tariffs that, in a weak and corrupt state, could be easily circumvented for a huge profit. It had got to the point where slowing production and distribution inside Kenya became an economic strategy, creating strange bedfellows as cartels in the Kenyan government forged links with Somalis connected to al-Shabaab, all with a shared interest in keeping the trucks with their sweet cargo from Pakistan and Brazil running smoothly from the port of Kismayo and along the road to Dadaab. It was the darker side of globalization. People joked that sugar was 'the cocaine of Kenya' and it was reckoned that smuggled sugar accounts for a third of the Kenyan market. The illicit trade continued with the blessing of Kenya's most senior politicians, so the sugar trucks were one of the safest rides across the border.

With his fortuitous $20, Guled bought a spot on top of one and clambered up. There, he was struck by a curious sight: the bodies of dozens of other refugees lying flat on the sacks of sugar, staring at the evening sky where, burning above, high in the blue-pink of dusk, was a solitary white star. They were just some of the two thousand who would sneak across the border that November. In December, as the war and drought bit harder, the numbers would triple. In January, they would triple again.

Guled shifted around on the hard sacks and talked to no one. This was what the war did: it stole the possibility of trust. He was tainted now with the militant brush, even if only in his own mind, condemned to study each encounter with forensic para-noia. The truck bounced through the night. It stopped once, briefly, and there were lights, murmurings; it was the driver paying off the police. Traffic hadn't fallen since the border was officially closed in January 2007, the police had simply got richer. Guled breathed the cool clean air of the desert across which the 682 kilometre border is but a hopeful straight line on an inher-ited map. He twisted the ring with the red stone on his finger, looked at the cold brilliant stars, and thought of Maryam. When the truck eventually rumbled to a stop, the driver shouted at the travel-stiffened riders to get down. The new refugees looked about at the shadows of low buildings made of corrugated iron sheets and the high fence of thorns that encircled the garage and they settled to sleep on the foreign sand to wait for the day to break. The clear desert air was cut with the smells of the village: the sour scent of humans and the sweet odour of goat droppings. But even the night-time murmurings of the vast rural-urban slum hinted at the enormity of the city breathing beyond the garage wall.

A few hours later, the cry of the muezzin crackled across the tin roofs of the refugee camp and around three hundred thousand people stirred under the pinking sky. Back in 1992, the camp originally held ninety thousand Somali refugees fleeing the civil war. They had reproduced. Then others had come: more waves of Somalis, as well as Sudanese, Congolese, Ethiopians, Ugandans and Rwandans seeking asylum whom the Kenyans had shipped out to the margins of their country. And they too had had children. Three generations now called this giant cosmopolitan city made of mud, tents and thorns, home. That morning, 1 December 2010, Guled was the newest arrival in the largest refugee camp in the world.

4

Ifo

When he woke on the hard, oily sand in the garage just as it was getting light, Guled had two thoughts in his mind. He needed to find his friend, Noor, whom he had heard was here, somewhere, in a camp called 'Ifo'; and he needed to call home to check that his wife and sister were okay, that al-Shabaab hadn't traced them back in El-Shabiye. Both tasks required cash that he didn't have. But first of all he needed to work out where he was.

As the sun peeled back the night, behind the *kamoor* – the high fences made of thorn branches lashed together that define the camps – Guled got the first glimpse of his new world. The garage fronted on to a square patch of ground bordered by makeshift buildings made of shiny new iron sheets. From their shadowy insides, men emerged with crumpled dull trays and chipped cups of tea. Businessmen, their pockets bulging with phones and cash, bent their heads in talk. While already, at this early hour, throngs of young men squatted at the roadside and strutted about in their European soccer shirts, freshly laundered jeans, impossibly white sports shoes and cell phone headsets, taking in the passing show. The place was teeming with people.

The sugar truck had brought Guled to Hagadera, the south-ernmost of the three camps there were then. Designed in 1991 to house 30,000, Hagadera, like the others, had now swollen to a medium-sized city of over 100,000. The other two: Dagahaley and Ifo, his fellow travellers told him, were fifteen miles to the north, on the other side of Dadaab town. The people gave him some coins and pointed at the minibuses in the road outside. He would need to take a bus to Dadaab and then on, north to Ifo. No one would offer him a phone to call Somalia; at nearly a dollar a minute that was a favour too far.

Guled walked towards a bendy pole overloaded with home-made electricity wires that hovered perilously above the road. Opposite, vehicles had scored an arc in the deep fluffy sand around a limp Kenyan flag on a pole. It stood to attention before a low orange-mud building painted in stripes of black, yellow and red with the words 'Hagadera Police Post' in an ornate hand above the door. In the middle of the road trucks were lined up ready for dispatch across the region to Nairobi, Somalia, Ethiopia; around them crawled other, smaller, battered minibuses that plied the sandy road to the northern camps. Guled climbed into the first minibus in the line. When it was full, the vehicle bumped through the heavy dust for nine miles until it joined the main road from the south and rattled into Dadaab town, just ahead of the morning rush hour.

The town of Dadaab clings to the flat red plain a hair's breadth above the equator. Thorn trees stretch in a stubborn thicket for hundreds of miles in every direction. Here, the main road from Nairobi to Mogadishu makes a short dog-leg through what was once a sleepy Kenyan border settlement, established in 1954 as a borehole by the British. In the local dialect, the name Dadaab means 'the rocky hard place', because two inches below the red sand are sheets of diamond-hard stone. Those first inhabitants had no idea how appropriate the name would become.

Vehicles approaching from the south, from Hagadera and what they call in North Eastern Province 'down Kenya', are halted on the crumbly ochre road by a pathetic chicane of bent metal spikes in view of a little hut from which bored police officers glare at the baking road. As the minibus slowed, Guled's heart rate picked up but an officer simply waved the refugee bus through. Behind the checkpoint, on the left, Guled noticed the police camp with its scrubby trees, wooden sheds and broken chain-link fence. On the right, he saw three rows of razor wire spaced with spotlights. Aloof, behind its blast walls lay two square miles of heavily fortified compound housing the operations of the United Nations High Commissioner for Refugees (UNHCR), the World Food Programme (WFP) and the other aid agencies that supply the camps. Ahead, a cluster of low buildings made from metal sheets, wooden spars and, in a few cases, concrete, crowded the edge of the high street.

Opposite the heavy white-steel gates of the UN compound, Guled dismounted one minibus and was directed to another. Dust briefly whirled about his head and stung his eyes and then the vehicle was off, through the funnel of shops down which the wind blows a steady blast of sand. On the right were the government offices with their barbed wire and police guard and the abandoned bus of the deposed dictator Siad Barre, still rusting where he left it twenty years ago beneath the lilac jacaranda tree, its bulletproof windows cracked like icy puddles and birds nesting in the gun turret. A little further on the road arced past the town dump, where, like customers at a garage sale, stinking marabou storks pick through the acre of debris thrown by the wind into the thorn trees all around. On the very edge of town, painted on the variegated brown of the endless hostile scrub was a single stripe of black tarmac, the airstrip.

Most foreign visitors arrive here by plane. And it is from the air that the scale of the refugee complex is best appreciated. Spread over thirty square miles, the camps look like huge black-and-silver moons shot through with a web of red veins orbiting Dadaab town. The red is the grid of unpaved roads, the silver is the glint of tin roofs in the punishing sun and the black is the ubiquitous building material of the desert: the acacia thorn. But it is a perspective that few refugees ever get to see. For the inhabitants, the size of the camps is not so easily grasped. From the southern camp, Hagadera, to the northern one, Dagahaley is, for someone with no bus fare, a walk of several days. There were no fences around the makeshift city that Guled could see: there was simply nowhere to go. On four sides for hundreds of miles in each direction, the desert burned. North and east was war and south and west was Kenya: forbidden. The road south was choked with roadblocks manned by greedy police. Within and between the camps, though, there was freedom of movement.

At the airstrip, Guled started as the minibus was suddenly lost in a red cloud. At around eight every weekday morning, the United Nations and the aid agencies make their daily commute out of their fortified compound into the camps. The powerful vehicles cover the four miles north to Ifo quickly, engulfing in a fine red mist the herds of goats that totter forth each day in search of grazing and the battered refugee vehicles that ply the tracks between the camps. When Ifo was built, UN bulldozers had cleared the land without thought of the tree cover, and now it was a dustbowl.

Through the shifting dust and the fractured windscreen of the minibus, Ifo camp came into view. The first sight lifted his spirits, a football pitch on the outskirts! Beyond, roofs of huts peaked above densely thatched thorn fences and out of the alleyways in between, figures emerged, female mostly, covered head to foot in hijabs. The road spilled into a clearing next to the football pitch beneath a huge elevated water tank that towered out of the thorn bushes. It was the original borehole for the refugees that had made the one in the town run dry. In 1991 water was ten metres below the surface of the plain. In 2011 the engineers had to go down two hundred metres to find it. Next to the borehole was the UN field office although all that was visible to Guled was a high concrete wall and a huge steel gate. He would come to know it well. The sun was already high, and hot. Lines of people pressed into the narrow shade thrown by the wall, as they waited to present their grievances to the officials who would soon be installed on the other side of the red welded metal. The residents of Ifo had plenty to complain about.

The overcrowding here, as in the other camps, was acute. After twenty years, the camps were in need of a doubling in water capacity and shelter. Health services were at breaking point. The place where Guled had come seeking sanctuary was, according to Oxfam, a 'public health emergency', and had been for several years. It was a groaning, filthy, disease-riddled slum heaving with traumatized people without enough to eat. Crime was sky high and rape was routine. And the population was about to explode again. On the day Guled arrived the camps held nearly 295,000 people. Twelve months later, at the end of 2011, there would be half a million.

Guled's minibus plunged into Ifo camp, through a knot of tracks weaving in and out of the warren of sandy roads, past tin plates on steel poles marking the names of the blocks: A5, D6, A6. The roads were lined with great hedges of thorns, towering above head height and punctured with the tin gates to people's compounds until the road tumbled into the chaos of the market. Here, it rumbled along the narrow bumpy alleys thick with people and strewn with rubbish, until finally it came to a stop at the edge of the maidan, a wide open space about the size of two soccer pitches where people gather on important events.

In the rainy season, the maidan becomes a lake, but it was now a sheet of hammered sand across which the dry season twisters raced. People walking across covered their faces. On one side is the dusty, pungent livestock market of Lagdera where the camp's riotous herds of goats are divided into bleating lots in pens made of thorns. Looming over the other end is the telecoms tower. Variously powered by shards of solar panels, a whirring wind turbine and a hulking generator all encased in barbed wire, its tall red-and-white beacon is the camp's lifeline to the outside world.

Ifo camp had a mobile signal but since al-Shabaab confiscated his, Guled had no phone. He had no way of contacting his friend Noor and no idea where he lived. He wandered hungry and aimless around the huge market heavy with the stench of decomposing meat and vegetables, in and out of the narrow alleyways between the stalls made of flattened steel sheets – it was a market made from scraps. But Guled was surprised to see that you could buy everything: food, clothes, radios, generators, mobile phones, long blocks of ice. He would come to learn that some of it, like the ice and the pasta, was manufactured in the camp, but that most came from Somalia on trucks like the one on which he had hitched a ride. The sun blistered on the tin roofs. The market was all bright light and, beneath the roofs, inside the stores and under the sacking, impenetrable shade. His eyes constantly adjusted, smarted; it made him dizzy. And everywhere he thought he felt the eyes of al-Shabaab, in the shadows, watching him: 'That bad thing in my brain makes me think that everybody is looking at me. I know it is not true. But I think that they look at me different ... sometimes they do.'

At prayer time he went to look for Noor in the central mosque. Squat and low, it had been built of mud and thorns nineteen years ago and painted green and white. It sat on a bend on the edge of the market where donkey carts nodded in the ruts of the road and the ceaseless pedestrian traffic of the camp poured past in a river of colour. Most of the inhabitants were, like Guled, Sufis, the moderate mystical kind of Islam full of syncretic additions with room for traditional wisdom and remedies. But thirty years of investment by Saudi Arabia in the Horn of Africa was paying off. Wahabism, the strict literal Islam of mistrust and division that has flourished in the fertile grounds of war-racked Somalia, was winning converts in the camp. Most al-Shabaab members practised a variant of Wahabism. Guled's instincts were right, they were here, although the militants had bigger concerns than tracking down a scrawny deserter from the mujahedin; Dadaab was full of runaways. Al-Shabaab's presence in Dadaab was a watchful one. It didn't have the strength or the desire to start kidnapping refugees and picking a fight with the UN and Kenya. At that time, it saw Dadaab primarily as a place to get medical treatment and stock up on food. All that would change though with Kenya's invasion of Somalia ten months later. Then, Dadaab would become a battleground and one of the first bombs would be placed here, outside the Sufi mosque, targeting a police car: the apostates and the infidel invaders all together.

Dadaab felt very different from Somalia. In Mogadishu, Guled had been accustomed to 'Shahad'; according to religion and custom, if a stranger was in need, people shared, unquestioningly. In Ifo he felt only hostility. The inhabitants eyed him nervously. Guled had come from a place of fighting and fear; as far as they were concerned, he was capable of anything; he was a murderer, a terrorist, a bandit, until vouched for otherwise. Then, in what he felt was a second act of divine intervention, he saw a face he recognized passing in front of a shop.

'Noor!' he called. A small boy in borrowed clothes turned towards him. The two boys embraced. Guled couldn't stop smiling with relief. They had been at Shabelle primary together in Mogadishu and he had helped the boy in the days when he had work and money. Now the tables were turned. Finding a friend was, literally, a lifeline: according to the Somali custom of sharing, Guled would not go hungry so long as Noor had food. His friend showed him around and, slowly, the camp began to make sense.

He learned how to distinguish Noor's small hut of sticks covered with mud and roofed with plastic in block C3 from among the identical huts divided into compounds by thorn fences and arranged in huge rectangles — what the refugees called 'the blocks'. The blocks are marked with tin labels and separated by narrow alleys just large enough for a car to pass down. The alley on which C3 was situated was also home to Horseed primary school, a white concrete structure. Thus it was a little wider than the others, its rutted tracks holding stagnant puddles of sewage that turned green in the heat; at each intersection a small tin box had been constructed by enterprising refugees with capital — a corner shop selling small amounts of kerosene, matches, sandals, the things the UN didn't hand out for free. At one end of the alley was the market, and at the other, nearly a kilometre away past countless geometrical blocks of huts, the road simply stopped, giving out on to the wild bush.

Noor explained to Guled that as a new arrival he was supposed to register with the UN High Commissioner for Refugees — to claim asylum — in order to be given a ration card, personal items like a blanket and a bucket, and a plot and a tent to sleep in. Tents didn't last though, and after a year most people built their own hut with the twigs and the mud of the plain. In the meantime, Guled slept in Noor's hut and shared his rations but Noor couldn't help him with what he really wanted: money to call home. When he asked about work, Noor laughed. Guled learned that employment in Kenya was forbidden. Like many governments anxious about asylum seekers, Kenya didn't want Somalis taking Kenyan jobs, so all formal work with a decent salary, with the agencies and the

UN, was reserved for Kenyans. Most of the camps' economy is informal, however, and in the grey economy it was possible to get work in the market, driving, butchering, teaching in the private colleges.

The other way the refugees raised cash was by selling the food rations that the UN issued every fortnight. Guled was lucky. Registration of new arrivals had only just opened again for the first time since 2008 when the Kenyans had declared the camp full. If he had come a month earlier, he would have been unable to get the ration card that entitles residents to food, education and health care and would have been entirely dependent on sharing with Noor. Five days after they had met, Noor escorted Guled down the alley, through the market and along the wider, busier roads of section A to the UN office beside the water tower on the outskirts of the camp that he had passed before. He left him with others to line up in the sliver of shade cast by the wall before the sun got too high. An hour later, Guled filed through the red-steel gate and joined the lines of men on the benches beneath the tin-roofed shelters inside the fence. In a concrete block whose cracked roof was home to dozens of birds and whose walls were replete with warnings about services being free, and corruption illegal (in English, Swahili and Somali for the benefit of the 20 per cent that were literate), a UN official took his name. The woman asked no questions about what had happened in Somalia. 'Insecurity' was the reason Guled gave for his flight and, after a medical, a photo and a fingerprint, he received a laminated ration card and the information that there was no plot or tent for him. They were reserved for families. Due to the overcrowding, single people were simply absorbed into the compounds of people they knew or assigned as lodgers in the compound of someone else. Noor would not be happy. And indeed, after two weeks he would find him an alternative arrangement.

All people arriving from Somalia are treated as *prima facie* refugees. The UN operates on the assumption that no one would willingly become a refugee – an assumption that failed to take account of the hunger and deprivation among the Somali nomads of northern Kenya. In the early days, although not fleeing war, many ethnic Somali Kenyans claimed asylum too. To be added to the distribution manifest one need only appear to be Somali and state that you were fleeing conflict. In the UN vocabulary Guled was 'family size 1' and he would collect his rations once a fortnight.

On his appointed day, Noor showed him the way out north across the maidan to the large white warehouse complex on the opposite edge of the camp to the UN. Inside several perimeters of barbed wire was the distribution centre for Ifo. Each camp had its own. The centre looked like a cross between an airport hangar and a prison: a line of nine huge, numbered, white warehouses dusted with red sand like a sugared cake. Painted along the side of each warehouse were letters ten feet high, although upside down on one, announcing the beneficent owner: WFP, the World Food Programme. Thousands of people passed through the chain of warehouses every day. The 'food cycle', as it is known, is like a machine. And every fifteen days it turns over, feeding the whole population.

Two blue welded-steel gates, lazily guarded by armed police and aid agency staff, faced a wide open area in which the sand swirled in circles around a single tangled thorn tree that had somehow escaped the hatchet. Several hundred men and women squatted on the ground in lines in the hot morning sun, waiting to be called to collect their food. For the poorer ones among them, their last square meal would have been several days ago. According to the fundaments of Dadaab's economy, with only rations for income, the price of anything in the camp is hunger. Some of the women in the line wore their cards protectively on strings around their neck and in their fists they clutched empty rice sacks, plastic bags and jerrycans, waiting to be filled. Gripping his new blue ration card with its days and distributions marked out like a contraceptive pill packet, Guled joined the line.

A policeman with a stick and a machine gun marched up and down keeping the 'clients', as they were called, seated, docile, ready to be corralled through the system, 'processed', like sheep being dipped. It was a ritual humiliation. After an hour in the sun, the policeman waved them up.

Through the blue gate the men thronged the entrance and pushed into the warehouse that was fenced into two parallel cages: one for each sex, about a thousand people in each. The women lined up calmly but the men were all bunched down one end pushing and shouting, their voices echoing in the huge hall. The mood was febrile and Guled hesitated. A turnstile regulated the outflow but a security guard had opened the fire exit and a tide of men was stampeding through into the courtyard beyond. A soldier watched the men stream past, his gun hanging limp by his side.

In the middle hall the men swarmed around the bulletproof windows, shouting and arguing. Behind the glass, World Food Programme staff received the ration cards through a small slit, like bank tellers, checked them against the manifest and returned them, punched: the bearer duly authorized to collect their rations. The mob pressed all around. Guled darted in among the bodies.

His card punched, he moved into the warehouses to collect his food. An old man wearing a hi-vis jacket directed the refugees into different sheds. 'Number nine!' he called, waving towards a hangar, the one that he would later learn was famous for corruption. Guled entered the huge dark warehouse with his plastic bags and presented his card to the two black-veiled girls writing down the numbers in a ledger at the door. At a small welded hole in the locked red-steel cage flanked by piles of white sacks of food with international logos, a woman in a hijab dipped a cup into a sack of rice and Guled held out one of his plastic bags. At the second, a wiry man dusty-white from head to foot, scooped cups of wheat flour from a bin. At the third, a woman gave him a spoon of salt. The last two windows yielded a cup of beans and a cup of oil that a scowling woman poured into his jerrycan, sucking her teeth as it spilled.

The final stage, outside the cage, was the checking. A drawn man with thinning hair, pointed beard and dark glasses all dusted with flour, snatched the bags of each refugee in the line and placed them on an electronic scale. The mandated amounts were written in green pen on a huge white board mounted on the side of the cage and he evened up the flour, rice, beans and salt with sharp stabbing motions of a tablespoon. All eyes watched the numbers flicker and still. He was fast. Blink and you could be cheated. There was much shouting as people shuffled continually through. The scales were hot with friction. The whole operation was close and fierce. The weigher's feet rested on a concrete lip around the base of the scale – the result of lobbying by the community to keep feet away from the scales and decrease the opportunities for the workers to cheat the refugee clients. As Guled's food was weighed he watched the man's toes flex in their plastic sandals but they didn't touch the scales. Watching too were two supervisors, well dressed in clean shirts, scarves and nice shoes, also in sun-glasses. They were smiling. There was a game here, if you could spot it.

The refugees didn't trust the WFP staff. They had lobbied for a separate community scale at which a gentle old man in a white skullcap took his time with everyone weighing bags to verify their amounts. The standard WFP ration per person is a finely measured and costed 565 grams per day providing 2,241 kilocalories per person. For Guled for the coming fortnight, this translated as three kilos of wheat flour, two of rice, one kilo of beans, half a litre of cooking oil and a cup of salt. In a strange incentive to reproduce, the amounts are the same per person, regardless of age. At the exit, a woman in a veil punched his card again and he emerged clutching his bags into the blinding midday sun.

As soon as he got outside, he sold some of his food. Traders lined the street buying up the rations cheaply. Two kilos of rice yielded 100 shillings ($1.2). So finally, ten days after he had arrived, Guled went to the phone shop in the market and called the three numbers that he carried in his head: those of his wife, his mother-in-law and his sister.

Maryam had almost lost her mind with worrying about him. But she and the others were fine. Overcome and emotional, Guled recounted, with an optimism unrooted in experience, all the benefits of the camp in an effort to persuade her to join him. He simply repeated what Noor had boasted of: that the camp was safe; that there was plenty of food, free housing, health care and education and even the chance of resettlement to America. He didn't mention that he found the sun so hot he couldn't open his eyes at midday or that the dust of Ifo caught in the back of the throat. Nor did he describe how the sewage stood in the street or how the overcrowded camp was still expanding.

Maryam was easily convinced. The heavy fighting in Mogadishu had continued. On 2 December an extra 8,000 troops from Uganda and Burundi had been deployed to the AMISOM peacekeeping force in the city. During the following three days over 100 people were killed. Plus, she carried within her a secret. One that she wanted to tell Guled in person. Without any idea what she was asking of him in a refugee camp full of people forbidden to work and reliant on international handouts to eat, Maryam told Guled to send money so she could come.

Guled was overjoyed, then instantly distraught. In Mogadishu he could have hustled the fare of $50. In Ifo camp he had no idea where to start, how to get money. He had sounded so confident to Maryam on the phone. So confident, in fact, that she would count the rosy unrealistic picture he had painted as the first betrayal.

5

Nisho

At the centre of the grey economy of the camp, where Guled hoped to earn some money, is the market. Business starts early in Ifo. At four a.m. every morning, on a cold slab of concrete, half a dozen camels are slaughtered. As the knives flash across their throats and the blood spills into polished bowls, the muezzin calls the faithful to the dawn prayer. By the time the market opens at seven a.m., skinned legs, ribs and camel intestines are hanging from metal poles in scores of makeshift butchers' shops across the camp. Livestock has always been the mainstay of the Somali economy, and, along with sugar, so it is in the Dadaab camps. The markets in Dadaab sell everything from tomatoes to trucks and turn over at least $25m a year; it is a black market in technical economic speak but, in real terms, it is a quarter of all economic activity in North Eastern Province and everyone wants a piece of it.

The anarchy of the border country is, for those with capital and connections and the ability to exploit it, a giant opportunity. On the Somali side, the traffic is controlled, and taxed, by al-Shabaab, and on the Kenyan side by the police. Higher up the chain, Kenyan politicians and Somali businessmen take their cuts leaving the workers of the market to speculate about the deals being transacted above their heads. The traders of the market are the middle class of the camp and the middle men; in touch with both sides: paying off the police and al-Shabaab alike. Among them there are dollar millionaires who have made fortunes out of the humanitarian economy: smuggling sugar, pasta, rice, milk, shoes, cars and all manner of other things into Kenya; renting vehicles to the aid agencies, supplying food and drink, constructing offices. These entrepreneurs have usually started from small beginnings wired from relatives abroad. But for the thousands scrabbling just to raise some extra cash, the market is a cauldron of competition, struggle and uncertainty. This was where Noor advised Guled to try his luck to earn the money for Maryam's fare.

The central market in Ifo camp is called Bosnia, named in the Somali tradition for something significant occurring at the time of its founding. Later in the year, it would live up to its warlike name, but not yet. In January 2011 the threats to life were economic, not martial. The drought and the war meant that trade was slow. The sugar convoys, the biggest business, were thinning out due to the competition between the rival cartels of Hagadera and Ifo camps. And the unskilled porters who fought for the chance to unload the trucks were starting to resent the rising tide of hungry young men like Guled muscling in on their business.

Guled asked around and was directed to the shop of Abbas, the most prominent trader in the centre of Bosnia, where the porters congregate on a concrete veranda, their wheelbarrows resting on the dirt. Here the fences of thorn are replaced by shacks made from opened-out oil drums in all colours – yellow, green, blue, red and brown – hammered flat and pressing in on all sides. Slender alleys hive off in many directions, and in the shadows crouch lines of men in sandals, grubby trousers and loose shirts, some with turbans, some with beards, young and old. These are the workers of the market and they stare at everyone and everything passing; evaluating, judging. It wasn't long before a crowd of them had gathered around Guled. Who did he think he was? Didn't he know there was a process for becoming a porter? They had an association. He couldn't simply show up just like that. Job opportunities were viciously defended in Bosnia. In the coming months there would be many fights, and challengers to their territory would be hospitalized. The porters' faces were hot and angry. One of them was Nisho.

Nisho crossed the road back to the siding where his colleagues were clustered around the back end of a truck. The lorries in the unloading spot in Bosnia were blue with red-and-white stripes down the side. They had green canvas awnings secured with ropes and Kenyan number plates. One was fully loaded with sacks of rice, the back of the other was down, a legend in Swahili painted along the bumper: *Haivutiwi na kamba* (No Towing). The lettering on the other truck was in English: 'No Pain No Gain'. A bicycle weaved past, its bell trilling an alarm. Inside the back of the truck, Nisho and the other porters were pulling and rolling sacks down a wooden ramp into handmade wooden wheelbarrows accompanied by much shouting, heaving and whistling. The roof of the truck was open and beneath a lattice of steel, black against the sharp blue of the morning, Nisho tugged at a sack of potatoes that had had another sack sown on to the bottom to extend it and a white net of twine woven around the top to cram more in, the whole lot stopped up with grass to prevent the potatoes from bruising. His grey trousers were dirty and his red plastic flip-flops magically clung to his feet as he danced on top of the sacks, slipping down, clambering up, swinging from the bars of the truck. His T-shirt, also grey, a free gift from some distributor, said 'Golden Instant Cup' in yellow letters. He grabbed a sack and called to his colleagues, 'One, two, three, heave!' They strained.

'Push! Push! That way!' The sack slid down.

'Kheylio is not working hard, he's not lifting his end!' The sack continued to slide. Nisho smiled, happy, enjoying the burn of his muscles and the pleasure of the work. The sack upended and landed with a thump on the wooden wheelbarrow. A plump-faced woman in a magenta hijab stood by the open tailgate of the truck squinting into the sun and shouting orders. Nisho jumped down, pushed another porter out of the way and grabbed the handlebars of the wheelbarrow. He grinned, a small gap between his teeth, sweat beading on his shaved skull, his eager eyes roaming around the street.

'Take it to Ferdoza,' the woman in magenta said. Immediately he turned and wobbled with the weight of the sack on the wheelbarrow. Another porter appeared in a blue shirt and a white turban with a hand to steady the load at the front. Together they set off through the crowded alleyways, one pushing, the other walking ahead, sandals slapping against bare heels, the frontman calling out: 'Give way! Give way for Nisho!'

Nisho is not a big man, but he handled the loaded wheelbarrow dextrously; it is his 'daily bread', as they say in the market and he knows it well. Nisho liked to claim Ifo as 'his' since they share the same age. In the story his mother tells, he was born en route to the camp when his parents fled Somalia in 1991, arriving in Ifo just as the grid of squares was being carved on the plain and the pioneers were cutting thorns and mudding them with the red earth for huts. Although if you ask him how old he is he'll most likely just blurt out a number that sounds roughly accurate, seventeen, eighteen, twenty. He has no real need to know.

The front porter laid a hand on the top of the sack, guiding, and Nisho pushed the 220 kilos of potatoes fast down a narrow passageway, too narrow for a car now, into the heart of the souk. The sprawling nest of shops is covered by sacking hung from the illegal power lines to soften the hammer blows of the desert sun. The wheelbarrow glided along, past clothes hanging from poles and jerry cans tied together in bunches, on hard-packed sand where the rubbish had been ground into a confetti of plastic and paper.

A woman in a full burqa stepped nimbly into a stall as the wheelbarrow wobbled past her. Then down another alley lined with curly mangrove poles holding up a tin roof from which hung nets of plastic footballs: pink, yellow and green. They hurried on into the butcher's area with its ribbons of meat strung on nails above heavy brass scales slimy with fat and down a side passage where the tomato-sellers construct impressive towers according to size, spread on sacks and cardboard. Makeshift tables covered in cloth sported pots of local honey opposite a small metal stall made into a box and filled waist high with second-hand shoes. Dresses, shirts, children's flip-flops, galvanized cooking dishes, pots and pans, all the manic commerce of Bosnia flashed past in a blur as the front man shouted out a continual warning and Nisho maintained the steady trot that he has learned to be the most efficient.

Nisho hadn't wanted to be a porter, but after his father died and his mother went mad, he felt he had no choice. For a while he went to school in the morning and worked in a tea-shop in the market in the afternoon for a kind woman who bought him books and paid his school fees. But one day she got selected for resettlement abroad and within two months she was gone 'up there', America, Europe, wherever they go, those people lucky enough to be plucked from the miseries of the camp. Nisho hadn't heard from her since. That was in 2004, when he was thirteen years old.

For Guled and the others who stayed behind growing up in Somalia, the camp had been talked up as a haven of opportunity; a gateway to health care, free education and resettlement to America. For those raised in the dusty prison of the camp, it was a very different world. A world with its own rules, its own boundaries and its own histories. Governed by the UN and the humanitarian agencies, it was a society weaned on food aid and the international vocabulary of rights. It was also a baking hot slum where new names had to be invented for every corner, where new legends were born. The war over the border was both close in the stories of the people who came to the camp and yet very far. Nisho and the generation born in the camp had not seen fighting and they feared what they heard about Somalia with the terror of the unknown. By 2010 the camps were nineteen years old and Nisho, never having set foot outside Dadaab, had been working in the market for more than half his life.

The first day that they put a sack on his back, he stumbled about from left to right and then fell in the mud completely. The other porters were encouraging; they told him he'd learn, that he was a man, and they comforted him with other sayings that made his new role seem more bearable, like 'a man must struggle to survive', and 'when you sweat, you eat'. Going from house to house and begging is shameful and Nisho didn't want to stoop that far. Back then, al-Shabaab did not exist and now that he was accustomed to earning a living, the lure of easy money promised by the al-Shabaab recruiters held no attraction. Besides, the nickname his mother had given her last born – Nisho: 'little one' – so suited him in his new employment he soon grew to think that fate had assigned him the role. 'My life is carrying a sack,' he declares these days with a kind of fragile pride.

Around a bend, the porters passed an open-fronted stall painted green stacked to the roof with reams of photocopy paper. Next door were freshly planed wooden boards with carved tops upon which every refugee child would practise Arabic calligraphy and learn the all-important verses of the Koran. And then, next to a stall selling spices and medicinal roots and powders, collision. Another wheelbarrow was coming the other way. Nisho, trembling, lowered his handles and inched forward as the Koran-seller steadied the potatoes on their way, keeping them from upsetting his wares.

Nisho and his wheelbarrow emerged in an open space among

onion-sellers on another road about a kilometre from where they had started. Bosnia is huge, serving not just Ifo camp but the others too and a large part of Kenya's North Eastern Province. They navigated around one woman selling clothes from a wheelbarrow and another tall one sashaying down the centre of the street in expensive grey cloth, and finally arrived at their destination. Nisho set the barrow down and put both hands on his load, hanging his head to breathe. Sweat popped out of every pore on his head. It ran down his face in streams. He bent his back, hands on hips, and grinned, mouth half open to reveal his gapped front teeth and drew his fingers down his face as though he were cleaning a window. He complained about the weight, and about the wages: 150 shillings ($1.9) the owner of the goods would pay him for moving them. It used to be 250 shillings ($2.5). Sometimes he used to have enough even for the crushed ice laced with syrup chipped from the huge rectangular slabs that emerged like sawn timbers from the ice factory in Bosnia. Those days were memories now.

Lunch would be seventy shillings, leaving only ninety to take back to his mother to supplement the dry UN rations with tea, milk and sugar and the occasional tomato or onion. She would be disappointed, if she was in her right mind. Nisho wasn't sure which was worse. She had taken to wandering about the camp again and he hated having to tie her up. He had forgone school to care for his mother and she needed regular visits to the witch-doctor which were expensive, plus, if he ever wanted to marry – he had needs now he was older – portering wasn't cutting it.

Nisho and his front man backed their wheelbarrow of potatoes into Ferdoza's shop. The mangrove poles holding up the tin roof were polished smooth by decades of hands. Hanging from the walls and the counter were long strips of seasoning mix, '100% Power Glue' and children's flip-flops. A man in a black-and-white striped shirt, grey hair and a grey beard materialized out of the murk behind the counter. He was the store manager. He helped them upend the sack for it took all three of them. 'Easy! Here! This way!' they shouted. And with that, Nisho's last paid load, his final hope of income for that day, was tied with string to a pole in the corner.

At the turn of the year, trade in the camp was unseasonably bad. Nisho really needed to find himself another line of work. He wondered whom he could approach for help. There were no kingpins from his clan, the Rahanweyn, but his faithful service over many years to the sugar barons should, he thought, count for something. Nisho was an important part of the chain: the main-stay of his income was offloading and rebagging the smuggled sacks, mixing it with Kenyan sugar. The traders of the market don't call it smuggling though; it is what they have always done – to them it is simply 'business'.

And business in Somalia is a family affair. Nisho lamented that he had no godfather, no well-connected uncles. 'Can a man push-ing a wheelbarrow be rich?' he was fond of asking, of no one in particular. There are four major clans among whom political power in Somalia is traditionally divided and then several minor ones. The Rahanweyn clan are treated as second-class citizens, the ones who do the dirty jobs: the cleaning, the carrying, the butchering. Abbas, the owner of the truck of potatoes, had started out just like Nisho, with a donkey cart. Now Abbas is not only rich, but 'triple rich!' That's what ten years and a helping hand from the right clan can do; Abbas was from the Aulihan, a sub-clan of the majority Ogaden clan. Bosnia is a closed shop, controlled by the refugees with links to the host community of Dadaab who are also from the Aulihan who dominate on both sides of the border. Nationality here is mostly just a slip of paper; clan is what counts. The other cartel that operated out of Hagadera was from the Marehan. Both cartels wielded considerable power. There are men in Dadaab who can order whole ships to dock at Kismayo, kingmakers who control access to their home towns in Somalia and who have the power, through their influence within the clan, to nominate members of the Kenyan parliament. Huge sums of money are at stake.

Mapping the networks of economic activity and political influence in the Horn of Africa is a lesson in political economy: the two are almost indistinct. Politicians in Kenya just like everywhere else need campaign contributions and elections in Kenya are particularly expensive: they took a keen interest in the sugar trade and maintained their share. Keeping the border closed, tariffs high and yet the sugar flowing involved a range of compromises with the clan, the traders, police, customs and al-Shabaab; all of which carried a transaction cost. Nisho's meagre wage was part of one of East Africa's largest illicit networks that reached, so they said, right to the heart of Kenya's State House.

Abbas and Nisho used to sit and chat but Abbas didn't have time for him any more. Like the other sugar barons, Abbas lived in Nairobi and drove a big car with black windows and knobbly off-road tyres. He had achieved the ultimate refugee dream: citizenship. He had followed the path of the wealthy and bought himself a Kenyan ID card – everything is for sale in Kenya. The card allowed him to live where he liked, obtain a passport, vote even. Abbas came to the camp only to check his trucks and his business. He was a Kenyan. He was free.

Nisho wasn't rich enough to be free, but he hovered a little way above the bottom rung of the market's hierarchy. And freedom, like wealth, is relative. While Nisho looked up to Abbas, it felt good to have someone looking up to you. Things seemed better now he had acquired a protégé who really was on the bottom rung, at the level of the dust, whose struggles put Nisho's worries in the shade.

Mahat was a short boy stunted with malnutrition who had spent so long clawing a living from the earth of the market that he fancied his skin had turned a shade darker because of it. Mahat tried to act tough, wearing a dirty white vest under the men's shirts that hung on him like a dress and that he tucked into jeans with an oversize Chinese plastic belt, but he had a lopsided smile of pure childish innocence and a halting stutter that belied his swagger. Nisho said the vest looked like he'd laundered it in a pit latrine. Mahat had come to the camp with his grieving mother in 2004 after his father was killed in Somalia, and he entered the market aged seven. Having an audience was precisely what Nisho needed to harden his nervous bravura into an act in which he himself could believe: 'He's like my son,' he declares, throwing an arm roughly around his small friend, and Mahat smiles shyly.

Nisho had taken Mahat under his wing and offered career advice. First he suggested shoe shining. Then later, a more promising line: firewood. For miles around the Dadaab camps there is a halo of stumps, the trees ravaged by the raiding parties of refugees gripping their insistent axes. Several hundred thousand cooking fires burn a lot of wood. Nisho and Mahat negotiated the rent of a donkey cart and Mahat joined the convoys that trundle out into the scrub in search of logs. While the others made 1,200 shillings in a trip of three or four days, little Mahat was only managing to load half a cart. One day the five men in his group met a lion with two cubs sitting on the path, just watching. Mahat sweated and shivered – it was the first time he'd seen a lion. An old man made them hit the donkeys and drive right past the lion as it watched them, looking but not stirring. Another time they saw a hyena. Another, a leopard. Mahat was scared. 'I made a decision in my brain,' Mahat said, and quit. He turned instead to collecting water.

Every block in the camp has a tap stand fenced with thorns and locked with a key at which, each morning, there is a long line of people, usually women, usually children, with large yellow jerry cans jostling for position. It is the most frequent source of fights. Those who can afford to avoid the indignity of the morning squabble, hire children to fetch their water for them. A lady paid Mahat 500 shillings ($7) a month to get her water every day. But Mahat quarrelled with her and, too small to join Nisho and the porters, he had recently returned to his original job of shoe-shining. He had prudently kept the polish and brushes, stashed in the rafters of Nisho's house. 'Life may change,' he said, justifying his foresight. Nisho nodded approvingly.

Mahat was now looking to Nisho for another hustle while Nisho looked up higher still. It wasn't going well. The anxiety dulled Nisho's usual volubility and he was aggressive towards Mahat. Neither Abbas nor Mrefu, 'Mr Tall', in Swahili, nor any of the other wealthy traders, were able to offer any alternative to portering. He and Mahat slept together on a straw mat in a hut next to his raving mother and sometimes swapped stories of 'an aeroplane full of money'. New arrivals such as Guled looking for work always made Nisho anxious. Every day now, four hundred people were arriving in Dadaab, driven by the drought and the war, coming even from Baidoa, his mother's home town from which she had fled in 1991, the traditional breadbasket of the country. He knew that there would soon be even more of them, roaming the market with the vacant, willing eyes of the hungry, and that they would do anything, at any price.

6

Isha

The great rivers of southern Somalia, the Juba and the Shabelle, never dry up. It was uncommon for there to be famine even in the breadbasket at the centre of the country. This was where, traditionally, people came when times were hard. But even as the water in the river dribbled past, the old Italian sluice gates to the irrigation canals controlled by al-Shabaab – whom the locals called 'the River Barons' – remained closed, for want of cash. Land ownership and control of the harvest have been a source of conflict since the beginning of the civil war. While the civil war in Mogadishu was, in the words of the novelist Nuruddin Farah, a sacking of the city by urbophobic herdsmen who saw it as 'alien and parasitic', in the countryside it was a war for land. Many of the residents of Dadaab, like Nisho's family, had been driven from their farms in the original waves of invasion in 1991. In the militarized capitalism that is the economy of Somalia, harvesting crops and taxes and harvesting the aid brought by the NGOs is the core business of the militias in the countryside, including the latest one, al-Shabaab. 'When the corn is ready, they come,' said one farmer. 'For four years I have been paying tax to al-Shabaab: one goat, two cattle, a percentage of my crops ... now I have nothing left,' said another. Al-Shabaab, desperate for funds for its massive war in the city, had taken too much.

The farmers couldn't pay for irrigation and so the crops, for the third consecutive year, lay short and stunted under a film of dust.

The farmers mourned the soil that they had tilled with their own fingers and as it dried and was sucked into the sky, the atmosphere itself went brown. In one village the milk in a mother's breasts dried up and her baby died. In January 2011, though, Isha still had hope.

There was still a little water in the oasis not far from the town of Baidoa that the nomads call 'Paradise' where Isha's husband took their animals. There, the exuberant aquifers bubble up from beneath the quaternary rocks into the sweetest spring. In the dry season, the pastoralists gather like birds around a pond and swooning palms throw shade over the sandy banks. The wells this time were overcrowded and, her husband reported, the people talked of going to Dadaab. Isha, though, did not want to leave. This was not the first drought she had ever seen, nor, in her opinion, the worst.

When, twenty years before, the first of her neighbours had left for Dadaab, Isha had stayed. She was a young, unmarried woman committed to her people. Since then, she had given birth six times in the place they lived called Rebay, between Baidoa and another town called Dinsoor. *Rebay* meant 'stay' in the Somali language and Isha had taken it as an invocation. She had a connection, she said, with the red soil of that land. As well as her crops she had animals, a foot in two worlds, and among her people she was something of a leader. During national service in the army she had learned to read and write. In the romantic, nation-building exercises of the former communist government, she had been sent out to teach the pastoralists literacy and now people referred to her as 'teacher'. She had relished the job, she was patriotic, but beneath a heavy hooded brow, her hard eyes still held a faraway look: she had the patience and the steel of the nomad. Nomadism as a way of life, though, was on its last legs.

The clouds raced above, gathering, building and then burning off like the froth on a boiling pan. In the night, the sky flashed and crackled in the distance. But still no rain. The animals had mowed the desert until it was hard and flat, and the sand was cracked into little canyons. The thorn bushes had been nibbled spare, and the thorns turned from black to brown to white as the water left them. For days, the white clouds built and built, turned grey into rain-heads and blackened the earth with their shadow, but then a wind got up and the clouds sailed calmly east scattering only a few drops as they went.

The animals withered, their skin slack over bones too tired to keep looking for water or food, until they started to drop. The vultures whirled. And then the desert was spotted with carcasses, rotting to dust, until all that was left was a ribcage of fingers reaching upwards from the sand.

Prices in the market in Rebay started to jump. Isha heard it was the same in other towns. By the turn of the year 2011 staples were up eighty per cent. In earlier lean times, Isha had relied on the government that had brought maize, oil and trucks of water but now, under al-Shabaab, there was little. In Isha's view, life under the dictator Siad Barre had been good, all the politicians since had been hyenas. Sometimes al-Shabaab brought food to Rebay but usually it only gave it to its fighters. 'God will provide,' they told the people. But God was not omnipresent.

The radio said that aid was coming but Isha saw none. Due to a corruption scandal the US had stopped funding the World Food Programme, plus al-Shabaab was restricting the access of NGOs across much of the south, including Rebay. Instead the little aid that was being unloaded in Mogadishu pulled food prices lower than in al-Shabaab areas and for those who didn't own land or whose animals had already died, the exodus from the countryside began. Patterns of flight followed the grooves of memory: places people knew or had been before, or about which they had heard tell: enough of a story upon which to pin a thread of hope. Isha watched some go to the city while others looked south, to the camps. These were the people who were making the numbers in Dadaab jump and causing Nisho to worry.

In Rebay, those with animals still alive were circling in the bush, hunting for the barest shoots of greenery for their goats and camels. Each day, they had to search further. Al-Shabaab was taking the remaining cattle by force. Only the *Gu* rains of March stood now between hope and certain death.

When he was younger, Isha's husband had been stocky and short and his peers had nicknamed him '*Gab*', shorty. Now thicker with middle age, the steady attrition of the drought on his crops and live-stock had drawn itself in tired lines around his gentle eyes and drained the colour from his hair. Over three years, all twenty of his camels had to be sold for food. He and Isha had debated fiercely the sale of each one; it was a finely balanced decision of diminish-ing returns and among the most important judgements a pastoralist will ever be called upon to make. Not once had he considered working for anybody else. He was employer, not employee. Now, at a loss, Gab said goodbye to Isha and took a final, desperate, gamble. He walked resolutely out with their eldest son and the remaining goats and cattle into the bush, ten nights on foot, where he had found grazing in hard times before.

Isha stayed behind with the other five children, feeding them whatever she could find. The neighbours shared without words; everyone knew the situation. Isha cooked once a day, grinding sorghum with a stone to make porridge, and some days not even that.

For the past three years, hunger had become a normal thing. Isha was familiar with the bleeding gums, the inflamed limbs, the cramped pain of drinking, the torture when the empty stomach eats itself. When the mind achieves a lucidity departed from the body, perhaps closer to God, and the world acquires a glassy sheen. Isha knew the lethargy like an old friend; when the brain shuts down and desire sleeps and the love between a man and a woman goes. Maybe the man says 'they are your children' and leaves, but a woman cannot abandon her children. The people of Rebay looked at the sky and worried. They looked at each other and they had nothing to say. Before, when someone told a story, they stood. But a hungry man will just sit and cry. Hunger keeps you awake. You cannot sleep. It was said that the mind of a hungry person goes gradually mad.

But Isha had grown used to being hungry; it was not enough to make her leave. To leave meant to lose everything. If she went, no one would protect her land: it would go the way of all the others who fled before; there would be new claimants by sunrise. The refugees in Dadaab had long ago stopped sending emissaries to check on their property back home. If you asked about their former farms most would simply smile and shrug and say, 'Hawiye,' or 'Darod,' whichever of the large clans was not theirs; and thus the complicated history of the war was reduced to a single word. And so Isha placed her faith in God instead. When the nomad astronomers, the rain watchers of the place, said the rain was coming, she and the rest of the village wanted to believe them. It was easier to hope than to face the truth. 'The rain is coming,' they repeated to each other, like a consolation, even as the animals dropped.

Isha could keep going, so long as there was no news from the bush, from her husband with their safety net: the animals. No news allowed the imagination space to roam, to live beyond the hunger. With their crops and their animals, Isha's family had been well off, but if it didn't rain soon, they'd have neither. She wished her husband and son well and she girded herself to wait; she was determined to hold on as long as she could. She couldn't bear the humiliation of having to beg for food like a refugee. In her mind, she was rich, she was strong, she was proud. Three things that were all about to change.

7

Hawa Jube

Alone, and thus ineligible for a plot of his own, Guled needed to find a family to take him in. Some people charge rent to single men, others simply take a share of their rations. Noor's place was cramped, barely big enough for him to lie down himself. In N block, on the other side of the camp from block C3, Noor had heard of a woman he knew, also from Mogadishu, who was looking for a lodger. He took Guled to meet her.

They walked out to the very edge of Ifo camp, along the wide, sandy road from the central maidan past the service area of the camp: the WFP warehouses, the teachers' barracks behind a loose barbed-wire fence and the bright white-and-green chlorinated buildings of the hospital guarded by the laconic G4S private security guards who enjoy a monopoly protecting all aid agency buildings in the camp. The G4S employees are paid a mean wage, and they are often drunk, but it is a formal job, and as such, they must be Kenyans. This was the toughest billet: the gates to the hospital are usually swarming, no matter the hour of the day, and the guards had a habit of shouting.

The neighbouring rectangular blocks of the camp are less densely populated here, interspersed with patches of bush thick with green thorns. The border of the camp is marked by the graveyard where mourners have ringed the sad mounds of orange sand with thorns to keep the hyenas from digging up the corpses. N block is the last of the blocks of the formal camp, known as

Hawa Jube – named after a woman called Hawa (Somali and Arabic for Eve, the wife of Adam), who lived here and who was shaped like a bottle, Jube. To the north, behind a razor-wire fence, you could see the newly finished, empty overspill camp, Ifo 2, with its virgin roads, taps and shelters fitted for 40,000 and intended to decongest the other camps. To all the refugees, the very sight of the empty camp was an affront. Trembling in the heat in the distance, it made the foreground seem poorer, harsher in comparison. To the west was bush: dust and hyenas.

Hawa Jube is the tougher end of town, the bad neighbourhood. It already had a reputation for bandits – a reputation that wasn't helped by the slow accretion of a new slum, in the adjacent bush bordered by the cemetery on one side and the new Ifo 2 camp on the other. With the formal camps full up, this was where the newer arrivals had encroached on the bush, and carved their own space out of the desert, beyond the UN's original lines in the sand. They were the people of Guled's generation who arrived with restless reddened eyes: the war breathing down their neck. They stripped all the trees, and now new huts made of bent sticks and woven thorns were going up, as if in a property boom. The blocks of Hawa Jube are numbered N1, N2, N3 ... up to N9, so the newcomers had christened their informal slum 'N Zero'. The UN called these informal settlements 'self-settled areas'. It was a nicer name than that given to the illegal town on the edge of Dagahaley camp: the inhabitants called that one '*Bulo Bacte*', the carcass dump.

Over ten thousand people were living now in Bulo Bacte and N Zero. The wind tore at the frail shelters and the people who lived on the very edge of N Zero avoided looking at the wilderness, they turned inwards. To face the constant snapping wind that bore a fine charge of sand out of the relentless yellow sky was painful. It hurt the eyes. When another line of huts pushed the boundary of the camp further out, it was as though civilization had made a little victory.

The dividing line between the slum of N Zero and the formal camp was in the geometry. The houses of N9 were grouped in squares and backed on to each other. N Zero had no pattern. Guled's new home was a large compound on the corner of block N9 bordered on two sides by an alleyway. Behind it the road ran out to Ifo 2 and the cemetery, into the chaos of N Zero. It was a square homestead with an enormous satellite dish in the middle of a hard-packed compound and a round-domed hut where most afternoons various men sat on threadbare mats engaged in the habitual male activity of the camp: chewing the narcotic herb *khat* and drinking tea. The satellite dish no longer caught the news or the football: the wires had been chopped and sold. The woman herself lived in a tin-roofed house at one end of an L-shaped mud building containing a line of three rooms. She let Guled have the last one in return for the expectation that he would share his rations and help her out. She had a clutch of children and her husband was in Somalia. Guled didn't ask too many questions. She told him to call her 'auntie'.

For over a month Guled had trailed around the bus stops and garages asking for work that he knew how to do: driving, but without success. For a young man without connections, a new-comer to boot, the labour market in Ifo camp was all but impenetrable. He was desperate to raise the money for Maryam's fare. When he could afford to call, the voice on the other end of the line sounded increasingly frantic, frustrated with his slow progress.

Near his new lodgings, Guled discovered another small market where, untroubled by the mafia-like controls of Bosnia, he was able to begin his apprenticeship as a porter. Opposite the hospi-tal is the food distribution centre for the whole of Ifo camp where

Guled had collected and sold his rations. By the exit gates is a bat-tered-steel turquoise box with a narrow slit in it barely wide enough for a single sheet of paper. It reads, for the benefit of the literate, in English and Somali: 'Complaint/Suggestion Box, Ifo camp'. And if you knock, it rings hollow. Next to it, in a rough line like a beauty contest, the porters jostled for business. Those with big families could not carry all their rations, so they traded some of their food in return for help with transporting it home. It presented another chance for a boy with only his strength to sell to earn a little extra.

According to the laws of supply and demand, the food sold by the refugees is among the cheapest food in all of Kenya. WFP can source less than a fifth of the monthly 8,000 tonnes of food locally. The rest must come across the sea and up the long dusty road from Mombasa in great clanking convoys of trucks that take three days to reach this burning spot. In the rainy season the journey can take six weeks. The majority of food is in-kind donations, surplus wheat and maize from the USA. It weighs heavily on the market price for the whole region. A family in need of some cash like Guled for a phone call or a finger of sugar will sell a few kilos here to the traders. Next to their scales, large white sacks printed with WFP or USAID 'not for resale' steadily fill up again on their way to fetch higher prices inside Somalia or back again, to Nairobi.

For the food that stays in the camp, Guled discovered that the rule of the market is 'one kilo per ton'. The customers give the porters one kilo of rice or flour per fifty-kilogram sack trans-ported. A fifty-kilo sack is called 'one ton' and it is the same as the entire food parcel for a family size 7. Guled watched the porters carry and did some calculations in his head. If he worked hard at portering, he thought, he could raise the fare for Maryam to come within a week. But first he had to lift the sacks.

Now, boldly, he walked up to the other boys and tried. The

smaller family sizes, 3 and 4, up to twenty-nine kilos, he managed okay. But family size 5 and above, his body let him down. Thirty-five kilos was over half his own body weight. He watched in awe as other boys shouldered fifty and staggered off to walk perhaps a kilometre to someone's home. Guled was slender but he was determined. He came back the next day and tried again. And the next, for a week. No advance on twenty-nine kilos. 'Is this the friend of Noor?' The other porters made fun of him. 'Why is he killing himself?'

In the end, Maryam ran out of patience. When he confessed to his mother-in-law on the phone the kind of work he was doing she worried that he might injure himself and told him not to do it again. 'Don't break your back,' she warned him. 'We'll pay for the trip.'

Several weeks later, on 11 January 2011 Maryam was suddenly there. When she stepped out of the packed minibus there was something different about her, he thought. She was a big girl, but her curves were changed somehow: her body announced her secret.

'You're pregnant!' he said. 'You didn't tell me!'

Maryam grinned. She was five months by then. But her smile didn't last. The poverty and destitution of Hawa Jube, the place that Guled had described in such positive terms, shocked her. It was a bad start to their new life. Guled's small room of mud and tin in block N9 was barely big enough for the furnishings he had managed to scavenge in anticipation of her arrival: a second-hand mattress that he laid on the earth, and a mosquito net. And now, Maryam informed him that her mother, persuaded by Guled's description and anxious for her daughter, had decided to come too. When she arrived in a month's time, he feared he would have to sleep outside.

The weather made Maryam uncomfortable; she was having a

difficult pregnancy. She hated the heat and the dust. She drank water constantly and demanded Guled bring her juice – that cost money. Most of all, she mistrusted the increasing clamour of poor and desperate people from unfamiliar clans who were her new neighbours in N Zero. Like Guled, she had seen displaced people in Mogadishu in the cathedral, in the makeshift camps. They were beggars. She didn't consider herself one of them.

Maryam was registered along with 9,861 other newcomers in January, 9,285 in February, and many more arrived unofficially. These were historically high numbers; if they didn't slow down, soon there were likely to be riots. Yet still the people came. The drought was unrelenting: the sand blew in ever tighter circles and the sky acquired a tinted brown colour behind which the sun glowed white with menace.

8

A Friday in Nairobi

In the green hills of central Kenya, far from the dry red plain of the north, a light rain fell. In the capital, it slid down the glass sides of the skyscrapers and trickled along the neat concrete pathways of the offices of the aid agencies. It collected in the potholes of the streets. After twenty-eight days of record heat peaking at thirty-two degrees, the downpour on 18 March was a blessed relief. From the air-conditioned offices in Nairobi, it was difficult to imagine still-parched Dadaab, where the temperature was hitting highs of forty-five and the UN staff in the camps were struggling to cope.

As the warnings from Dadaab reached Nairobi, the agency people watched the rain slide down their windows and contemplated the situation across the region. Somalia was too dangerous for them to work, even, in most cases, to visit. They relied on reports from their partners and sub-contractors in the 'field' whom they regarded with varying levels of mistrust. The reports from the field were not good. For six months, since August 2010, the news from Somalia had been getting steadily worse. Médecins Sans Frontières (MSF) in Somalia had been broadcasting an impending crisis since June and the acute malnutrition maps coming out of the Famine Early Warning Systems (FEWS) offices were blanketed red. The next shade, black, was famine.

The FEWS Food Security Alert for 15 March 2011 said: 'substantial assistance programs should be implemented,' and

warned that 'large scale contingency planning should begin immediately given that the failure of the March–May rains would result
in a major crisis.'

The agency people forwarded the email to their headquarters
and to the donor countries but nobody, it seemed, was listening.
The aid they asked for didn't come. In Nairobi, they had meetings
and worried about what to do.

'The map of Somalia turns red every year,' one of the more
experienced among them said. Crisis in Somalia was a normal
thing: 'all we can do is hope for the best.' The warnings had almost
ceased to have any meaning; in political circles distant suffering had
long ago become simply another kind of noise. In London or
Washington or Geneva, an official who had actually read the FEWS
alert email said that the latest warning 'was not useful to unlock
resources'; the rich governments needed numbers, lives on the
brink. The timing was inconvenient, hadn't they seen the news?
On 11 March, an earthquake and tsunami had devastated Japan.

Some of the agency people in Nairobi felt bad they couldn't
help. Others got angry and went in search of things to blame: 'It's
because of the US Patriot Act and the OFAC [US Office of
Foreign Assets Control] sanctions that criminalize us for paying
fees to al-Shabaab,' they said. Headquarters didn't appreciate the
compromises that had to be struck in order to work in these areas.
Or, 'It's because of Haiti – the world can't cope with more than
one disaster at a time.' Or, 'It's because the industry is geared
around disasters, a famine averted doesn't generate profile.' But the
cynical ones didn't bother to find excuses, for they had heard it all
before: early warning was a waste of time – there would have to
be people dying on television before the money from rich governments would flow. And when it finally did, it would come in
a flood. And the markets for the local farmers would collapse
entirely. The same thing happened every time.

What the aid workers didn't stop to consider was the complicity of some of their number in the looming disaster. Foreign aid has always been a key ingredient in Somalia's conflict economy, an object of taxation and fighting. The year before, a UN monitoring report had accused the WFP of colluding with Somali NGOs in diverting over half of official assistance. The price of the agencies' corruption and complacency was now being felt. The US had stopped funding the WFP in Somalia as a result of the scandal. Now there was suspicion in some quarters that the UN was simply crying wolf.

As the battle of Mogadishu pounded on and AMISOM and the TFG slowly pushed back al-Shabaab street by street, the city that had so recently emptied of people fleeing the fighting now filled up again: hundreds of thousands ran headlong from the countryside into the war in search of help. The displaced constructed plastic and paper huts in the settlements as Guled had done and watched as the urban warlords and fake NGOs took the lion's share of the aid for themselves and sold it in Bakaara market. Some agencies were so desperate to be on the frontline that they were indiscriminate in their distributions, sometimes giving over three-quarters of supplies to the very warlords fuelling the conflict in order to reach their 'customers'. They turned a blind eye, wrote down their losses to 'corruption', ticked their boxes and trumpeted their impact while, back home, their over-enthused cadres shook people down in the street for more cash.

Meanwhile, in the countryside, in Bay and Bakool, Gedo and in Juba regions, the animals grew thinner and the people too. The European Union had spent hundreds of millions of dollars in recent years on irrigation and 'food security' projects in the riverine areas all, it seemed now, without any effect. By the end of March the ground was still dry and food prices were up 130 per cent. The land groaned with a great unease as people gathered up their possessions and readied to flee. The UN said 2.4 million were at risk: a third of the population of the whole country.

FEWS sent another warning saying, 'famine possible if April rains fail,' but still the rich governments did nothing. The technical parts of the humanitarian system were working, delivering the warnings, but the political side was either sceptical or asleep. The agency people in Nairobi didn't know what else to try. They'd sent eleven warnings and requests for funds since August 2010. But there was no glory in a famine averted. So they did what they usually did on a Friday.

At five o'clock sharp, they left their cool offices and their computers glowing with warnings and got into their cars – so loud on the outside, so quiet on the inside – and the doors of the vehicles closed with a luxurious 'thud'. Their drivers piloted them through the streets wet and slick to some house party or restaurant glittering with laughter and money, and the lights of the city sparkled in the puddles.

9

Maiden Voyage

By May in Somalia, it was clear the *Gu* rains were not going to come. Over 20,000 people had arrived in Dadaab during the past two months. N Zero and Bulo Bacte now had over 15,000 residents each. The hospital in Hawa Jube was struggling to cope and had called in reinforcements to deal with the drought victims. The stabilization centre that normally looked after one or two children was suddenly full. And then the extra ward they had cleared for the malnourished kids was full too. Among the starving children, Maryam was having a long and complicated labour.

Guled paced the narrow hospital courtyard in the moonlight as he listened to the sounds of the maternity ward, the disembodied cries into the night. The sleepy G4S guards watched him go up and down. Finally, on 9 May, a baby girl weighing 4.3 kilograms was delivered safely by Caesarean section. But instead of being grateful, Maryam was furious. She felt she had been cheated of a natural birth.

'No lifting,' the doctor told her.

'How I am supposed to live?' she complained to Guled. A woman in the camp needed her strength: cooking, laundry, fetching food rations. 'When you have a C-section you are disabled,' she said. She blamed the climate, the heat and dust of Dadaab that had caused her to drink so much and that, she thought, had made the baby too big. And she cursed her decision to come.

Maryam and her mother struggled to see the benefits of the

camp. 'It's only the bullets that are the problem back home,' Maryam complained. In Mogadishu, the fighting was still intense, but once a week or so, irregular trucks carried people back there. Going home to visit relatives, to do business, to check if a house was still standing. 'At least in Mogadishu we had a washing machine!' she said. And the muttering about going home began.

Half a mile away in Bosnia, Mahat was unhappy too. There was a new gang in town. Seven young boys who had helped each other to purchase shoe-shining equipment were steadily cornering the market. At the end of the day the seven of them rented one motorbike to take them home to N Zero. 'We are the *kala-mashorto!*' they called out as they rattled past. Mahat didn't know the meaning but he was grudgingly impressed. 'They are young and tough. They know how to make business,' he conceded. 'If you work hard, the world will love you.' Mahat was forced to charge as little as five shillings ($0.06) for buffing the eternal dust off a pair of shoes.

The Imams in the mosques were preaching compassion, telling the people to help the indigent newcomers who were coming to beg in the market every day. But Mahat wasn't feeling charitable. 'I cannot help them if I am near to begging myself,' he said. 'I was wondering at them, why not work instead of begging?' Many of the wealthier traders felt the same. When the new arrivals who slept among the thorn bushes of N Zero without enough water to drink, let alone wash, appeared in the market, they held their noses against the smell and turned away. There was one shop owner, though, who didn't. He was Professor White Eyes.

'When I saw a mother and father carrying seven children walking barefoot in the market, I felt like crying,' he said. 'I felt bad and so I resolved to help them. They go all round at the beginning and then at the end they come to me because they know that I would give them a few extra onions, or a potato.' White Eyes had several reasons to be sympathetic. He knew what it was like to be marginalized. He was from a minority clan, the Habr Ade: 'Our whole tribe could fit in one car!' And he had a close and personal relationship with *nasib* – luck or fate. Up until the age of seven he had been completely blind.

When, as an infant, his eyes crusted over after a measles infection, he heard his mother say, 'It's better for him to die than to go blind.' But after a while he stopped hearing her voice. His grandmother fled with him to Dadaab. Several years later, he was sitting on the sand listening to children playing when he felt the skin on his right eye cracking and a little light seeping in. He tried to pull apart the other and, to his joy, it split open. Of course, there was no money for spectacles, but if he sat very close to the blackboard and squinted he could learn to read and write.

His eyes are off centre and still partly cloudy, as though holding a tiny splash of milk. His doctorate he earned through his first hand study of survival in the ways of Ifo camp; he is, he wants everyone to know, a 'professor of daily bread'. Ever since he left school, because doing homework by torchlight hurt his eyes, he has been a fixture of Bosnia. From humble beginnings fetching water, he progressed to wheelbarrow work and then selling ice creams from a mobile fridge: 'tip-tops' bought in bulk from a factory in Bosnia. 'The ladies of Somalia, they love it so much!' His talent for talking to the women meant business boomed.

With profits of 1,000 shillings a day ($12) he rented a shop and opened the grocery. Officially, all the land of the camp has been leased from the host community by the United Nations for the benefit of the refugees, but long ago the majority clans monopolized the permits for stalls in the market and a property market evolved just like in any Wild West town. Professor White Eyes rented his space from one of the major businessmen and traded in a specialist niche: serving the lower-caste clans who were happy for a chance to patronize the business of one of their own. Even shopping in Bosnia is a tribal affair.

While life at the bottom of the food chain for Nisho, Mahat and Guled was made harder by what the aid agencies were calling 'the influx' of drought victims, for those who didn't depend on smuggling or their own cheap labour, it was a boon. More people meant more business. White Eyes was saving money for a dowry. He had in his sights a strikingly beautiful, illiterate girl called Habibo whose mind he intended to shape. If the influx kept up like this, he thought, she might be his wife by the end of the year.

Nisho, meanwhile, was rapidly losing patience with the market. 'My back will give out soon,' he told his friends, but the real reason was something else. Portering was fine for the small expenses of daily life, but it couldn't cope with unforeseen events like the expenses of marriage or a medical bill. Nisho's mother was in a bad way again and the witchdoctor's treatment would be expensive.

Nisho's mum is a short, crooked woman with a misshapen head that sits unevenly on her neck. Her speckled eyes are set deep in her skull as though driven in with a stave. One of them doesn't fully open. She was fifty-one years old then and she shared the compound with her son. When, in the night, she shouted to herself or to other people, 'What have I done to you? Why do you want to kill me?' and banged the window or the door of their hut, Nisho had to calm her down and remind her that there was no one there. 'It's just Satan,' he said, or, as she preferred to think, 'it's just *shetani*' – spirits. In the daytime Nisho sometimes tied her by the wrists to a neem tree in their compound to stop her running away. Once, he found her three miles away in the bush.

'What are you doing?' he demanded.

'I just wanted to visit where I used to come with the goats,' she said.

'Well, you could have told me where you were going!'

At the hospital they had no suggestions, so he had tried the witchdoctor who lived in A2. It had been his mum's idea. 'I don't believe in his medicine,' said Nisho. 'But if you believe a medicine is going cure you, then it will.' And that was what she believed.

The witchdoctor lived in a normal house, but he had another hut in his compound where he did his work. He called it his office. People visited him there and told him their problems and he scattered objects on the floor or consulted a book and offered his diagnosis. Nisho didn't like going there. The man gave him the creeps. The strict Muslims called him names, insults like 'Christian'; superstition was frowned upon in Islam but the wealth of the witchdoctor betrayed the pastoralists' enduring faith in the old pagan ways. The witchdoctor was tall and black, walked like a camel and had a rare gold tooth. He was known for dressing entirely in one colour. The last time Nisho had counted out the 6,000 shillings ($75) he had begged and saved for his mother's treatment, the man was clothed completely in black.

Nisho had been sent to the bush to gather leaves from a special tree whose name he didn't know. His mother told him later that while he was gone, the witchdoctor had recited verses of the Koran over water and told her to drink it while he slaughtered first a white hen and then a black one. When Nisho brought the leaves, the witchdoctor mixed them into a paste with honey and butter and poured it into the small blue plastic lid of a water bottle. Nisho's mother drank. There was muttering and smoke and some words she didn't understand. But for sometime afterwards she slept through the night. She even cooked. But now she was back to shouting and waking up the neighbours; Nisho needed to find the money for another treatment.

He had heard that there was more cash to be made travelling on the trucks rather than unloading them and he badgered the people he knew for a position. It was only when he got the sudden news that a truck was going to Somalia the following day and he had accepted the job that he reflected on what he had agreed to. All he had heard of Somalia was war and he feared he would not return alive. But a small part of him wanted to travel, to see Somalia, his family's homeland, and to glimpse something of the world other than the flat horizon of the camp.

At four p.m. on the day of departure, he climbed into the cab of a long ten-wheeler truck with a cargo of cooking utensils, most likely repurposed from the United Nations, bound for Mogadishu. The driver, a forty-year-old clean shaven man, large and fat, and his assistant, a young, skinny, confident boy, had both just come from Somalia. Nisho's habitual restlessness was not suited to confinement in a vehicle. Forced to sit, Nisho will talk or sing or hum to himself, his fingers working a small padlock key attached to his trousers by a rope. He will roll his head and crick his neck and look around, peering into everything, his mouth hanging open in enquiry. 'I am used to carrying fifty kilos,' he once shouted, 'I cannot sit idle!' He had underestimated how much portering had shaped him. Up in the cab, he shifted in his seat and calmed his fears of fighting and his hopes of the money he would earn by losing himself in gazing at the landscape, the unending arid bush of the border country.

The Dadaab camps are surrounded by a fierce desert across which, without water or milking animals, it is often suicide to walk. The road south and west to Nairobi is interrupted with checkpoints and a bridge, the de facto border between Somalia and Kenya, over the fat wide brown loops of the Tana River. On the bridge, at the checkpoint they call *halak* – 'the cobra' – the Kenyan police sometimes collect money from everyone without a movement pass. On other days, they throw refugees attempting to escape Dadaab in jail before returning them to the camp. In many ways, things haven't changed since the '*Kipande*' system of the British who controlled the movement of the nomadic Somalis in the rangelands with their hated 'pink slips'. The camp is a bounded world. To send your imagination out beyond the horizon of the plain is a dangerous enterprise, fraught with disappointment, and Nisho had blocked the idea from his mind. The way to Somalia, however, is clear.

A straight road runs through red-and-brown brush, the soil thinned and sifted into furrows of dust, to a little border town struggling on the plain called Liboi. Its sole landmark is the bare rusting pin of the abandoned telecoms tower. On the Somali side is Dhobley.

As the truck crossed the border, Nisho's face was glued to the window, alert for signs of conflict. There were none. The first time Nisho's feet touched the soil of his native country, he felt a strange sense of peace. By the roadside in Dhobley, the three travellers cooked rice on the ground and then the boys climbed up on top of the load to keep watch during the night. Annoyingly, his new colleague went straight into a deep sleep while Nisho struggled to stay awake, under the stars and alone in this new country that his mother had talked about his whole life.

All the next day as they drove through the stunted thorn trees, they passed people coming the other way, weak and malnourished, women and children mostly. Some, Nisho was shocked to see, without any clothes at all. He had never seen people in such a state before. The memory haunted him. And the graves that flecked the roadside through the forest left him pensive and quiet.

At a place called Afmadow they met their first al-Shabaab checkpoint. Old men in military uniform and beards – the younger ones were doing the fighting – took six million Somali

shillings from the young boy and gave him a stamped letter of permission and a message: 'Tell the driver to let his beard grow.' The
fat driver laughed but that night he didn't shave. They were in al-
Shabaab territory now and they were headed for their stronghold,
the source of all the sugar and contraband that Nisho unloaded in
Bosnia most nights, the port city of Kismayo.

Near the city, the convoys of military trucks brimming with soldiers increased. At that time, Kismayo was on high alert in the grip
of rumours that US, French and British forces were capitalizing on
the drought to squeeze al-Shabaab. Unattributed airstrikes and
mystery shelling that seemed to come from the sea were common
and in the city al-Shabaab scanned the sky, listening for the whisper of drones.

In the distance, above the rusting corrugated roofs and the
ancient limed walls of the old Swahili port city, Nisho spotted a
band of blue that at first he thought was 'moving water'. Then he
changed his mind and considered it to be 'water that had stayed for
a long time'. The driver told him it was the ocean and Nisho felt
proud of his country for the first time; whatever its problems, at
least it had a beauty to speak of.

The next day they turned north, to *Xamar* – the local name for
Mogadishu meaning 'the red place', perhaps referring to the earth,
perhaps to the skins of the cosmopolitan people from India, Persia,
Zanzibar who have inhabited the ancient city for millennia. In a
ruin that had once been a petrol station, and still sold fuel siphoned
out of huge steel drums, they spent the night. Nisho asked the
driver why all the buildings they were passing had collapsed and
the whole final day of driving was taken up with the answer; it was
the first time Nisho had heard the history of the war narrated from
beginning to end. When the long truck came out of the tall trees
and onto the dusty white soil of the coast near Mogadishu, Nisho
braced himself for gunfire.

The truck aimed for Bakaara market. For Nisho, who had only heard the name on the radio as a place of constant mortar fire, the word itself spelled fear. The truck bounced along the shelled roads coated with white dust and littered with the burnt-out carcasses of cars. Huge beige AMISOM armoured cars, of a design pioneered in Soweto and Baghdad, crawled along. In the harbour, tankers and cargo ships waited like basking sharks for their turn to dock at the port while the dark windowless sockets of beachfront hotels watched them, like skulls. The tree-lined ocean boulevard was now a parade of stumps amputated for firewood. Rubbish smoked in little piles on the roadside. The city appeared calm and stable to him that day, not tense. Apart from the ruins everywhere, there was life, it seemed, threading its way through the destruction. When they dismounted in Bakaara the place was bustling with money.

Bakaara was not one market as such but a whole district, with different streets for different goods. One street sold only medicines and the walls were painted with pictures of pills, another sold shoes, another meat, another vegetables, charcoal, scrap metal, weapons. In the place they called *Cir Toogte* – literally 'sky shooter' – hundreds of traders hawked AK-47s, pistols, RPGs, mortars and ammunition which eager customers tested by firing into the air. An AK-47 at that time cost $350 and bullets fifty cents each. Despite the official arms embargo, the regular European and American shipments of guns to the Transitional Federal Government kept the price low. There were around half a million unregistered small arms in Somalia; nearly every gun found its way to Bakaara eventually.

In a wide, dusty open area, the truck pulled up. Nearby another truck offloaded rice onto blue handcarts. Stacks of yellow jerrycans filled another cart. In comparison to the market Nisho worked back home, the volume, the noise, the colour, was 'double

Bosnia'. Mogadishu seemed peaceful, it was not like the media reports that Nisho had seen and heard and the experience challenged his faith in television: 'The problem is not just Somalia, all over the world you have the media saying one thing and the truth is completely different,' he said. In fact, he was just lucky.

A few days later, on 2 May, the TFG and AMISOM launched the 'Bakaara offensive' to oust al-Shabaab from the market. For two months there would be almost daily battles, sniper fire, mortars and suicide attacks as the frontline moved every few hours. The TFG and AMISOM failed to take the market, but not before they had lost a senior Ugandan commander, the Interior Minister, fifty soldiers to al-Shabaab's thirty, and at least eighty civilians.

While the driver disappeared into the city, the boys took it in turns to look after the truck and explore the market. The skinny assistant was away for a long time. He knew the place, and clearly he had means for he came back sporting new clothes: a shirt, trousers and a hat.

'I bought clothes,' the boy said to Nisho. 'Why don't you?'

'With what money?' Nisho thought to himself. When it was his turn, Nisho never let the truck out of his sight. He talked to no one. His memory of Mogadishu was the food that he bought with the small amount of Somali shillings the driver had given him: injera, pasta and all types of fruit, many that he didn't know. At night he lay rigid in the hotel in the market listening to what he discovered in the morning was the whoosh and roar of aeroplanes. He was glad they were going back to Kenya that day.

The road south was clogged with dozens of minibuses, trucks and cars, all brimful of people leaving. The driver had strict instructions not to carry any passengers; the truck was supposed to be returning empty to Kenya. But by Afmadow the human flood was impossible to ignore: hundreds and hundreds, walking doggedly south. 'If you look at them, you will not ask them anything,' Nisho said. The whole story was written on their grey faces: the desperation, the hunger, the journey. The driver was a good man and they managed to fit around a hundred into the bed of the ten-wheeler and took them as far as the border.

It had been five trying days to Mogadishu and five risky days back again for which Nisho was finally paid 500 shillings ($6). He had been expecting at least 3,000, for the witchdoctor. He was furious. The truck owner claimed that this had been only a trial run, that there would be more next time. But contemplating those bumpy dangerous roads thick with misery, Nisho loudly told his friends, 'never again'. And from that point, his expression increasingly took on a kind of tragic weariness: the door to an imaginary room had been closed.

When the truck finally rumbled into Bosnia his heart sang. He pointed and babbled out the names of familiar places, as if seeing them for the first time. He was delighted to be coming back safe, 'where my work is'. It was the longest he'd ever been away from the camp and the only time he hadn't slept in the hut with his mother. She was pleased to see him. There was a lesson in his maiden departure from the camp: 'Ifo felt like home.'

10

The Silent March

The kindness shown by the driver of Nisho's truck was in fact an exception. Many of those moving along the roads at that time were not so compassionate towards this new wave of displaced people. A car from Kismayo to the camps was $100, from Barhdeere in Gedo region it was now $200. People were selling food, animals, all they had for a lift. Those without money, walked. From Luuq, Dinsoor, Baidoa, Bu'ale, Jilib and Jamame, they came. Ragged groups moving silently through the bush found others, joined forces, and soon there were crowds, whole villages, thousands of people dragging themselves, their children and each other along the roads. These were the people that Nisho had passed on the road south. He didn't know it then, but among them was his future wife, Billai, and ninety-three others from the village of Salidley. Another of those walking towards the border, her hope broken and her pride in shreds, was Isha.

It was at the beginning of June, when the first child in the village of Rebay died, that people began to stir. News from Isha's husband came soon after. A boy who had been with the herders in the bush for the past three months brought a message: 'The animals are dying and the others are going also. Your husband and son cannot come here, they have nothing and they feel ashamed.' With forty cattle gone, Isha decided it was time.

For three years as the militants had taxed the community into privation, there had been no help. But as the situation in Rebay became critical, even al-Shabaab showed compassion. The group had a network of social workers who kept an eye on the community. In Rebay, the social worker was a tall dark man who spoke the Rahanweyn *af-Maay* dialect. He knew everything, including which families had nothing left. In other areas, al-Shabaab prevented people from going to Kenya to seek help from the infidels, but the tall dark man was not so cruel. Isha and her neighbours didn't fear to tell him their plans: they were desperate. When he heard, he gave the families who were leaving a twenty-five kilo sack of rice saying, 'Take this and go to the camps.'

Isha packed one cooking pot, one kettle, one cup, one plate, one twenty-litre jerrycan full of water, one mat and five children, and then along with seven other families on the edge, she said goodbye to the neighbours who still had camels. Camels allowed you to try and stick it out a while longer, although many of the neighbours would leave, too, in the end. She took 'no books, no photos, no memories', she would later recall.

The plain was hot and dry. The low scrub provided little shade. They walked when it was cool, by moonlight, until the children wailed and would not go on and then they'd make a fire, some tea, maybe a little food. The seven families shared one donkey cart. When Isha carried her youngest daughter on her back, she put the twenty-litre jerrycan on the cart, taking turns. When the jerrycan got to about half full, they would have to beg to get it filled again. 'It was hard to carry, so hard, but your children will die of thirst if you don't do it.' During the heat of the day Isha arranged the children in a row, their heads on the mat, their feet resting on the sand, their thin little bodies inside a circle of thorns to keep the lions out.

After the town of Saakow where they begged a little maize, the ground was unfamiliar. For three nights the seven families wandered lost in a forest of tall trees and cacti, convinced that they would die. Isha was wasting away, walking on nothing; the food and water was running low. Hunger made her terror worse: that her children would die before they could get to the refugee camp. Finally, by chance, they came upon a road and, defeated now, they sat down to await their fate. They decided, if no one passed by soon, that would be the end of it and they would bury their children and each other among the foreign trees.

And then occurred one of the many divine moments that people walking out of Somalia would recount, a miracle, but for the grace of which they would not be sitting here, telling the tale. Almost immediately, a group of people came walking down the forest track. 'Are you trying to find the refugee camps?' they asked. They took the men who had strength to walk to the nearest town and sent them back with hot food and with directions to the main road at Afmadow.

Forced to start walking again, the children were complaining and dragging. The sand had taken all the skin from their feet. So Isha took a small piece of cloth, wetted it with the valuable water and wrapped a child's red raw soles and gave it a rest on the donkey cart while the others walked, each one taking their turn. They were in a bad way. The adults took to scaring them: 'There's a lion coming! Don't sit or relax, keep moving!' although they themselves walked slowly, conserving energy. It was the same with the others they met along the way and so, quietly, the group grew bigger and bigger: a silent battalion, marching.

Somewhere on that road, at the same time, perhaps part of Isha's column, were thirty families from a leper colony near Jilib who had walked for fifteen days, sleeping in abandoned homes. They had the lightness of death about them. One said, 'When a human being has something maybe they are afraid and keep themselves separate, but when you have nothing you can move anywhere and you are less scared about yourself. You are free.' But when the group met the al-Shabaab checkpoint at Afmadow and the men in black asked, 'Where are you going?' the refugees feared to admit the truth: to Kenya, to the infidels. The males among them were ordered to return and fight for their country and the rest of the people took to the bush. Al-Shabaab turned back many.

The refugees learned to avoid the roads in the government areas, closer to Dhobley, as well; armed men of all stripes were a menace. One group of refugees stopped by government soldiers was robbed and held at gunpoint through the night. The men and women were separated and in the morning when the women returned, 'their clothes were ripped and their faces were sad,' and then they carried on their journey. Rape of asylum seekers was epidemic. And they might have considered themselves the fortunate ones: they were alive. Whole families were left behind. 'The animals go first,' said one old man, 'it's the children next.' Over ten thousand children were dying each month by then, many of them buried along the way: little mounds beside the road, foot-long bumps in the sand.

Isha's little troop from Rebay were lucky. None of them was raped, and none of them was left behind. Eighteen days, Isha counted until, finally, their huge crowd, the adults at the back, picking up the children, arrived at the town of Dhobley.

An elder came and met them on the road, 'Don't worry,' he said. 'No more walking. UNHCR will take you to the camps from here, and you will eat very soon.' It was just as well. The valiant donkey was on strike. He had had no water the whole way and at Dhobley he finally gave up; they decided to leave him there.

At that time the Somali telegraph was in full cry, with lists of the villages on the move gathered and broadcast down the line to the camps; nearly one thousand arriving every day now. 'People from here, and there, and so and so, spotted on the road!' The refugees who had relatives on the way sent out parties to meet the newcomers and to search the police stations of Liboi and Dhobley. To the police on both sides of the border, the influx was a once in a lifetime chance to get rich. Many people only arrived at the camps after two or even three attempts, having been turned back by al-Shabaab and then robbed by TFG or Kenyan police. Again, Isha's journey was unusual.

At the camp, a committee of existing refugees organized themselves to help the newcomers, cooking food and making collections of money and clothes. Although five, six, seven UN trucks were bringing people from Dhobley every day, it was taking over a month for new refugees to get cooking utensils, blankets and tents and nearly two weeks to receive the first food rations. Wrangling between the UN and the Kenyan government was still keeping the new Ifo 2 camp closed. As always with humanitarian emergencies, it is the people on the ground who are the first responders. The internationals, if they come, are always late.

When Isha's bus stopped on the main road, the older refugees gave her and the kids blankets and showed them to a tree, under which they would sleep with half a dozen other families for the next three days. In a makeshift house in the new suburb of N Zero belonging to someone distantly related to them by clan whom they had never met, Isha's children ate unground American yellow maize for the first time but they were too hungry to complain.

When the family was strong enough, they stretched a plastic sheet they had been given over a frame of sticks gathered from the bush and set it in a little spot of cleared sand next to the others. There were close to 400,000 people in Dadaab now and nearly 25,000 in N Zero, and the frontier of the city crept a little further towards the hyenas and the bush. Daily, the plain was studded with numberless female figures stripping thorns for houses, their coloured dresses bright against the implacable brown sky, the wind whipping their skirts about them.

11

Muna and Monday

The wind that sweeps the plain during the Hagar season is called *kharif*, and it is strong enough to loosen the tethers of a tent. It blew sand into the huts of N Zero, and it pulled and tugged at the long line of new UN white plastic tents on the edge of Hawa Jube, making them vibrate. By June there had still been no major airlift of aid, no international response. Still, near the hospital, the UN had set up a temporary complex to register the extraordinary numbers arriving. Along with the constant droning of the wind, the guy ropes made an eerie rhythmic whipping like the snapping of halyards against masts in a harbour. It elevated the tension as the hungry people huddled in their lines against the wind.

After three days under the trees and thirteen in her makeshift house, with barely enough to eat and no more than three litres of water a day given out from UN trucks, Isha had heard a message broadcast from a loudspeaker calling new arrivals to the reception centre. And she and the children had been waiting there since five a.m. There was a backlog: 2,000, 3,000 a day were being registered, but 31,109 new refugees had reached Dadaab along with Isha that month.

People were shaking the fence now. G4S guards struck the metal links with batons. 'Get back!' It was the only registration centre for the three camps – all the procedures had been amalgamated – and some people had walked for up to twenty miles across Dadaab to reach the place. Along the line, community leaders marched up and down with clipboards and lists waving their arms and barking at the people, 'Yow! Yow! Yow!' It was the same command with which they herded goats. A man with a megaphone arrived and then police, with low-slung guns. The hubbub simmered down.

The G4S guards were collecting bribes of between six and twenty-four dollars a head to get into the reception centre during the emergency. Although Isha saw money changing hands, no one asked her for any; she assumed it was obvious from her face and the state of her children that she had none. Eventually, they filed through the wire gate and took their place on narrow wooden benches beneath an awning. Isha wore a long dress with a tight-fitting hijab that folded over her temples pinched by the sun. Her face was smooth and reddened from exposure, like fired clay. The angles of her bones showed beneath her skin. In their small brown sandals her toes had shed their nails, but her eyes were no longer filmed with panic. All her children were alive. Sixteen days after they had arrived in Dadaab, international help was finally at hand.

Out of the holding pen and into the first in the long chain of tents, Isha sat down with her children to watch the welcome video, a new innovation since Guled had come. Somali music accompanied the face of a man who spoke slowly in Somali: 'Welcome to Dadaab, the largest refugee camp in the world. While in Dadaab you are under the protection of the Government of Kenya and UNHCR. Today you will begin the process of integration with camp life.'

This was the moment of encounter. The meeting point between the two contradictory arcs of the twenty-first century: the rule of law that had spawned the international humanitarian system, and its other legacy: the chaos unleashed by the end of the colonial project to subjugate and carve up the globe. It was also the moment of the bargain. When you traded your name for a ration card number. When you surrendered your autonomy to be processed into the faceless bureaucracy of the UN system. Isha surrendered willingly. She needed the protection of the camp. Therefore the camp was good. And she was grateful.

Isha's name and those of her children were entered into the manifest on the computer. A wristband showed their family size in permanent marker. They smeared their fingerprints on the paper one by one and then a string around their upper arm graded their malnourishment. Isha had got them there just in time. Down the production line they went: interviewed about what had caused them to flee, immunized, wormed, injected with vitamin A, photographed with the web-cam and issued with a health card. Then the video again, commanding: 'Wash hands! Seek medical help! The camp is designed to support your needs! Camp services are free!' This last concept was a constant battle. The timid watchful people processing through the tents were easy prey for poorly paid security guards, bullying refugee leaders and rotten agency officials.

Everyone had been quick to apprehend the opportunities afforded by the influx: from the G4S guards asking for bribes, and a system of recycling old refugees, to a sophisticated process of identity theft. Many of the older refugees had purchased Kenyan ID cards but new software was weeding them out, matching the fingerprints, and so they needed a 'clean' refugee document with fresh prints to keep in with a chance of the resettlement lottery. For a large fee, officials were double-dipping famine victims' fingers. Unaware of the money being made all around them, Isha's family shuffled through the line of tents until they emerged into the blast of the wind, blinking and newly stamped, like cattle.

Next to the Somalis was another line of tall, black, stern-looking people, passing through. Some had dashes of scars ribbed across their forehead and on their cheeks. The Somalis eyed the strangers warily. They chattered.

'They have our colour of skin. They're tall like us.'

'And thin!' someone shouted, and the others laughed.

'Why have they come here?'

'They are Somalis, but they are from the west,' someone said.

'No, no, they dress differently, they don't have the culture of Somalis,' said another. Nobody knew. It was Isha's first time to see a foreigner. She asked one of the men in the line, 'Are these people Somalis?'

'They're Sudanese,' he said. 'They're also refugees.'

The chattering stopped. The Somalis stared. Somalia was not the only conflict that season. Fighting had broken out again along the border between North and South Sudan at an oil town called Abyei and in the Nuba mountains. Hundreds of Sudanese refugees had been shipped from Kenya's western border with South Sudan on the other side of the country. Kenya liked to warehouse all its refugees in one place where someone else could be relied upon to feed them and where they were easily surveilled. This created unusual communities and unusual conflicts. Although 96 per cent Somali, Dadaab was, in fact, a cosmopolitan city and Ifo was its most international quarter.

In Ifo there were Ugandans who had fled with the revolutionary Acholi spirit medium, Alice Lakwenna, the 1980s insurgent whose mantle was taken up by Joseph Kony and his Lord's Resistance Army. There were Congolese victims of Africa's other endless civil war and even some Burundians and Rwandans still afraid to go back after the original genocide in 1994. Over 20,000 Ethiopians had come too, victims of the government's brutal land clearance schemes, its secret war in the Ogaden region and its harsh treatment of the Oromo majority. There were also an estimated 40,000 Kenyans in the camps illegally, who had come for the free food, free education and health care that their government did not provide.

The Sudanese in the line had elected to be shipped to Dadaab rather than the other refugee camp in Kenya, Kakuma, because they had compatriots here from Abyei who had fled earlier iterations of the conflict. As they filed through the tent and were interviewed by the UN staff, some of them wept and embraced their interpreter: a tall middle-aged man in a UN T-shirt with a kind face and smiling manner. He laughed and hugged the people he had known many moons ago before he had fled Abyei as a teenager. He was a refugee himself, living in Ifo. His name was Mayar which meant, in the Dinka language, 'white'. But he was, like his people, among the blackest human beings on earth. 'Maybe I am white on the inside?' he used to joke. Working with many nationalities at the UN he found it easier to go by the nickname given him by his mother whom he had not seen since one night in Abiyei in 1996. She had called him Monday, because he was born on a Monday.

Working with the UN was not Monday's first experience of the challenges of multiculturalism in the melting pot of the camp. He had taken the position of interpreter because at his last job his Somali colleagues had threatened to kill him. And that morning he had arrived at Hawa Jube in a UN vehicle specially tasked to collect him from his hut in the camp because, a few weeks prior, a Somali mob had jumped him on the way to work. It was not a random lynching. Twenty years of living cheek by jowl with other nationalities had done much to soften the notorious mistrust of the Somalis towards outsiders, but it had not yet corroded the conservative laws of clan and religion. Monday had violated the Somalis' first commandment: thou shalt not touch our women.

*

You had to feel sorry for Monday. There were not that many Sudanese girls to choose from. And the marriage arrangements of the Dinka people that he came from involved three or four hundred head of cattle – a challenge even in peace time and impossible in a refugee camp. He was from a group that in Sudan they called the 'Lost Boys' – those who had been orphaned or displaced during the civil war, many of whom had famously walked hundreds of miles into neighbouring countries to escape the violence. Although to call them boys was no longer accurate. They were now thirty-five-year-old men. Monday was one of 16,000 when they first came to the Kakuma camp, on Kenya's border with Sudan in 1987. Some had since been resettled in the United States to cold places like Minnesota, others had melted into foster homes or returned to Sudan, or found their own way to the West. The majority though, were left behind in camps in Ethiopia and Kenya.

While the Somali refugee population in Dadaab is predominantly female, among the Sudanese it is the opposite. The war had ended a few years before and most of the women had gone back. The Lost Boys, however, were still traumatized and afraid. When he first came to the Kakuma camp, Monday lived in a block of a thousand boys – all orphans, all former child soldiers. He had been kidnapped from his home in Abyei by the Sudan People's Liberation Army (SPLA) in 1995, when he was thirteen. After a year on the battlefield during which he had seen his friends 'killed, shot! – like on TV!', he managed to escape and return to Abyei. He was just in time to witness an attack by the Janjaweed of the North in which they shot his father in front of him and his mother and younger brother disappeared. The bullets, by God's grace, missed him. He ran.

When he met the Somali girl Muna, fourteen years later, after living in three different refugee camps in as many countries, he was a plumber with the German development agency GiZ, inside the large, secure aid agency compound in the town of Dadaab. Because the Kenyan government does not allow refugees to work, the UN had cooked up a compromise in which they were permitted to volunteer. The agencies called them 'incentive workers' although they were, in effect, interns paid a stipend far below what Kenyans received for doing similar work. In the camp where hard cash is scarce, competition for such positions is fierce. Monday had got his job through a connection with a Congolese guy who went to the same church. For her part, Muna came to GiZ as a cook, as a result of an experiment in gender balance. It was an experiment that horribly backfired.

Christine was the head of the kitchen at GiZ. She was a handsome Kenyan woman, broad and strong. At six feet tall she towered over the diminutive Muna and felt sorry for the younger woman. She was trying to be, as she put it, 'gender sensitive – we had so many men in the kitchen at that time'. During the interviews for the job, Muna did not excel. Nor did she have much idea about cooking. But something about Muna called out to Christine that caused her to suspend her professional judgement. 'I felt Muna really needed a job at that particular time,' she said. 'I took a chance.' She was right to pity Muna. By that time she had been widowed, divorced and had two children by two men. She was only eighteen years old. What she needed though was more than a job. She needed to escape.

The kitchen in GiZ is a low wooden shed, blackened on the inside, that stands in the middle of a wide compound planted with palm and neem trees surrounded by circular concrete buildings with thatched roofs made to look like traditional African huts. Painted on the side of one of them was a colour map of Germany. It was a pleasant place and Muna thought it beautiful. In an open canteen behind the kitchen, the staff came to take their meals.

Afterwards, when a tall muscly 'incentive' plumber called Monday would linger and make jokes with the cooks, Muna, at first, ignored him.

Monday can't remember what it was about Muna that drew him to her. There were other Somali women working in the compound. 'You know,' he said, 'you get a feeling.'

Muna was one of the very first Somalis to arrive in Dadaab in flight from the civil war. When the soldiers of the United Somali Congress of General Aideed arrived in Saakow in southern Somalia in 1991, Muna was an infant in her mother's arms. They shot her uncle and raped her elder sister but the presence of the baby in Muna's mother's arms saved both of their lives. That first night in the camp they slept in the bush, under the stars, where the airstrip is now. 'It was like a zoo,' Muna's mother recalled, 'animals everywhere,' and the first refugees used to hunt gazelle, zebra and giraffe. Soon, Muna's father succumbed to disease in the camp and her mother began collecting firewood to support her children. 'Life is hard,' are the first words Muna remembers her mother saying.

The baby who came to the camp aged six months grew up to become a fiercely independent young woman. She had come looking for a job at GiZ because, in the relative safety and limited opportunities of the camp, her schooling and her grasp of her own rights had brought her into conflict with the diktats of the clan, with her uncles who attempted to control her life. She was part of that first generation raised entirely in the camps exposed to Kenyan education and the liberal ideals of global NGO culture. She felt safe. Safe enough, in fact, to rebel.

Muna was clever and strong-willed, but she also possessed a quality that can be such a liability in the hands of someone unaccustomed to its power: beauty. Big brown eyes beneath two smudges for eyebrows filled her almost perfectly symmetrical face and she walked with a lazy swish. Her skin shone with health and the satisfaction of mischief.

Her family was happy with her first marriage. Falling for your maths teacher in a primary school in Dagahaley at the age of fourteen was a common enough event in the refugee camp, even back in Somalia. When Muna was six months pregnant, her husband Aden returned to Somalia to visit his father who was sick. One day soon after, she was called to the 'Taa' – the VHF radio station that was the way news reached Dadaab from the bush in the days before mobile phones. Aden had contracted cholera, his father told her. He was dead. Three months later, she gave birth to a girl. The infant's long curly hair and striking face with its high cheekbones would forever remind Muna of her handsome, lost, first love. She named her *Umaima*, which means 'my heart'.

As the tradition goes, as soon as Umaima was old enough to stand, the clan sent Muna to live with Aden's elder brother, a middle-aged man called Mohammed to whom Muna took an immediate dislike. She refused the match. Her mother pleaded with her uncles but in vain. Soon after the forced wedding ceremony, she became pregnant again; she doesn't like to recall how. She fled back home with Umaima to her mother. Her uncles threatened to kill her but the pregnancy earned her a reprieve.

After the second baby, *Hodan* – 'prosperity' – was born, Mohammed filed suit; he wanted his beautiful young wife and his child back. Muna's family's honour was at stake. Negotiations between the families lasted months. Death was frequently invoked: Muna threatened to commit suicide and Mohammed said he'd kill her himself if he didn't at least get his child. In the end, Muna's clan gave way and, as the custom dictated, when Hodan could walk, the child went to live with the father in Hawa Jube. Leaving Umaima with her mother, Muna ran to the main

UN compound in Dadaab looking for a job that required employees to sleep on site, inside the razor wire, away from a husband who continued to stalk her. The woman that caught Monday's eye in the kitchen of GiZ who smiled coyly at his jokes was in fact broken with grief at her stolen daughter and intent on revenge.

The staff quarters in GiZ were a low square of simple rooms with green numbered doors and wired windows surrounding rough grass where laundry dried. Muna stayed in number M26. Monday stayed in M9. Their rooms faced each other across the grass and Monday would often make his way over the quadrangle to sit in her room and talk. Gradually, Monday pressed his case. He had a winning smile and he was, Muna told a friend, 'Very tall . . . Very black.'

'I love you,' Monday said early on, with the disarming openness of the Sudanese. 'What have I got to hide?' he said with his big booming laugh. 'He was a good maker of stories,' she thought. But when he came and told them in her room, and she explained that there would be problems with her family, problems he could not imagine, Monday was blasé: 'We will run away to Sudan,' he said.

Then, the way Muna tells the story, she simply decided to let him have his way, saying, with audacious naiveté, that she believed after sex he might leave her alone. It was only once, she insists, and they were unlucky. Monday, however, remembers things slightly differently: 'She fooled me!' he said. 'She is very clever!'

When she started getting sick, at first she claimed it was malaria and Monday bought her medicine. When she didn't improve, Monday insisted on taking her urine to the clinic in Dadaab. After he came back with the result and challenged her, she told him the truth: that the greatest insult to her family would be to have a

Christian baby and she had done it to shame them. Monday was not pleased. But he had a good Catholic boy's sense of responsibility and he promised to stick by his girl. He had no idea of the price he was agreeing to pay.

That the relationship would be frowned upon was clear to him. But he underestimated the scale and zeal of the culture wars that have gripped Somali society since the rise of conservative Islam during the war. After the terrible ethnic cleansing based on clan that characterized the ignition of the Somali civil war, clan identity had become both supreme but also more fragile. Before, a woman traditionally married outside the clan, to reinforce the clan's ties to others. But with the violence coursing along clan lines, communities looked increasingly inward. A community under threat is rarely known for its tolerance. To marry outside the clan was now a scandal; a Christian in-law was unthinkable.

Muna, on the other hand, knew the zealots very well; she was related to them. If she failed to sneak out of Monday's room before daybreak, she would often have to spend the whole day hiding inside, peeing in a bottle to avoid being seen. The wooden chalets of the staff quarters were not designed for keeping secrets. The woman who lived in M8, next to Monday, had put two and two together and the rumours were beginning to thicken like soup.

Christine called Muna into her office, in a small wooden building next to the kitchen. Muna was now always late to work, sometimes not showing up at all. Christine had issued warnings, and counselled Muna. Then she began to see some changes. 'Muna became temperamental. Sometimes she wouldn't feed, sometimes suddenly she wanted meat.' She saw Muna as her own daughter and sat her down. 'I am suspecting that you are expecting,' she said. 'Be sincere, Muna, please.' Muna lied.

Leaving the office, she went straight away to her family's round fenced compound in Dagahaley camp, where her mother was surprised to see her. On the hard-baked sand between the kitchen made of sticks and the well-mudded house, the two women faced each other. Twenty years in the camp had been unkind to the older woman. She had the humped back and sideways shuffle of someone to whom life had not kept its promise. Her hennaed toes were split. Her face was cracked and two bottom teeth were missing. She had pale-brown skin and wide-set, light eyes that glowed with personality: she too had been a deadly beauty, once.

'Aren't you supposed to be working?' she asked her daughter.

'I have a leave,' Muna lied again. 'I am sick, I have got malaria.' It was a half-hearted attempt.

'Really? I heard you got a Christian pregnancy,' her mother said.

'Where did you hear that?' Muna said.

'People called me on the phone.'

'It's not true.'

'You're lying! We're going to take you to the hospital to be checked.'

'Fine,' said Muna.

She was indeed a clever woman. The second urine sample that her mother took for testing was in fact that of a neighbour. Having mollified her mother, Muna went back to work at GiZ. Lying, however, was not in Monday's nature and when he was confronted by his boss about the rumours, he confessed. From there the issue, as they say in the camp, went 'international'.

The Somalis working for GiZ called Muna into the office and advised her to have an abortion. They even offered to collect contributions to pay for it: 'Don't say we didn't warn you,' they said. Others were more forceful: 'You can say you were raped, then we can go and arrest him!' But she thought that God might be annoyed with her if she killed the child and, besides, Monday's religion forbade it. One night, unknown men broke down the door of Monday's room. He was not there, having been warned that the Somalis would try and kill him. After that, the managers of GiZ sent him home. 'If you die here it will be a problem', they said. And so, he had found the incentive work of interpreting for the new arrivals instead. Christine sent Muna home to her family's compound then too, falsifying her attendance sheets and forwarding her salary. But Muna was even less safe there than Monday.

In public, Muna took to wearing big clothes and a full niqab, covering her face: what they call in the camp 'ninja'. People called her foetus a 'mutant' and Muna's own brother threatened to kill her: 'You have ruined our family's name!' he yelled, sending her scrambling with her six-month bump over the fence behind the toilet. She ran to the Sudanese block in Ifo, S3, where Monday lived and that's where she was hiding now: afraid to go out, watching for a mob or a hit man.

Block S3 is inhabited by the tall, austere Dinka people from South Sudan, their black-blue skin welted with scars called keloids. The Dinka are bigger and stronger than the Somalis but they have built a tall fence around their block all the same – their church of mud and sticks has been burned down by a Somali mob three times. This was a new phenomenon. The rise of al-Shabaab over the last few years had shifted the centre of gravity in Somali society towards harsher strains of evangelical Islam like the Wahabis of the market, and the camp was not immune to such currents. Preachers were now regular fixtures on the Maidan on Fridays and in their speeches, Christians were increasingly vilified as scapegoats for the country's troubles. Recently, the little cosmopolitan island created in the camp had become more and more volatile.

The Sudanese put a guard on Monday's gate at night and deputed twelve warriors to sleep in the compound, spears by their side. 'They will kill me first,' Monday told Muna, when he got back from the long days at the reception centre. 'You will not die alone.' Now, though, as Muna's term neared, there was a new threat doing the rounds. Christine had told them of a plot hatched by the Somali nurses who worked at the Hawa Jube hospital to assassinate Muna's baby with a lethal injection in the delivery room, the moment the infant was born.

12

Live from Dadaab

On 20 July 2011 the United Nations finally declared a famine in southern Somalia and the food security map blinked black. It was the worst famine in the region for decades. Up to 1.2 million people were at risk of starvation and 12 million needed food aid, among them 2.3 million Somalis. In July 40,434 arrived in Dadaab, peaking at 2,000 a day, and thousands more were on the way. Suddenly the sleeping donors found their cheque books. The UN started airdrops inside Somalia. One hundred tonnes of tents were shipped to the camp. The wheels of the emergency business began to slowly turn and the NGO Oxfam accused the rich governments of 'wilful neglect'. It was a famine that should never have happened.

The situation in the camps, according to MSF, was, 'catastrophic'. Fully equipped emergency feeding stations in Hawa Jube were only just coming on line and the three camp hospitals were filled with women and children clinging to life by the thinnest of threads. The mortality rate was seven times over the emergency threshold. Half of the children and over a third of the adults arriving from Somalia were seriously malnourished, and one in five was on the brink of death. And then measles struck in N Zero. Every spare inch of the grounds in the hospital in Hawa Jube was crowded with tents and the wards were stuffed with as many beds as they could fit. The air inside the green and white buildings was thick with the cloying sweet smell of malnourished flesh and the earthy rot of death.

One nurse, a veteran of the 1992 famine when the camps were first established, said he'd never seen anything like it. Two years later he would still be unable to talk about that time: 'You don't want to remember those things,' he said, tears running down his face. Every day they lost one or two children in Hawa Jube alone, but the greatest challenge in dealing with the new arrivals was convincing the wary mothers accustomed to medicines of herbs and roots that intravenous drips and needles were not going to harm their children. Many refused the treatments, tore off the oxygen masks and pulled out the drips and then the staff had to write the name of the child in the 'death book'. All of this alongside the six hundred or so normal daily admissions, and the thirty women delivering babies, that you'd expect for a city the size of New Orleans. The hospital staff worked for fifty-six days straight then had two weeks off. 'Your brain is fried. It's not working actually,' said the nurse.

On 19 July, tipped off that the UN was about to declare a famine, the US television network ABC News launched a campaign called 'A Cry for Help: Disaster in the Desert', ushering in two weeks of intense and disturbing coverage of the emergency. The media frenzy began. By 25 July the UN compound was crawling with journalists. Isha's neighbour was interviewed by some white people with a large camera. She didn't know where they came from. They didn't give her any food. Every day at the reception centre, Monday saw another crew from another country, eager to film the thinnest children, the ones with the rapid breathing and bulbous eyes, skin shrunk to their skulls, bones light as balsa wood. They toured the hospitals and did pieces to camera in front of the long lines huddled by the tents. The doctors at the hospital hired a public affairs officer to deal with the visitors and were forced to spend two hours of their precious time each day preparing and giving briefings. They even had to seal off the intensive care unit because on some days there were more journalists than patients. Even so, one intrepid German photographer broke in through the window to capture the all-important deathly shot.

The roads in the camp were a constant fog of dust as the private vehicles hired out at up to $250 a day rattled around. The market was loud with goods unloading and vehicles arriving, ten-wheelers boiling up the long road through the desert from Nairobi. Hundreds of new incentive workers like Monday had been hired to deal with the influx; everyone was an aid worker now. One of the young men who was making thousands of dollars a week working as a fixer for the media crews overheard them calling the emergency 'Haiti part two'; the nickname spread like fire in Bosnia, among the older refugees and those able to retain a sense of humour despite the tragedy.

In the midst of all the activity, Muna decided to risk an excursion. Although she was heavily pregnant and walking was tough in the forty-degree heat, she set out from block S3 to the UN Ifo field office. Somalis in block D6 that neighboured S3 had discovered her presence and the daily torrent of insults hurled over the thorn fence had become intolerable. She gambled that she would be safer if the UN knew where she was. With Umaima by her side, she waddled slowly to the UN office to lodge her complaint. She had grown up under the suzerainty of the UN and the Department for Refugee Affairs (DRA) and, for better or worse, she believed they would protect her.

It was the middle of the morning and there was the usual crowd outside the UNHCR field office shouting through the metal grille in the wall, pressing to get in. One of the UN staff had even stepped outside, trying to calm them down. As Muna walked along the road with Umaima directly in front of the building, she didn't see her brothers and sisters coming.

'You are beautiful and strong!' one of her sisters shouted. 'But you married a Sudanese, why did you do that?' Her family hit her head and then her body, until she fell on the road. Then other women joined in. 'Prostitute!' they screamed. The women continued to hit her while the crowd outside the UN office stared in amazement until staff came rushing out and her attackers ran away.

At first, Muna wasn't sure if it was the pain of the beating or of something else, but, three days later, on 29 July, after a long and difficult labour during which they had to cut Muna twice, a bruised but healthy baby girl was born a little early. Christine had arranged for her to give birth in the health centre reserved for citizens in Dadaab town with Dr Naila, a GiZ doctor that she knew and trusted. If she'd gone to Hawa Jube, Muna might have found herself on television – one of the many mothers and children in the background, mixed in with the famine victims in the maternity ward.

One mother who gave birth the week before in Ifo recalled a room crammed with fifty beds and even the floor space between them occupied. Although it was punishingly hot during the day, at night the desert temperatures dropped. That was the time the nurses feared. They stocked the wards with heaters to keep the malnourished children warm. Some of them, the new mother remembers, 'were very thin, smelling bad', sleeping on the floor next to her. Two beds away, a little boy, about one year old, called out one night and then was silent. His mother said, 'It is over,' and the other women in the ward listened to her quiet crying in the dark. In the end, an estimated 260,000 people died in the famine, half of them under five. Reports afterwards placed the blame firmly on the delayed response by the international community. But, as the rest of the world was finally waking up to the humanitarian tragedy of the hundreds of thousands of new arrivals, the older refugees were focused on an entirely different scandal: the birth of Muna's mongrel Christian–Muslim child. The famine was an obligation, an inconvenience and a business opportunity; it was, in that sense, part of daily life. But the mutant birth, as far as the elders were concerned, was an insult and a crime. And they were bloodthirsty for a sacrifice to assuage the sin against their own, most beautiful, flesh: Muna. 'Have you heard?' 'What did they call it?' 'What's its religion?' 'God will punish them.' 'It's wrong.'

Monday and Muna named the dark and chubby infant Christine Abuk Omulkher. Christine for the woman who had given Muna her job and helped them so much; Abuk was Dinka for Mary, the mother of Jesus, and Omulkher was Somali for 'God with us', despite what the mob might say. After three days, Muna was discharged and the new young family locked themselves inside the house in S3. They feared for baby Christine's life. They didn't sleep. And they trembled behind the Lost Boys, their spears glinting in the moonlight.

Although no longer boys, those remaining in Ifo were still, in many ways, waiting for their adult lives to begin. Their homeland of South Sudan had gained its independence, but the Lost Boys were unwilling to trust the fragile peace in the world's newest country. So they spent their days dozing like leopards along the low boughs of a mango tree at the entrance to the block, next to the stagnant green pool that spilled over from the communal tap. The tree had been planted twenty years ago when the first Sudanese had come to Ifo, but it seemed as though little else in their lives had changed. Time in the camp was monotonous, and therefore elastic. 'Something you are used to, you don't take it seriously sometimes,' said one of them, called William. He could have been speaking for the whole refugee population.

Those who had come of age in the camps, like Muna and

Monday, who had seen so many of their peers resettled abroad, lacked respect for the present: as though one's actions in the here and now had no relation to the great hereafter, abroad. Life was only a process of waiting. And this was their problem too: in such circumstances, people are more inclined to act without consequences, without limits, to be caught by a hedonism of the senses or the indulgence of emotion, or the violent righteousness of religion. Nothing had any permanence, there was no building anything, since both the people you loved or the people you hurt could soon be gone. The older refugees with a grounding in school or community had a better chance. But still, in such a situation, life can lose its meaning. Hence the temptations to slip into khat and drink, or into ideology, or further, across the border to join al-Shabaab.

Of all the fears of the Sudanese, al-Shabaab loomed largest. Its alienation was something the Lost Boys well understood. But it was a fear with no face. No one in the camp admitted to being a member of the group. There was only rumour and the occasional story of a relative who had gone missing, 'back to Somalia', with a raised eyebrow or a knowing grin. Someone in the community had once had a phone call warning them not to mention the name of the group and that had spawned a new vocabulary: 'those guys'. It is a story of rising religious tensions the world over. Under threat, the Lost Boys could not differentiate between the conservatives and the terrorists: to them, Muna's zealous family and 'those guys' were the same thing.

After a week, Monday and Muna relaxed a little into their new routine in S3 and Monday ventured back to his work as a translator in the reception centre. The UN needed all the hands they could get and Monday needed the money to supplement the family's rations. He wasn't paid for the days he didn't attend.

On a hot, still afternoon, the Lost Boys having drifted off to their own business, Muna was preparing food. Umaima was playing in the compound outside and ten-day-old Christine was asleep on the bed in the house. Muna was happy. She had a man who looked after her, who brought money, and she felt at home among the gentle Sudanese who didn't judge her, whose liberal values were more in line with those she had imbibed at school in the camp. Then she heard Umaima scream.

'Mama! Mama!'

She rushed outside to see a Somali boy holding Umaima to his chest while another came at Muna with a knife. 'We're taking her away, you're poisoning her,' he snarled. Three others stood around, menacing. Muna turned and ran, scaling the six-foot-high thorn fence of the compound with uncommon agility for a woman who had just given birth. She started shouting. She had left baby Christine in the house, she prayed they wouldn't look inside. Just in time, the Lost Boys came running down the alley with their spears. The Somali boys dropped Umaima on the sand and ran.

Monday came rushing back from work and they called the UN protection team for Ifo camp. Five miles away, in the main compound, the staff who answered the phone were overloaded. Not just with the emergency, but with all the visitors that had decided to come and witness it. Now that Dadaab was world news, it wasn't just the journalists; celebrities had started coming too. It was 9 August. The previous day, the wife of the US Vice President, Jill Biden, had visited. On 11 August it would be long-time UNHCR supporter and Goodwill Ambassador, Angelina Jolie. Later that month, ministers from various countries arrived as well as the Somali-Canadian rapper K'naan, US political wife Cindy McCain and the actress Scarlett Johanssen.

K'naan was the only one Muna had ever heard of. When K'naan visited the hospital on 23 August, Professor White Eyes abandoned his shop in Bosnia and ran all the way there to try and glimpse possibly the most famous Somali on the planet: 'The man that I only see on screen,' he said, 'I needed to see face to face!'

In spite of the celebrity visitors, the harried staff of the UN immediately moved Muna, Monday and the girls to a part of Ifo called 'Transit'. It is the place where, historically, people were housed while awaiting a plot somewhere else in the camp or a plane ticket out. Over time, it had been increasingly used as a holding pen for refugees at risk. Transit is a fenced-off area on the edge of the camp across from Ifo's police post and two of the Ethiopian blocks, E1 and E2. Green thorns have strangled the broken chain fence encircling rows of tents and the two latrine blocks for hundreds of people. There was a single G4S security guard asleep in a tin shack by the gate. Muna and Monday were assigned a tent next to an older woman who had HIV/AIDS and her children and another younger, beautiful woman with large gleaming black eyes who greeted them in a sing-song melancholy voice and said her name was Habiba, but everyone called her Sweetee. Later, Monday would claim that from the first time he saw her, he knew Sweetee was trouble. He would blame her for all the problems that came after. Although it was supposed to be a temporary safe haven, Transit would become their home for the next four years.

That night, Muna struggled to sleep in the tent on the hard ground. She missed her bed from Monday's place. The noise of so many people in such close proximity was disorienting, like sleeping on the deck of a ship sailing through the desert night.

Meanwhile, inside the heavily fortified UN compound in Dadaab town, the normal staff who service the camp had been overwhelmed by a tripling of capacity as reinforcements and journalists swelled their ranks. Each night journalists set up their lights and their cameras for the evening news bulletins. White people in identical khaki combed their hair and powdered their faces.

CNN's Anderson Cooper broadcast his whole show, *360 Degrees*, 'Live from Dadaab!' pacing up and down in the UN car park. In the background, the white 4×4s with the big blue UN logos were lined up in their sheds, resting after a hard day's work: a clichéd symbol of the heft that the international community is capable of deploying, when it chooses to do so. Finally, the famine relief poured in. It had taken television to bring it here.

13

Billai

The little aluminium pot perched on three stones above a meagre fire. There was not enough firewood to go round, and Isha and some other women from N Zero who had gone looking for kindling had met competition from locals on the plain. They retreated to N Zero beaten and bruised. The aid workers who came to the outskirts, when they came, told the newcomers they'd be issued with firewood when they were relocated to the new camp, Ifo 2. But when would that be? the people asked. The aid workers didn't know.

Isha's children sat in a circle and watched the pot boil. She and Gab watched with them. He had got the message from the boy in Rebay that his family had left for the camps and he had joined them at last. The animals hadn't made it. He had borrowed money and paid for a lift. But he was not yet registered and the food was stretched thin. It was interminable, the cooking, Isha hated it. Every now and then one of the children would peek under the lid. 'Has it cooked? . . . Has it cooked yet?' Isha teased them, trying to make a joke of it. Every day the younger children complained. She was grateful though for the elder ones, they understood.

Now it was Ramadan and the stronger ones among the refugees had begun to fast and even some weak ones. An old lady who collapsed and was taken to hospital said, 'What's the point? I have no food anyway, I might as well fast and die clean!' Fasting made the waiting worse. For more than a month they'd been living in

N Zero, waiting in line for food, waiting for the food to cook, waiting to move to Ifo 2. And every day N Zero grew.

Clanking through the huts, churning up dust, water trucks now came on rounds for those on the outskirts of the camp. The dust, pushed up by the wind against the sides of the huts, settled in clothes, in hair, on the skin. They gave out three litres of water per person per day, but they didn't reach every part of N Zero every day. Seventy thousand people were now living, without toilets and without running water, outside the formal bounds of the camp. Isha conserved her water carefully to afford her a wetted sponge once a day with which she could remove the film of dust that permanently coated her children. It made her angry. Dadaab made no sense to her.

Next to N Zero, the brand new complex of Ifo 2 lay empty. When the new arrivals complained that the water given out by the trucks was not enough, they were urged patience. There were four water towers in Ifo 2, the humanitarian staff said, enough for the basic international minimum of twenty litres per day (the UN right to water says thirty to fifty), three schools and hundreds of latrines. But when will it be open? they asked, 'Soon,' the agency people said.

'Talking, talking!' Isha grumbled. She was right. After an international outcry, Kenya's Prime Minister, Raila Odinga, himself promised that Ifo 2 would be operational by the end of July. But, at the beginning of August, it was still closed. Odinga's public excuse was that his announcement had not been approved by cabinet and the matter required collective approval. The truth was that local MPs, habituated to profiting from misery, were holding the process hostage.

In return for their approval for new land at Ifo 2 and for the other camp south of Hagadera called Kambi Os, the MPs wanted generous contracts for their own firms and a second, brand new,

UN compound, on the other side of Hagadera camp at a place called Alinjugur. The UN knew these manoeuvres for what they were and vainly tried to resist. The sole purpose of a new UN compound would be the opportunities for grabbing part of the $25m it would cost to build and the contracts needed to clean, cater and run it. But, collapsing under the weight of the desperate new arrivals, the UN blinked first. The MPs got their deals and the refugees, at last, after nearly four years of negotiations, got their new camp.

Ifo 2 was meant to be state of the art. The UN had spent a lot of time developing a new product: Interlocking Stabilized Soil Blocks (ISSBs), bricks made of mud, that could be used to build cheap houses in refugee camps. It had planned to build 15,000 such houses in Ifo 2 but only managed to construct 116 before the Kenyan government visited in December 2010 and ordered the building stopped. The houses looked too much like houses, better even than houses that Kenyans lived in, said the Department for Refugee Affairs, not the temporary structures and tents that refugees were supposed to inhabit. It would embarrass the government. So, when Isha's family was eventually relocated from N Zero, she and the other new arrivals moved from their makeshift huts into even more temporary UNHCR dome tents laid out over ten square miles in great squares and long white lines stretching into the haze of the horizon.

The geography of a refugee camp is about two things: visibility and control – the same principles that guide a prison. The refugee camp has the structure of punishment without the crime. The crime is implied. And, by and large, the refugees, docile, disempowered, do as they are told; they hesitate before authority and plead for their rights in the language of mercy. Ifo 2 had wide roads for police patrol vehicles, long avenues of tents that hid nothing and no private space. Into the huge grid of blocks, the new arrivals poured. All that was left of the temporary stick city of N Zero was the bare skeletons of abandoned hut frames. And within days, even these were gone for firewood.

Isha's plot and a tent were in block M2 at the far north-eastern corner of Ifo 2 on the windblown outer edge of the camp. Along the northern perimeter, there was a road separating the camp from the denuded plain of roughly chopped stumps, with a shiny new white plate that announced the name: 'Forest Road'. A timid police car could occasionally be seen patrolling Forest Road but it was not a popular beat. The real forest was to be found inside Ifo 2, in the thorns planted in the sand to demarcate the boundaries of each ten-metre-square plot that was allocated for families sized 4–7. Isha and Gab and six children made eight but Gab had arrived after the plots had been allocated. She took her time preparing her home. She found a sturdy thick thorn for her live fence, a once common species called Commiphora. It was the nomad's friend. The bark is used to treat malaria, the resin for disinfectant, the burnt sap is an aphrodisiac and the amber 'tears' that weep from the trunk are the base ingredient for myrrh. The wise men who visited the baby Jesus in the stable likely came from the plains of the Horn of Africa.

In the corner of Isha's plot was a square tin box for a toilet like an upended coffin, the sticker with a Turkish flag still intact. Everything in Dadaab is 'donated by' or 'provided by' or 'funded by', as if to remind the refugees that they have nothing of their own. Even the police cars are 'donated by UNHCR'. Isha wondered for whom the notices, written in English, were intended?

Now that the world had recognized the famine as a crisis, everyone wanted to help, but only so much. Humanitarian agencies had requested $2.4 billion for the emergency. At the beginning of August they had received less than half that amount.

Europe and the US, Canada and the Gulf States led the contributions, but even Kazakhstan and Palestinian refugees in the Gaza Strip donated.

The biggest surprise of the famine – it made the traditional donors nervous – was the massive response from Turkey. The Turks – the ones who put the sticker on Isha's toilet – were popular for several reasons. Because they distributed cash directly to the refugees – the 2,000 shillings ($23) that they gave Isha when she moved into her new tent was the first money she had handled in the camp and the first time she had seen the Kenyan currency. And because, with their frenetic building of latrines, schools and mosques and the unloading of huge quantities of food, they were, after the UN, the second biggest employer of incentive workers in Dadaab.

The enterprising Nisho, only too keen to stop hauling potatoes at the market, was among the first to get himself hired. The mention of Turkey would afterwards always send him into raptures, shouting and pointing at the sky. 'I will never forget the help of the Turkish government! I will always pray for them!' But they hadn't only provided him with a job. 'My wife is very beautiful,' he would say, smiling and looking down, abashed. 'I was married by the grace of Turkey!'

The hub of the Turkish aid operation where Nisho worked during the emergency was a new mosque erected on the deforested no-man's-land between N Zero, Hawa Jube and Ifo 2. It was a huge building made of wood and iron sheets that looked like a giant tin foil sculpture topped by a weathervane of three loudspeakers rigged together on a flimsy pole. Whatever the intended name of the mosque, it was obliterated immediately by the success of the porters' nickname for the place: Istanbool.

During Ramadan the crowds spilled out of the corrugated iron walls and into the large fenced area surrounding it. Nisho was often to be found among the worshippers kneeling on the plastic mats with their backs to the wind and the sun. He had a lot to be thankful for and a lot to pray for too. The Turks had given him a red T-shirt with the Turkish flag on it and soon he had progressed from portering to measuring and distributing food. He had made good money from the famine, 2,000 shillings a day, enough to water his imagination and allow a seed, long dormant at the back of his mind, to germinate: 'I was thirsty for women at that time!'

With his own savings from the famine and pledges from relatives, Nisho amassed what he considered to be an impressive dowry of 70,000 Kenya shillings (about $800). Thus armed, he dispatched his uncle to go and speak to the parents of a girl from Ifo 1 whom he had been trying to seduce in the market. When his uncle came back from the meeting with the bad news, Nisho was heartbroken. The family had wanted 500,000 shillings ($6,000). 'I will never marry, not in twenty years,' he wailed. He was a virgin. He feared, rightly, that if he played around and got a girl pregnant, he would have a whole clan on his neck. But depression submerged his spirits only briefly. When he went to work at Istanbool the next day, looking at the malnourished new arrivals collecting the food, he had an idea. In Ifo 2, a starving bride would be cheaper.

The following Friday he summoned his confidence, telling himself with characteristic drama (he was not an orphan), 'orphans have to have a big stomach and a big head,' and he took a walk among the wide grid of blocks of Ifo 2. Down the rows of tents desperate people wearing sheets, rags, some nothing at all, peered out. Nisho was continually shocked at the state of the new arrivals, but, holding fast to the idea that he was poor and not in a position to help anyone, he didn't part with any of his hard-earned money to people he didn't know; he contented himself with praying for them instead. Five blocks south of Isha's place, near a new metal sign that read 'S1', he spied a pretty girl whose luminous beauty was undiminished by her torn clothes and skinny frame. Billai would have been beautiful anywhere, anyhow. Nisho made a joke. She was terribly shy and hid her face but he managed to make her laugh. They talked. Nisho was jumpy, words bubbling up out of him as they do when he is nervous or high. His desire was naked, so close to the surface he couldn't hide it, so he decided not to. After ten minutes he said, 'I love you.'

'You're mad, just go away,' she said.

'I'm serious!' he pleaded.

She went back inside her tent. Billai's shyness was proper. Somali girls are famous for making an art out of womanhood. Karen Blixen, in *Out of Africa,* remarked on her Somali employees' 'exquisite dignity and demureness'. In Billai's case though, it was also, in some measure, fear of her own tongue. She had a kinship with Nisho in that she too struggled to conceal her emotions. The anger in Billai was quick and overflowing; she had a contempt for the world and for her situation. She had been happy in Somalia, but the war and the drought had torn her from childhood too fast and she was full of sadness and regret.

Nisho returned the next day. And the third, and the fourth. On the fifth, he changed tactics. He had done his research. Billai was also from the Rahanweyn clan and they were, distantly, related. She had come to Dadaab in a large group, walking for a month from a town called Salidley. They had been more than ninety-three when they left. Some of them had died along the way, but there was a new addition too: one woman had given birth three days' walk from the camp and arrived into the health centre with the umbilical cord still hanging from the infant.

Billai and her family were very malnourished but they were improving slowly. Recovering from malnutrition takes a long time.

In the last days of August, the levels of malnutrition in the camp were still well above emergency levels. Thousands of children were still in supplementary feeding programmes and over a quarter of all children showed signs of wasting. The food rations were supposed to last two weeks but were, on average, gone within ten days. Not enough.

When Nisho visited Billai, he pressed his suit with sugar, vegetables, whatever he could do to assist. He talked to her older sister and explained the clan links between their families. And that, or perhaps the groceries, decided it. Billai and he were officially courting. She was fifteen years old. For the young shy girl with only one set of clothes, the relationship made the disappointment of the camp bearable. Everyone in southern Somalia had heard of Dadaab and believed it to be a proper camp 'with everything there', she said. Instead, she found 'nothing'. Under less pressing circumstances, Nisho might have thought twice about a bride so disdainful of his beloved Ifo camp, but no sooner had Billai's family agreed to allow their daughter to begin talking to him than things took an urgent turn.

At Istanbool the Turks were getting ready for Eid-el-Fitr, the end of Ramadan. It is a time of feasting and of alms for the poor. The Muslim world had mobilized, sending food and money to Somalia and Dadaab. The Turks had an ambitious – and highly popular – plan to distribute camels for Eid and they had contracted Nisho's friend, a trader from Bosnia called Hassan, to supply them. The livestock market always jumps in the run up to Eid. Now it was red hot. Hassan was buying camels from Dadaab, from Garissa, from as far away as Somalia. The Turks agreed to set aside fifteen camels to be given as dowries. The community was very concerned that a generation of refugees with no hope of raising a bride price would go unmarried. Among the older refugees there was even a marriage lottery to combat the problem, where interested singletons would toss a shoe into a special basket at the mosque and an Imam would match one shoe from the male entrance and one shoe from the female. Hundreds were married in that way. Nisho had not got that desperate yet. When news of the camel scheme spread, he went straight to Hassan. A camel for a wedding was undreamed of. No family could resist. He was determined to get on the list.

'Don't worry,' said Hassan, over a cup of tea in Bosnia. 'When the time comes, send your uncle to me so that I can tell him what to do.' Suddenly, Nisho's courting had a deadline. Eid was only three weeks away.

For Nisho, the influx that had begun as a challenge to his prospects was now beginning to transform them. The market was booming. He had more work than he could handle and, if God willed it, he would soon have the most beautiful wife, acquired at a bargain price. In hindsight he was convinced that God had already made the match. 'It was written,' he claimed. At the time though, he was less assured. Every day he worried if Hassan would keep his word. When his uncle went to Ifo 2 to talk to Billai's parents, Nisho bounced around their compound in block B, unable to focus. He needn't have worried.

Billai agreed to the match perfunctorily: it wasn't clear if she felt joy as well as duty, or if indeed she felt she had a choice. Marriage is, in Somalia, a relationship between two families and the feelings of the individual, while a consideration, are not all-important. For Billai's exhausted and impoverished family, there was nothing to discuss. Even when Nisho's uncle pressed for the wedding to take place unnaturally fast – the camels were coming – they raised no objection.

And so, when Eid came and the camels arrived, Nisho led one of them from the market across the no-man's-land where so recently had stood the makeshift shelters of N Zero, past Istanbool and along the lines of tents of Ifo 2 to Billai's compound. It had already been swept twice since dawn. There, a sheikh, the uncles of the two young people and about two hundred onlookers watched as the camel was slaughtered and Nisho bowed his head to the Imam reciting a verse from the holy book. The formal part of a traditional Somali wedding is a male affair. Billai was waiting in her elder sister's tent nearby. The women's role is to dance. Once the legalities were completed, while the smell of the roasting camel meat beckoned the new arrivals from nearby blocks, Billai's relatives danced the traditional Rahanweyn dances of Salidley in the af-Maay dialect that few in the camp can speak:

This is the wedding for our beautiful lady
This is the wedding for our son
Praying for the newborn fruit of the union

Raised in the camp, Nisho had never heard the songs before. But he had been taught how to memorize and recite a verse and even though he heard it only once that day, he sang it frequently ever after.

By the time the meat was ready, the compound in S1 was overflowing with onlookers, coming to stare at the dancing and watching the food with anxious eyes. Inside the compound, in circles on mats, dozens of eager hands dug into the mounds of rice and meat, and hundreds more crowded into the open space along the road where Billai's family ferried platters of food. A guest was never turned away from a wedding feast; the Turks had known their camels would be shared.

Nisho himself didn't eat. He was happy, in his clean white clothes, his chest pushed out as far as it would go, drinking in his success. Some people made fun of him for marrying on charity, but most of his friends were full of admiration. 'He has a sharp brain,' they said, 'he timed it well.'

In the evening, a vehicle with its hazard lights flashing took Billai from her compound across the wasteland and through the scrub, past the grave site and the hospital, to the older camp, Ifo 1. Down the twisting narrow alleys banked by high, unruly thorns the car nodded slowly over the ruts while a gaggle of women circled it and danced, dust playing up into the beams of the headlights. Inside his small one-room hut, the walls freshly mudded by his friends and the ceiling adorned with the names of famous soccer players – in marker pen, 'TEVEZ' – Nisho sat on his bed and waited. He was happy. He was now a man. He used to like sleeping alone, but from that day on he never could again. Billai and he had both been advised about sex by their parents and about respecting each other. 'If one needs it, then you do it, and if the other, the same,' Nisho summarized. Someone else had told him that if he had sex on a day other than Friday he would die. But that year Eid had fallen on a Tuesday and Nisho was not inclined to listen to that advice.

The noise of the singing and rhythmical clapping approached. Soon it filled the night and flooded the little house. At the tin door with the 'USAID' pattern came a timid knock. The crowd roared and danced. The dust rose in ribbons cut with torchlight. Despite the famine and the suffering and the death, life was continuing. Marriage was a bet on the future, on the next generation: maybe this one would be the one. The one that would make the change.

PART TWO

Rob – Rain

14

Kidnap

Finally, at the beginning of October, it rained. For several days the heat swelled to an unbearable clamour. It hurt the head. The wind barrelling from the north hesitated and when it came again whispering then rolling and somersaulting it blew from the east, cooler and with a humid scent. The brown clouds thinned to grey and then darkened. The first drops kicked up spikes of sand and for a moment the air was fresh with the wet wooded smell of water on dust. Then out of a smoke-black sky came a muscular wind. A heavy threshing of the trees preceded a shot, thunder, and then the roar; the surround-sound blast of the equatorial deluge that set roofs rattling like machine guns and puddles bubbling red.

In Somali culture one wishes others *bash bash* – the blessings of the rain – but no one does that in Dadaab any more. For the farmers and the nomads the rain was the rhythm and compass of life. But in a makeshift city, atop hard stone, with no drainage and no sewage, water brought new terrors: flooding and disease.

The rain transformed Ifo 2 into a glistening sheet of wet clay that was treacherous to walk on. Isha, Gab and the children built small dams of mud to divert the water away from their tent and piled up mats along the edge to stop the water coming in. Isha was a tough woman: she laughed at the irony. For months, they waited for rain. And now, 'We pray to God not to let the rain come!' The roads turned to slurry and Ifo 1 became a bog. In Bosnia market donkey carts and wheelbarrows strained through pools of liquid mud. Nisho had hated working there in the rain.

'You must push the wheelbarrow with heavy force,' he complained. 'It pains the chest.' Another reason that, this year, he was glad of the Turkish.

Most afternoons, around dusk, the falling water slowed. The birds would begin again, louder, hysterical almost. The last of the sunlight filtered through the tangled shadows of the scrub and out of the ground came the bugs. Fierce squadrons rose in clouds: mosquitoes, winged ants, beetles, moths and daddy-long-legs whirling and zipping into the thick and heavy air like static. After a day or two, the red sand acquired a green tint. Another day and it was a thin beard, and then a proper coat of grass. The thorn trees unfurled soft little fists of iridescent lime and within a week the desert was a riot of colour stippling with life. Lilac flowers showed along the hard plasticky bark of the camel thorn and on the acacia were little yellow flowers that smelled of paper.

It seemed as if the lid had been lifted from a pressure cooker. People breathed easier. Instead of a suffocating blanket, the sky billowed soft clouds. The light came clearer; the haze was gone and at sunset the plain was bathed in a pale fire of crimson and pink. The night was windless and silent apart from the steady drip of trees.

An old man in Dadaab town with a hennaed beard that he washed and stroked lovingly when performing ablutions, picked his way gingerly among the puddles beneath the wet neem trees near the government offices. 'Al-Shabaab. They like the rain,' he said, to no one in particular.

In August, after over a year of intense fighting, AMISOM had successfully pushed al-Shabaab out of most of Mogadishu. And in the countryside, the drought had hit them hard. Some were in fact among the new arrivals, fighters posing as refugees who had come with their families. It was not lost on them that, as a result of the emergency, the camp was brimming with white people – the largest concentration of potential kidnap targets within easy reach of Somalia. For a battered rebel group in need of foreign currency, it was a tempting scenario.

The rain did not signal the end of the famine though. Herds that had taken three years to die could not be replenished overnight. The abandoned farms in Somalia would not yield harvests straight away and besides, many had fled not only drought, but fighting too; and the war didn't stop for the weather. The rain simply made the humanitarian operation harder. Vehicles got stuck. Latrines collapsed. Epidemics raged.

By the end of September, 63,000 had been relocated to Ifo 2. The overnight city had tents, schools and taps, but no hospital. The sick and malnourished refugees trekked instead to Hawa Jube and to the Médecins Sans Frontières hospital in Dagahaley, to the north. MSF-Switzerland who ran the facility had already doubled their capacity since the beginning of the emergency, but it was not enough. Another section, MSF-Spain, arrived to help.

Among the volunteers from Spain who heeded MSF's call to come to Ifo 2 were two women, Blanca Thiebaut and Montserrat Serra. They had arrived in Dadaab in August. Serra, aged forty, had taken a leave of absence from her job as a schoolteacher in Girona. Thirty-year-old Thiebaut, an agricultural engineer from Barcelona, was beginning her second stint working in Africa. It didn't take long to become known in the camp, and for the refugees to form an opinion of you: they knew each officer working for the agencies, and they discussed their characters. After two months, the women were popular. People remembered Thiebaut fondly because, when feeding the malnourished children in Ifo 2, she had been unconcerned about being covered in vomit as the babies struggled to hold down the enriched milk.

Around noon on Thursday 13 October 2011, Thiebaut and Serra returned to the site of a health post on the outskirts of Ifo 2 in the no-man's-land between the new camp and Hawa Jube. That morning they had unsuccessfully negotiated with an angry group of locals, several of whom all claimed title to the same plot of land, and thus a share of the meagre compensation MSF would pay for siting a health clinic there. As ever, the local community would not let an opportunity for squeezing some cash from the internationals pass them by. Just before lunch, the Spanish women got a phone call from one of the local leaders urging them back again; the community had resolved the dispute, they said.

The details are hazy, but soon after the women's car reached the site, four men carrying hand guns and satellite phones, shot their driver, Mohammed Hassan Barre, in the neck, pulled him from the vehicle, and sped off. Twenty miles beyond Dadaab, the car hit a depression and broke an axle. The kidnappers abandoned it, the engine still running, amid the endless scrub of the border country. Footsteps led away into the bush and then divided. At regular intervals shreds of white tissue paper dotted the red sand, like a game of paper-chase, until the footsteps disappeared into the freshly filled rain gullies of the desert and the tissue paper ran out.

Almost the moment Mohammed was shot and the car driven off, the local people phoned the authorities, reporting what had happened. Information travels fast in Dadaab, faster than the police. The UN security team were alerted and the police informed within minutes of the kidnap, but it took them over an hour to get out the door and on the trail of the hijacked car. When journalists called, the police told them they had launched a manhunt and sealed the border when in fact the vehicles were still in the compound.

That morning, Nisho, back at work after a week's honeymoon with Billai in his own hut, was distributing Turkish food in

Istanbool. The hijacked car would have raced nearby on the other side of the fence but he doesn't recall seeing it. He was busy. The first he knew, about an hour later, was many police cars speeding across the no-man's-land towards Ifo 2. The supervisors at Istanbool told them to pack up the food. The news crackled through the crowd and the hundred or so beneficiaries in the line didn't wait for the distribution: they ran. It didn't pay to be around when the police were under pressure. Nisho and his colleagues locked the supplies inside and discussed which way to flee. The only place he could think of was home and he started running. Thousands of others did the same – everyone wanted to be off the streets, expecting the police to come charging through the blocks in angry revenge.

In the back of one of those police vehicles crashing through the sodden desert was Sergeant Barnabas, a rather large officer with a laconic air. His tour in Dadaab had been longer than most and he maintained the unruffled insouciance of the weary professional. When the police vehicle got stuck, his group steadily tracked the stolen car on foot in the rain, finding it eventually at three a.m. The patrol slept in the bush and in the morning turned for home. They didn't bother with the paper trail because, Barnabas said, 'It meant nothing, in the rain.' In a lonely concrete house somewhere in southern Somalia, the two Spanish women spent the first of 644 nights in captivity.

Al-Shabaab denied responsibility for the kidnapping, but it is unlikely that hostages would be held in their territory without their permission. Al-Shabaab needed money which it got from taxing business in its area, including the business of sub-contracted kidnapping. In recent weeks, one British and one French woman had been taken from the tourist hotspot of Lamu archipelago on the coast. It seemed to be simply the latest act of piracy by pirates who had had their maritime operations curtailed by EU warships.

If the emergency had an end point, this was it. Within hours, the aid agencies had suspended their activities. Registration of new arrivals stopped. Vehicles were called in, staff evacuated. The very people who had come to help were running away in fear. And three days later, on Sunday 16 October, Kenya declared war, for the first time in its history as an independent country, on al-Shabaab.

15

The Jubaland Initiative

The office of the Department for Refugee Affairs is located along with the other government buildings in Dadaab town inside a circular fortified enclosure called the 'Administration Police camp'. In his narrow low-ceilinged office, crammed with oversize furniture – a large black conference table and a bank of grey filing cabinets – the deputy head, Mr Lukingi, was having a bad day.

Like the rest of the town, he had been woken in the early hours of the morning of Monday 17 October, by a police siren tearing open the soft quilt of the desert night. Roaring through the dark came convoys of camouflaged green trucks, lights burning, their cargoes of three thousand soldiers swaying in the back. The whine of engines straining in the wet sand was the sound of a new front opening in the war on terror: Operation *Linda Nchi* ('Defend the Nation') was under way.

Now journalists had started coming and asking difficult questions. Mr Lukingi was a tall, earnest civil servant with an open face and sparkling eyes who had served in other towns in Kenya's troubled northern region. He had a kindly reputation among the refugees and in the beginning he had walked freely in the blocks without bodyguards. But in his view the kidnap was the last straw. He lamented the difficulties facing those helping the refugees, like the kidnapped women.

'Every time you try and build something, someone pops up and claims the plot. Money is everything to these Somalis,' he said. Under pressure, Kenyan officialdom was quick to abandon the distinction between refugees and troublemakers. Lukingi had come round to the view that the best thing for Kenya was to invade Somalia and make it safe for the refugees to go home. 'We've tried to have a good relationship with these Somalis,' he said. 'It doesn't work.'

Lukingi was a teetotal family man with good intentions, but he was angry. He was, in fact, resuming the stance of official hostility towards Somalis that marked the very history of the building he inhabited. The Administration Police itself had been created by the British in 1929 to fight 'tribal' insurgencies in northern Kenya. These subsided when Somalia became independent in 1960 and the Somalis living inside Kenya's Northern Frontier District voted in a referendum for the region to become part of the Somali Republic. But the British ignored the vote and when Kenya gained its independence three years later, the 'Shifta War' began. For nearly three decades, Kenyan forces waged another war against Somali insurgents, only lifting the state of emergency in the north in 1992 – the year that Ifo camp was built.

As he was being called upon to justify his government's actions, to Lukingi it seemed that apart from a brief hiatus the Kenyan government had never *not* been at war with its Somali population. He struggled to maintain the party line that the invasion was in response to the kidnapping even though the pace and scale of the mobilization belied the government of Kenya's claim.

Lukingi dismissed the journalist and tried to get on with his work. Outside his office, two policemen sat discussing the events of the previous night.

'There's always profit in chaos,' said one.

'Uhuh,' said the other, his eyes on a UN vehicle that was circling the tree in the centre of the police camp. Many people, police and refugees alike, thought the war was just an enormous business deal, that some in the Kenyan government were trying to control the smuggling business from Somalia's Kismayo port that kept Nisho employed. His sidekick Mahat wasn't even sure that the kidnap had actually happened: 'People lie,' he said; 'people talk a lot.' The conventional wisdom in the camp was that the kidnap was just an excuse: the Somali radio stations spat the news of the invasion with disgust. The more conspiracy minded thought the Kenyans may even have encouraged the kidnap as a pretext for war. But a war for what? The invasion, launched into the middle of Somalia's rainy season, seemed so plainly self-defeating that Wikileaks cables would later reveal even the US and UK had argued against it.

In fact, among the UN officials, diplomats and the Kenyan government, the war had been a long time coming; it was an open secret of which Lukingi was certainly aware. The invasion was, in some respects, a war against the refugees. Repeatedly since 1991, Kenya had tried to encourage the refugees to go back home. When the US-backed Ethiopian invasion of Somalia faltered in 2007, Kenya nervously watched the rise of al-Shabaab. In 2008 it had hatched a plan to carve a new country out of southern Somalia bordering Kenya. It would be called Jubaland. The thinking went that such a state, cut loose from the in-fighting in Mogadishu, could host the refugees from Dadaab and act as a buffer-zone against incursions by al-Shabaab into Kenya. It would be a state which Kenya could control, and, later, into which it could drive the refugees. Kenya liked the plan so much that the then foreign minister Moses Wetangula asked the Americans three times for their blessing. Three times the Americans refused. But Kenya went ahead with the plan anyway.

Nisho remembers young men joining up to fight for

Jubaland; the recruiting office was in a hotel on the main street in Dadaab town. It was something all the refugees wanted to believe in: a peaceful country in which to be free. The Kenyan recruiters promised the young men money, training and a gun. The gun was all they got. After a few border skirmishes and a year spent in an alcoholic barracks in a desolate place called Archer's Post, many of the young boys sold their weapons and found their way back to Dadaab. The so-called 'Jubaland Initiative' had failed. Now, with the influx of 150,000 extra refugees, the idea took on a new urgency. The invasion, then, was the Kenyan army deciding to do its own dirty work, to establish Jubaland itself.

Out of the opposite office from Lukingi's, across the sandy fore-court, the new District Officer emerged into the shade of his veranda and stretched in the heat. He was a young slim civil ser-vant called T. K. Bett with an upright bearing and a genial manner, less coy than Lukingi. He had only been in the job a week, yet, for a Monday morning following the declaration of war, he was remarkably not busy. He thought that the NGOs who refused to travel with police escorts, like MSF, had only themselves to blame for the kidnap. He had a not uncommon suspicion of white people; that they were naive, delicate humans, always smelling of soap, clutching bottles of water and afraid to walk in the street. There was resentment at the fuss made over the whites. A Kenyan driver kidnapped only weeks before had occasioned simply a report. Bett was proud of his government's plan to invade and create the new state called Jubaland. 'Al-Shabaab have been taking us for a ride,' he said. 'It is time for us to show them what we are made of!'

Above, the midday clouds boiled over. It rained all afternoon, a hammering roar that deadened the spirits and invited sleep.

In the evening, the Administration Police (AP) officers and the other government officials crawled out from their barracks and galvanized zinc huts inside the AP camp and made their way to the makeshift wooden bar at the back of the compound, next to the wooden church among a jumble of defunct generators, satellite dishes and beer crates. The government employees from the hills of central Kenya were, in some sense, also refugees here in the northern desert, clinging to their God and their drink.

Far from home the poorly paid civil servants huddled under a roughly constructed shelter and watched television on a set suspended from the ceiling. The leg of a goat roasted over a blackened oil drum sliced in half, filling the air with smoke. Men and the occasional woman tip-toed heavily on breeze blocks to traverse the lake that had sprung up between the TV hall and the bar. Then tottered back again carrying bottles of the Kenyan national drink: Tusker lager.

In baseball caps with round bellies spilling over belts, they sat on wobbly wooden benches and watched the news from Nairobi while the rain drilled on the roof. It was all about the invasion. Burning graphics declared 'Nation at War' and footage showed long lines of trucks rumbling past. There was no hint of what it might mean for the future. No intimation of the bombs planted in buses, in churches, in markets and in shopping malls. Of the hundreds of dead. When the TV reported the government claim that it had 'sealed the porous border with Somalia' a laugh rippled through the crowd. It was a ridiculous idea. The anarchic bush pulsed in the dark, metres beyond the fence.

When the government claimed that the incursion would be swift and victory certain, they believed what it said. They had to. They were targets now, somebody's enemy. Never mind that the Kenyan government was less a state than a corrupt collection of rival cartels, some of whom probably had an interest in prolonging the fighting: this was war. And the assortment of drunk and overweight police officers staring at the television were, God help them, the front line. The news finished, the bottles tinkled together and the laughter dribbled on as before. The smoke from the barbecue billowed out into the rain, not rising.

16

Tawane

The following day, Tuesday 18 October, in a little cafe opposite the entrance to the AP camp, beside the road that was turning to dirty porridge in the rain, Tawane frowned. Neatly framed by the straight lines of his exquisitely barbered hair and clean-shaven jaw, his face was grave. He glanced suspiciously at his goat soup and took a slurp of sugary tea made with camel's milk as he pondered the consequences of the weekend's chain of events.

Tawane was the youth leader for Hagadera, the largest camp. He had taken a minibus to Dadaab town at the request of UN staff, since they were confined to their base. In response to the kidnap, the UN had implemented a general 'suspension of all non-life saving activities'. The blocks were eerily quiet, crouched against the rain. The war the refugees had all been running from had finally arrived in Dadaab. And with the suspension in services, they were on their own.

A humanitarian catastrophe was looming, fast: food needed distributing, water pumps needed refuelling, health clinics needed to be staffed and stocked. The UN required nothing less than a volunteer refugee army. And the three elected youth leaders from Ifo, Dagahaley and Hagadera camps were the ones who could deliver it.

Tawane had arrived in Kenya on a donkey cart in 1992, aged seven. His whole family had fled together, apart from the ones they had not had time to bury, from a small town on the road to

Mogadishu where two old Italian bridges span the river Juba. It was the reverse of a journey his grandparents had made two generations before.

Tawane's grandparents had been born on the plain at a time when the camel trains trekked from the Red Sea to the mountains of Ethiopia and back again without any idea of borders, nations or checkpoints. Italy, Great Britain and the Emperors of Ethiopia of course had other ideas, and at the end of the nineteenth century they drew three very straight lines that met at a point where Tawane's nomadic family often visited for their summer grazing. But it was not until the twentieth century was well under way that the family that had reigned supreme in their native wilderness suddenly realized what had happened and found themselves colonized.

In their family compound in block E5, Tawane's grandmother tells the story without words but with short breathy whistles and chopping motions of her hand and a curling of the eyelids to show the whites of her eyes. Robbed of teeth, she can no longer talk and her tales become performances that attract an audience of her grandchildren who hoot at every scene.

She shows how she pleaded with the British not to rape the women in the northern Kenyan town of Wajir where they were staying at the time and how – an extended finger to motion shooting – she grabbed the barrel of a gun of a Kenyan soldier who tried to shoot her clansmen. Following the ancient logic of 'my enemy's enemy is my friend', her husband, Tawane's grandfather, joined the Italian police force in revenge and the family moved to the small, fertile town of Bengine between the bridges over the wide, brown delta of the Juba river.

When, sixty years later, the war arrived in Bengine, Tawane's father, Idris, was unprepared. Idris is not an imposing figure. He is short and slight. But his angular jaw with its hard mouth, his nose like a beak and his piercing eyes atop a strong wiry neck radiate a determination and authority that his children knew not to dispute. In later life he cultivated a sharp-pointed beard, dyed orange with henna like his hair; it gave him at least the air of dignity and authority, a kind of compensation for what he had lost.

Although the inhabitants of Bengine knew that the rebel militia of the United Somali Congress (USC) were coming down the road from Mogadishu, they thought they were still far away. That day in 1992, there had been some discussion about the exact position of the USC army but Idris ended it by ordering his two eldest sons to go to one of his three farms to harvest what they could before the inevitable attack.

Idris had not been born a farmer but he had worked hard to wring considerable wealth from his land and he was reluctant to leave it for the approaching militia. Idris had two seasonal farms that relied on the flood waters of the Juba river and one on higher ground where Italian bulldozers had pushed the soil into ramparts during the Second World War and where, after the rains, he would occasionally unearth bombs that he would dutifully hand in to the police station. When the river retreated from its annual flood, he was, he declared, 'the richest man in the whole world'. The land allowed his children to eat three meals a day and made him one of the wealthiest men in the town, a respected elder with a seven-room house roofed with iron sheets next to the tarmac road. Apart from the monkeys that lived in the trees on the river bank and occasionally raided his crops, he feared nothing.

For the past few months, since the collapse of government authority, a local militia had been causing trouble in the district. The leader was from a sub-clan hostile to Idris's, who called himself 'Rambo'. One day Rambo and his boys arrived at the family home and helped themselves to two sacks of rice that Idris had set aside for the difficult period that he reckoned to be ahead. When Idris made a fuss he found himself face down on the tarmac road. Two of Rambo's men took a hand each. They dragged him along the road leaving shreds of his clothes and several layers of skin on the blacktop. Soon after, they put a bullet in the head of his only milking cow and sent him a message: 'As we have done to the cow, so you will also be done the same.'

On the day the warlord General Aidiid's USC army came, sweeping all the sub-clans with their petty rivalries before them, Idris had expected to join his sons later at the farm but, around noon, he looked out of the window of his house. A convoy of trucks crammed with armed men and pick-up trucks with bazookas welded onto the back rolled past. Soldiers followed on foot. Far off, gunshots sounded as if coming from the outskirts of town. He waited for the army to pass on its way to the bridge and, as soon as the coast seemed clear, Idris raced to the farm. Along the earthworks the maize stalks were high. Here and there some had been knocked down in a rush; the cobs still clung to the plants, their wispy beards hanging down. He followed the broken stalks and, soon enough, he found his boys in the field. They still gripped tools in their hands, one lifeless body on top of the other, a single bullet in each. They were eighteen and twenty-two years old.

Idris climbed a tree and watched another convoy of vehicles loaded with rocket launchers, heavy machine guns and men moving along the road. He stayed out of sight and picked his way back home. There, he gathered up the other children along with his wife and his mother and went away from the road, to the river. At Bengine, the Juba river is nearly at the ocean and it is broad and swift. The family had no boat and the children couldn't swim so Idris found two drums and tied them together to make a raft for them to struggle across. On the road south a tractor picked them up and they joined the anxious throng that was filling Kismayo.

Idris was better off than most of the refugees: he had money. After two days on a truck that dropped them at the border, they rolled into Dadaab in a rented donkey cart and registered with the UN. The place Idris, Tawane and the rest of the family were taken was an area of uneven sandy ground, unimaginably hot and without natural water. The land was bush, nine miles from Dadaab town. The locals called the area *Hagadera*, the place of the tall trees. The sand of Hagadera is soft enough for feet to sink into the sugary red soil. The thickets of thorns are brown. When the wind blows the sand gets everywhere and turns everything: feet, shoes, tents, hair, a shade of red; it is a world with a limited palette. It was to be their home for the next twenty-five years.

The arriving refugees were told to build a traditional house – the local style was to make a frame of sticks and cover it with mud thickened with dung. But Idris refused. He insisted on constructing an *aqal*, the nomad's tent: a bent wood structure covered with blankets and skins which the family erected on the square of sand they were allocated amid the grid of the camp, block E5. After all, he reasoned, the family would soon be going home. Being poor is harder when you have known riches. Idris knew that the sand upon which he slept belonged to another clan and that fact burned within him like a fuse.

As more and more refugees arrived in Hagadera, the people organized themselves as they had done back home. Clans collected together in certain blocks. People who had been elders and elected officials back home slipped easily into positions of authority in the emerging forums of the new camp. Some appointed themselves 'block leaders' and would go to the authorities with complaints from their constituents. Businessmen and prominent farmers such as Idris were among the first to be offered plots in the new market that had been sketched in another grid in the sand. Again though, the proud man refused. The family, he was sure, would not be staying long.

Before the distribution centres were established with their system of warehouses, twice a month the World Food Programme would give out rations in an open space and Idris would go and line up with the others in the sun. One day, not long after the family had arrived, he saw a familiar face in the line. Rambo recognized him too. His old foe asked for forgiveness.

Idris told him: 'I know that here I can mobilize people for revenge but I will give you peace. However, I will not forgive you. You planned to kill me but it is only God who kills.' The next time Idris saw Rambo he was a block leader of E7, the one adjacent to his. They were to be neighbours for the next ten years.

Even as Idris got used to their new surroundings, learned his way around the grids and started referring to the tents and makeshift huts as houses, as homes, his mind rebelled and held itself apart. And that was really the only way that the reality of their new life could be borne. 'I had the name of refugee but I never had the mentality of settling here,' Idris said. Everyone in Dadaab has an original story. A story that has been retold so many times, the narrative worn smooth like a wooden handle. It doesn't matter that Tawane himself can't remember that far back, what's important is that the family has a story to make sense of their present predicament. And, for Idris, it had become a habit, a part of him even.

Somalia, for him, was still a hinterland of trauma that flashed and trembled on the horizon like the electrical storms that made the animals nervous. When Tawane finished high school in 2003 and requested permission to return to Somalia to look for work, Idris refused and Tawane became an incentive worker for the US agency CARE instead. And when, in 2005, the Danish Refugee Council offered Tawane a job in the relatively stable northern part of Somalia called Puntland – for '$900 a month', he still remembers joyously – his parents again advised against it. 'That place is not our home,' they said. 'It is under administration by another clan. In case of any incident in another part of the Somali world, even in Kenya or Ethiopia, they can kill you.'

Tawane's friend Omar took the job instead. When Omar came back to visit in 2009 he was earning $2,400 a month and driving a new car. 'He had completely changed himself, very fat! Very brown!' Tawane was sick with regret, but he didn't blame his parents. He had lost the battle for control of his own life long ago when he had allowed his mother to choose his wife.

A generation back, a drought had dispersed his mother's family and one brother, a pastoralist, had crossed the border back to Kenya in search of grazing. Her brother had ended up in the town of Haberswein, a small community seventy miles north of Dadaab. Even for a man rich in goats and camels, when his eyesight failed, the hospital of choice was the free one in the camp. When her ailing brother came to stay guided by his beautiful daughter Apshira, Tawane's mother saw her chance to keep her son close.

She talked to the young girl and convinced the fifteen-year-old child that her cousin Tawane would be a good match. Tawane was not consulted. 'She seduced her for me!' he says. For Apshira, it was a shot at freedom. Her family was most likely planning on giving her someone else to marry and she didn't trust their choice. She agreed.

Tawane cried and pleaded with his mum, he was eighteen then, not yet finished high school and with dreams of further education, he didn't want to marry. But his mother was implacable and crafty. She kept the plan from her brother. 'He is a very difficult one, that man!' she said. 'Very complicated. He would have asked for hundreds of camels and we didn't have that.' She plotted with Apshira: the girl would return to Haberswein with the old man and then Tawane's uncle would steal her back to the camp to elope with Tawane. A compensation dowry – an apology for a crime of passion – was much cheaper than a formal contract.

'It was a success!' the old lady cackles still, proud of her sub-
terfuge. In a week, Tawane's life had been transformed and his
mother's power confirmed. A year later, Apshira bore their first
child. Tawane's mother believed she was defending tradition
against the corruption of the new culture in the camp. 'It is my job
to ensure that the old ways are not entirely diluted,' she told
Tawane.

Tawane stood on a threshold. He was a new kind of person
from his parents. But the bonds of the old world were still visceral,
still strong. He was a prisoner of guilt and of fear. The fear
belonged to his parents but the guilt was his own: at having survived, at not remembering.

His whole life, Tawane had been cautious, avoided conflict and
done as his parents advised. He hadn't intended to get involved in
politics. He was, by instinct and upbringing, a businessman. He
had sought election to the youth umbrella, a consortium of community groups from sports to counselling, because he was
interested in the 'income-generating activities' that it supported;
credit and training for the youth to set up enterprises, and he had
been voted in as treasurer.

For a while, things had gone well and Tawane had become
something of a tycoon. There is no fixed power in the camps so
with credit from the umbrella, Tawane and several friends bought
a generator. They charged 220 subscribers, business owners and
some of the richer residents, a monthly fee of 1,000 shillings ($15
dollars) each. But there wasn't much to spend his earnings on in
the camp. He dreamed of buying a big house, but no permanent
dwellings are permitted. He had considered getting a car, but with
the movement restrictions safaris were limited. In any case, nothing of value in Dadaab stays nailed down for very long. So he did
what people do with their money in Dadaab: he buried it.

Dadaab's scruffy compounds hold billions of shillings just below the surface of the sand. His family was happy. But then the chairman of the umbrella had contracted meningitis right before the influx, and as the second in command, Tawane had stepped into his shoes.

During the famine, Tawane had frantically organized collections of money, food and clothes for the destitute newcomers and taught them how to cook the unfamiliar rations. Uninitiated mothers had mixed the white American flour with water and fed it to their babies thinking it was powdered milk. Little bellies had swollen up like footballs. At a coordination meeting with the agencies he had shamed them all into following the example of the older established refugees in contributing from their own pocket to assist the coming hordes. And when the Kenyan driver was snatched from Hagadera three weeks before the Spaniards, he had tried to help negotiate with the clans across the border to find a way to speak to al-Shabaab, which people suspected of holding the man. Now, as youth chairman, fate had cast him in the spotlight. It made his father Idris nervous.

Tawane saw immediately the dilemma facing the refugees. On one side was the Kenyan state that harassed and ransomed the refugees with impunity. On the other was al-Shabaab, from which many had already fled at least once. The refugees were, literally, between the rock and the hard place that the name, Dadaab, embodied. Taking another slurp of tea, his frown deepened as he offered his prognosis: 'Al-Shabaab will start bombing in the camps, pretending they are refugees, changing their clothes. The Kenyans won't know the difference. And they will make us all suffer.'

17

Heroes Day

October 20th in Kenya is called *mashujaa*, 'heroes', day. In the
national stadium in Nairobi, the President dresses up in military
uniform and the security forces march past. Traditionally a day to
celebrate those who fought for independence against the British,
from this year onwards it would be a day to commemorate those
who were at that moment losing their lives in Somalia fighting
Kenya's first ever war. The army was currently bogged down in
heavy mud ten miles outside the al-Shabaab-held town of
Afmadow. They would remain there for weeks. The headline in
an article in *Time* magazine that week read: 'Kenya Invades
Somalia. Does it Get Any Dumber?'

Meanwhile, in the aid agency compounds inside the UN base
in Dadaab, the televisions carried the celebrations live from the
capital. Bored aid workers slouched on sofas and watched the out-
of-tune pomp, the soldiers sweating in their white gloves and tight
chinstraps and the overwhelmingly Christian songs and rhetoric.
You'd have thought Kenya was a Christian country. Due to the
kidnap, the aid workers who had not yet been evacuated were
prisoners of their little bungalows, painted blue and white like a
holiday camp. Outside, the volleyball and badminton nets hung
limp on their steel poles in the afternoon heat. Dadaab was now
a security level 4. Only Iraq and Afghanistan were higher, at 5.
The compound was suddenly, uncommonly, quiet.

For the aid workers and the journalists, the emergency had

been a ball. The staff danced the dust off their boots at the UN bar called *Pumzika* ('relax' in Swahili), which throbbed into the early hours. 'At that time, there was a party every night!' the UN staff reminisced. 'Ahh, the emergency . . .' they waxed sentimental. The stream of visitors and all the extra staff made it like spring break. People crawled to work hungover, out of unfamiliar bedrooms. 'If you lifted the roofs off, you'd be shocked!' said one. Another aid worker recalled tripping over not one but two couples having sex in the bushes outside Pumzika. Free condoms are distributed inside the compound. The UNHCR main compound alone gets through an estimated 10,000 a year, and this is not a family station. And when it comes to cleaning out the septic tanks, the maintenance guys complain, they are invariably blocked with rubber. The kidnap had put a stop to all that. The bigger agencies, like CARE and Save the Children, pulled out all their expatriate staff immediately. By heroes day, 'it was as if there had been a nuclear strike', said one of the UN staff left behind. The compound was a ghost town while the UN figured out what to do.

Trucks were still delivering fuel to the agency generators, although not to the boreholes in the camps. The roads were quiet. The mud lay undisturbed, smooth and glistening in the ruts. The registration centres were empty and the hospitals had lost qualified doctors and surgeons. The suspension was supposed to be 'all non life-saving services'. No education, no resettlement, no counselling, no care for disabled people, no income generating activities, no protection for people at risk of rape or abuse. In the blocks of Ifo 2 some people who, like Isha and Gab, had only just cut thorns and mudded huts, talked of going home to Somalia.

The mood grew sombre as the agencies began to look more critically at their operations and how they might plug the gap in personnel. There were elected refugee leaders among the elders,

but the UN found them tricky to deal with: too many subter-
ranean politics and curious allegiances. The under-twenties were
an unpredictable, largely uneducated force, and in any case most
of them spoke no English. The '92 group, though, the UN understood: the ones like Tawane, Muna and the others who had arrived
in the first wave from Somalia who had grown up in the camp and
were now aged twenty-to-forty. They spoke the UN's language.
So, it was to them that the UN turned in their moment of crisis.

To Tawane and his colleagues in the youth centre, it was not
heroes day but a busy Thursday. Tawane arrived early at the white
concrete building in a rectangular compound of rubble, opposite
the hospital in Hagadera camp. The two G4S security guards lolled
in their corrugated-steel hut, feet up on broken chairs. The war
had made little adjustment to their posture. On the wall of the
main building was painted: 'Information Technology and Youth
Centre (funded by DANIDA)'. Inside, the computers donated by
the Danish government were already all occupied by kids willing
to pay 440 shillings ($6) a month for access to the internet, their
cheeks shining in the glow of Facebook and the English Premier
League. When he got to his office, Tawane found a line of people
waiting to see him. In the week since the kidnap, his authority as
the de facto camp manager had been almost automatically established. He found himself telling people what to do, and to his
surprise, they complied.

As the elected leader of the 'Youth Umbrella', Tawane had no
formal role to compel people to volunteer on behalf of the
refugees, but he had a respect that had been earned. The youth
who had come of age in the camp felt a responsibility to their
people and to the camp. They were not like the traumatized elders
of Idris's generation, shell-shocked, spending their days staring out
at the horizon. They had always seen themselves as separate. From

Somalia, but not of Somalia, they considered themselves uncorrupted by the war, not like the forty-to-sixty-year-olds whom they blamed for starting the conflict and the under-twenties whose naiveté and muscle, they thought, was responsible for sustaining it. They were a unique creation of the United Nations, an unwitting experiment in humanitarian social engineering.

In some ways, the camp had been good to them. Although a few, like Muna, had not finished school, most of that first wave raced through the Kenyan school system laid on in the camps and onwards, to correspondence diplomas and even degrees. They spoke English and Swahili and wrote it better than they wrote Somali. They had been raised on a diet of NGO culture, of 'gender balance' and 'rights mainstreaming', drilled in all the proper liberal values.

But adulthood in the camp for the '92 group was an unfamiliar place, for which the elders could offer no guide. Having acquired all the educational garlands possible, they had reached Dadaab's glass ceiling and were eager for a bigger life elsewhere. Many of their friends had been resettled to Europe and North America, before 9/11 caused the number of slots in the lottery to evaporate. The young men and women at the youth centre now were the ones left behind, who followed the progress of their friends abroad on Facebook – the cars, the clothes, the unveiled women. They marvelled and they were consumed with longing. Stuck in the camp and forbidden to work, they lived on the welfare of incentive jobs and passed the time playing at politics and civil society in the youth umbrella, preparing themselves, they believed, for a career beyond the camp.

They were a close-knit group: problems were shared, savings were pooled and work was communal. On any given day, some of them could be found at the youth centre, passing the time together as they had done every day for over two decades. Present that morning was Tawane's right hand man and best friend, a tall handsome soccer player named Fish who also worked as an incentive employee for CARE. He was the cabinet member of the umbrella responsible for sports supervising 143 football and eight volleyball teams, and had achieved fame as the organizer of the camps' most celebrated football league. The caretaker of the youth centre, Mohammed, nicknamed 'Africa', was the webmaster of Dadaabcamps.com – the portal that spread news about the camp, though the traffic was mostly from the diaspora outside, desperate for news from home. Owke (pronounced okay) was there too, a musician who played in the camp's most famous band: they borrowed instruments from CARE and sang mostly for the agency calendar: international water day, world toilet day, international day for zero tolerance of female genital mutilation, and so on, though they were also available for weddings. And 'Norwegian', whose nickname derived from a computer error on his ration card.

In the week since the kidnap, Tawane had already become accustomed to a new life: leaving home at six o'clock every morning and often not back until midnight. Meetings, organizing, mobilizing: committees for food distribution, for security, for health extension, for water, for rubbish collection, for the youth. It was like running a medium-sized city without a budget, and his friends in the group had rallied round. The camp was facing an existential crisis, the present, for once, loomed larger than the imaginary future.

Outside, under a neem tree that had struggled up from the rubble of the compound, the friends of the '92 group had assembled themselves on broken plastic chairs, an upturned jerrycan and a breeze block. When Tawane walked over to greet them, the talk was full of suspicion: that the UN intended the suspension as a kind of punishment to the refugees for hosting the kidnappers, a charge the loyal '92 group deeply resented.

'The trouble with the whites, they have no security, they have no clan,' somebody said, trying to pin their troubles on the foreigners' culture. But it was easier to blame it on the newcomers: those who had fled later iterations of the civil war, who hadn't been to school and who were thus, they assumed, more at risk of being radicalized. Among the group, education was held up as an essential value, one of the pillars of a more civilized world.

'Imagine, a child of ten or twelve,' said Owke, 'chewing khat!'

'At eleven in the morning!' said Tawane. The '92 group associated khat with degenerate behaviour and by extension, a propensity for other degenerate activity such as joining al-Shabaab.

'Life was good before. Security was good. Before they came,' said Africa. The kidnap was a watershed. Suddenly, the '92 group had become the old guard and the hot, hungry, miserable past had become halcyon days. They had all mobilized to help the new arrivals but the '92 group mistrusted them all the same. The kidnap seemed to have proved their natural suspicions right. The rumours of fighters visiting the camp were now thicker than ever but when Tawane and his friends made investigations their attempts at counter-intelligence drew a blank. They had no connections, no way in to the networks of the newcomers like Guled. The problem was, as the elected representatives of the youth readily realized: would the UN and the police understand the distinctions between the refugees? And even if they did, could they resist the urge to punish them all collectively? On the evidence so far, it appeared not. And this was the source of Tawane's current problems.

There were eight boreholes in Hagadera camp that relied on generators to draw the water up, but the diesel for the generators was in the CARE compound. The police had refused to escort the agency vehicles and the aid workers themselves were also refusing to come to the camps. So Tawane asked his friends under the tree

to arrange to fetch the drums with donkey carts. He would telephone CARE to tell them the volunteers were coming. They
would go to all the boreholes, a journey of many miles. It was hard
work, but minds that had been sick with dreams of America
would find a brief distraction in the urgency of the present crisis.

In the absence of any agency staff, the women waiting in their
burqas alongside Tawane's office had contributed money and hired
a car to survey the damage caused by the rains. They knew that the
UN trusted Tawane, so now they brought him a list of all the
latrines that had collapsed. And they came with a complaint from
the inhabitants of the new NGO mud-brick houses – they were
melting in the downpour. Tawane told them he'd report it, but he
could promise nothing else.

As he worked his way through his meetings, out of his office
window, across the sandy street, Tawane could see the welded
blue-steel gates of the hospital shaded by eucalyptus trees, the only
original 'tall trees' of Hagadera that had escaped the axe. Inside, his
wife Apshira was in a bad way. She had been due to give birth on
the day of the kidnapping. Five days later, the baby had finally
come, but Asphira had lost a lot of blood. She was in a critical
condition, breastfeeding the newborn and awaiting a transfusion
that was taking longer than usual to arrive. The Hagadera hospital was run by the International Rescue Committee and it was
operating beyond capacity, with beds arranged sideways to fit more
in, and patients lying on strips of cloth on the floor and in the
courtyard. Cholera had just been confirmed in Hagadera and the
staff were braced for worse. Tawane had spent the last few days flitting between his wife's bedside and his office.

At the end of the day he crossed the street to the hospital.
Apshira was asleep on one of the iron beds, her long body curled
in a protective crescent around her sleeping newborn, swaddled in

the green medical linen. Afraid to wake her, Tawane tiptoed out again and turned for home.

The house in block E5 in which he had lived all his years in the camp was on the other side of the camp from the hospital, a thirty-minute walk. He was a stocky, powerful man with a round head and a jaw that when it wasn't smiling could appear fierce. When he walked, he did so purposefully. He made his way now through the Hagadera market, not stopping, but nodding and greeting people chewing khat in their shadowy stalls, sitting next to unsteady towers of plastic goods, mostly from China. Everyone knew him.

As he passed a small tent made of sacking stuffed with men drinking tea and talking loudly, there was a shout. He turned to see a tall man in Kenyan police uniform cuff one of the men round the head several times then kick him in the behind. Apparently he had insulted the policeman. There were hundreds of men sitting around within sight. They could have seized the policeman in a second, yet they sat there, staring at the scene with the sullen gaze of the disempowered. It was the way they had looked at men in uniform for generations.

As the policeman moved on, a stone sailed through the air and landed innocuously on the sergeant's boot. He jerked his head up and took a few rapid steps in the direction of the stone. A gaggle of children shrieked and ran for cover. When the sergeant turned his back another stone whistled past his ear. Enraged, like Mr Wolf in a game of grandmother's footsteps, he wheeled again. The children bunched together, screamed in delight and retreated. It was a classic image, kids throwing stones at occupiers. In the hostility of the children to the policeman and in the sergeant's nervous bullying lay the beginnings of the war's arrival in Dadaab. Both the sergeant and the children knew which sides they were on.

Beyond the market, Tawane crossed the wide maidan in front

of the E blocks. Under a low, black sky, lapwings skittered with little crested heads bleating like goats. Schoolgirls' veils billowed as they walked home from class and smaller children wearing only T-shirts tugged and pulled each other to the ground. On the maidan boys played football threading between holes dug in the sand for building materials and two rubbish-piled skips, one of them alight. Between the blocks, long lonely alleyways stretched for half a mile. And all along the edge of E1 and E3 the gates into the compounds were painted in multicolour stripes, triangles and geometric patterns. One of them was plated with USAID tins and embroidered with a lattice of barbed wire. Inside were mountains of scrap metal scavenged from the camp – valuable loot.

Tawane's compound on the edge of E5 had a corrugated-iron gate painted in the colours of the Jubaland flag. From here, the view of the rubbish-strewn maidan was partially obscured by a single, well-chewed thorn tree. Inside were three donkey carts with steel and wooden boxes fashioned on the back. In red letters on each was the word 'MEAT'. Tawane's family had done well in the camp. They ran a chain of butcheries. A donkey blinked lazily, the rope tying it to the post of the thorn fence gently rocked. Lodged inside the fence were the accoutrements of the family: a kettle, a radio, a comb, children's shoes, clothes and toothbrushes. A thick blue cable snaked through the trees connected to a large satellite dish and a small house washed in pale-blue colours; inside was the family television set. Five goats lay in a pen made of thorns in one corner. Children played on the dust in the other. Tawane's grandmother was asleep in the shade of the neem tree. Hanging from the washing line, out of the way of the dogs and cats, was a small plastic bag of cubed camel meat. It would be dinner.

This was the tranquil domesticity for which Idris had struggled half his life and to which he clung with the force of the trauma-tized. Tawane, though, had the luxury of taking it for granted.

And now he had a chance to prove himself, to break free of his parents' anxious caution. His habitual longing for resettlement that throbbed like a dull ache at the back of his head, dissipated temporarily in the drama of the crisis: his energies were now focused on the opportunities that would flow from his present role. All his life, he had needed the UN; now they needed him. His talk acquired a note of bravura as the new power flooded his veins. 'I have been to trainings on democracy. I know what it is about,' he declared. 'I am an in-born leader!' He was in his element.

18

Kheyro

The refugees who came to the camps as babies were the youngest of the '92 cohort. Muna was one of these. Kheyro was another, although the trajectories of the two young women could not have been more different. While Muna had dropped out of school for love, Kheyro had struggled to stay enrolled because of the demands of providing for the family; she was often called on to help her mum and had fallen behind. Aged nineteen, she was only now in form four, poised to complete secondary school. The timing of the suspension could not have been worse and her hopes of graduation hung in the balance.

In a rented house near Ifo secondary school, Kheyro and the rest of class 4B watched developments in the camp with rising anxiety. The exams for the Kenyan Certificate of Secondary Education (KCSE) had begun on 18 October, the week after the kidnap. After the suspension, most of the fifty trained Kenyan teachers stayed away and more of the thirty-five untrained refugee teachers had to be mobilized from the camps to invigilate, supplemented by police. The authorities would not suspend or delay the exams for any reason. Fear of 'leakage', they said. For the students of 4B, this was the most important month in their lives so far: the KCSE has been their sole aim for the past four years, the culmination of the effort they'd put in long before that to become one of the 2,500 children in the camp to graduate primary school each year and one of the 500 to win a coveted place at secondary school. At the start of the school year, eleven months ago, they had elected a committee and a chairman and contributed 500 shillings ($6) each per month towards the cost of renting a house together, where they would have light (two bulbs between forty-three of them), tea, food, and peace and quiet for studying during their voluntary examination purdah.

Kheyro and her fellow students bent their heads over their exam papers in the low classrooms made of tin, broiling in the afternoon heat. Paramilitary police walked up and down the rows of desks and accompanied students of both sexes for their two minutes in the toilet, their rifles hanging loose as they searched the stalls. In the evenings, the form four pupils regrouped in their rented house and caught up on the news of what had happened while they had been cut off from the outside world.

Every day the radio crackled with new advances: Kenyan airstrikes kill seventy-three militants; Kenyan forces take border towns; France, Denmark and US pledge support for Kenyan invasion; forty-five al-Shabaab fighters ambush Kenyan convoy. And every day, the Kenyan military spokesman, a plump, soft-cheeked man with a mischievous gap-tooth called Major Emanuel ChirChir, tweeted updates as the war unfolded along the border, in locations the students knew. On 28 October events came closer to home: a landmine hit a police vehicle just outside the town of Garissa, a hundred miles further inside Kenya.

The girls prepared the food for the evening meal and then they all went back to studying. The exam was more than their life. The students carried with them the hopes and expectations of whole families.

Kheyro's mother, Rukia, had fled Somalia in 1992, walking for ten days with the infant Kheyro on her back. For nineteen years in the camps, as her young family had increased, Rukia had scavenged firewood from the desert and carried it on her shoulders in the hope that one day her eldest, educated daughter would be able to look after her in return. Kheyro's father had disappeared in Somalia and the family had no other relatives to assist them in the camp. A cousin of Rukia's, Ali, whom people nicknamed 'Ero', white-haired one, had come from Ethiopia recently with his son, Weli, but they were poor and struggling themselves and unable to assume the traditional duties of a male relative and take Rukia and her children under their wing.

Kheyro had a serious face with two large front teeth that took an effort to cover with her lips, and she felt the burden of her mother's effort keenly. It was the accumulated weight of nineteen years of wood: wood that had purchased two batteries for her torch instead of three kilos of rice; light that enabled Kheyro to study at night. Wood sold at ten shillings ($0.15) per load that went towards the cost of a school uniform (a white veil 2.5m square and a blue skirt) at 1,200 ($18). When Kheyro had got in to secondary school, she had waited at home for eighteen days, elated to have won a place but ashamed to be unable to enrol for lack of a uniform and ashamed that her mother had to sweat on her behalf. All for the exam and the possibility it opened up to everything else: an incentive job, money, even a chance to leave.

There are two official routes out of Dadaab to the rich world. One is the resettlement lottery, weighted towards the longer-staying refugees and the vulnerable. For this, the names of the lucky ones selected to go to the few countries that agreed to have them – USA, Australia, Canada, UK, Germany, Norway and Sweden – are posted on the tin wall of the Horseed Hotel in Bosnia market on top of the brightly coloured murals of amazing foods unavailable inside. By now, the list had shrunk considerably from the old days and most people only passed by the hotel to check out of habit. Kheyro's mother, Rukia, was one of these, so was Nisho. The other way out was the KCSE.

Every student who has won a place at one of the six secondary schools in Dadaab dreams of Canada. The World University Service of Canada (WUSC) offers around ten scholarships to young men with a grade B or above in the KCSE and ten young women with a minimum of C-plus – an effort to redress the balance in favour of the few girls that make it that far. Every year that the name of you or your family does not appear on the painted tin wall of the Horseed Hotel, the importance of the escape route of studying increases. Some paid 'morning bribes' to teachers, going early to school for extra help. Others have gone mad in the heat: 'Your head can get full up with reading too much,' said Abdi, a student in Hagadera. 'The temperature of the sun is too high, it is best to do mathematics in the morning, before it's too hot.' Others have committed suicide with the pressure, or the disappointment. Kheyro was vigilant in allowing nothing to upset her course. 'I will be hard-working and get a C-plus,' she vowed.

She knew almost nothing about Canada, but she devoted more energy to imagining it than Somalia. 'If I was in Somalia now, I would not have got an opportunity to learn,' she said, disdainfully. Like their militant brothers in Nigeria whose very name 'Boko Haram' ('western education is forbidden') was against the idea of secular education, al-Shabaab had done much to control or shut down schools in Somalia: banning certain subjects like English or science and appointing hard-line religious instructors or, in some cases, closing secular schools altogether. In its view, education was a religious practice, not a scientific one. The group well knew that their ability to grow and recruit depended on a fresh supply of unenlightened minds.

'I am not afraid of being lonely in Canada,' said Kheyro. She planned to buy a goat to stem the homesickness. And if the goat was not allowed to live in the house, she would buy another house for it, she said. Like her family, Kheyro was a pastoralist at heart.

But the war threatened Kheyro's plans. She was thinking a lot. Worrying about failing, and being trapped in the camp. Worrying that the exams would be cancelled altogether. That was her first fear on 5 November when she heard about the bomb.

The night before, she had returned home for Eid-al-Adha, the feast of the sacrifice, when Abraham prepares to kill his own son only for God to relent and replace the boy with a lamb. She woke in the dark at five and left the mattress on the sand that she shared with her two sisters in their own mud hut. Next door in the hut with the UN plastic tent on the roof that they had put there when the rains came, Rukia slept on in the bed that she shared with Kheyro's eleven-year-old brother, the only man in a household full of women. The boy cannot sleep with his sisters. She prayed and then took a broom to sweep the kitchen. She gathered some of the firewood that lies in a pile next to the kitchen and the fence and lit a fire for tea. The other girls had filled the jerrycans from the tap stand in the block the previous evening and Kheyro poured a little of it into a saucepan and set it to boil. She released the goats from their pen adjacent to the compound and took them to the corner of their block where the old man, the herder, collected them with others into one huge flock and drove them out onto the plain in search of grazing. For this, the family paid him fifty shillings per month, per animal.

As the low morning light fingered the sand through the twigs of the kitchen wall, Kheyro made breakfast: tea with *njera*, a kind of pancake. When the family had extra money they bought milk, and sugar, never meat. Kheyro could not remember ever eating meat. She crossed her hard hennaed feet on the mat, eating and drinking alternately while her sisters helped themselves. They called her by her nickname, Misaal. Rukia had lost five babies before Kheyro lived and, in awe and wonder at the miracle, she nicknamed the child Mithal – unique, an example. The way the

Somalis say it is Misaal. At six-thirty she went to the little tin stockade above the concrete dome with the hole in it that is the family's pit latrine and, taking a bucket of water, she had a bath.

The news came later that morning. A police car had struck a landmine buried in the sand beneath a cooking pot outside the Hagadera police post, on the main road to Dadaab. The bomb failed to explode. But Kheyro knew that didn't matter. Every day the teachers moved with their police escorts between the camps. If they refused to come that would be the end of everything she had worked for.

That year in Kenya, 411,783 candidates were sitting the KCSE. Only a quarter in North Eastern Province were girls. Kheyro was in a minority already. 1.3 million shillings allegedly changed hands nationwide to facilitate cheating in the KCSE, an illicit advantage for some that would raise the average and thus hurt the performance of the poorer majority. The odds were overwhelming against her, even without the insecurity.

Two days later, on 7 November, a car carrying exam materials was attacked near the border post of Liboi. Al-Shabaab was choosing its targets carefully: in the gathering war with Kenya, as it had been in Somalia, secular education would become a battlefield. Kheyro and her fellow students tried to focus on their studies not the radio and braced themselves for the worst. But the Ministry of Education held its nerve for one week more. The exams finished, on schedule, on 14 November. The first successful improvised explosive device (IED) attack in the camps hit the following day.

19

Police! Police!

On 15 November Tawane was eating lunch at home when he heard it. The explosion was so loud he thought it was right outside his gate. The ground shook and the sky seemed about to fall. The radio had been announcing clashes in Somalia daily and army spokesman Major ChirChir had warned residents of ten towns across Somalia to expect airstrikes, tweeting that they would be 'under attack continuously'. He also claimed that donkeys were being used to transport weapons and thus 'large movements of donkeys would be considered al-Shabaab activity'. The war was now here, in Dadaab. After a while, Tawane's phone started up. Everybody was calling him. But still he stayed inside, waiting. It was the first time he'd heard the bang of combat and, for the first time in his life, Tawane was deeply, viscerally, afraid.

When he finally made his way to the site of the blast – the strip of road between the truck garage and the police post where Guled had arrived almost exactly a year before – he found the whole place teeming with people and the two-metre crater cordoned off. A landmine had caught the back of a police Land Cruiser that had been at the head of a convoy of ten agency vehicles returning to Dadaab. A month after the kidnap the suspension of services had finally been lifted and aid workers were beginning to get back to work again. Two G4S security guards, who had been travelling inside the police truck, were badly injured. It was their blood that stained the sand.

Services were immediately suspended again. And Tawane spent his days going round and round the agency compounds, taking the bus from Dadaab and then walking in the sweltering heat between the offices designed for people who always travelled in cars. He arranged temporary contracts, discussed security, planned deliveries of fuel and medicine. But the situation was desperate. The mortality rate in the understaffed hospitals crept up and children that might have lived were dying.

The UN leaned heavily on the police to beef up security. Negotiations with the agencies to resume services again were tough but yielded tentative, limited, advances. After two weeks, some of the braver organizations went back. But then, on 5 December, came the second bomb, in Ifo this time.

That morning, Guled was in Hawa Jube collecting money wired by a friend in Mogadishu. Until the kidnapping, Guled had had a good famine. There had been a stampede of agencies giving out things in the camp. Desperate to demonstrate their reach and impact they had indiscriminately distributed extra food tokens, clothes, blankets, stoves, plastic sheets – all of which could be liquidated for cash. Another friend of his had come from Somalia, and there were new neighbours in the compound in N block. They had even received two goats for slaughter from the Turkish. It had been a party that day. But things were different now.

With the declaration of war, the flow of aid had dried up so only the food rations and skeleton health services remained. And the invasion had added another complication, extra checkpoints on the roads inside Somalia: the Kenyan army was making the most of the invasion to impose another layer of taxes. Life was cheaper when al-Shabaab was in charge over the border. Since the invasion, the price of sugar had jumped from 100 to 150 shillings a kilo. Guled had been forced to call home for help.

He was waiting in line outside the M-Pesa shop, the Kenyan money transfer service, when he heard the blast. The line dropped to the floor all together as though they were merely limbs of one animal. The shop's wire grille snapped shut and the customers who were inside burst onto the street, still crouched against the noise. When they stood up, they saw black smoke climbing into the sky above the road to Dagahaley in the west. A vehicle was on fire. Moments later, they saw three police cars speeding down the road towards Hawa Jube, very fast.

'Police! Police!' the crowd began shouting. Everyone scattered and Guled ran for home.

Nisho was racing along the same road, in the other direction. He had been in the market when he heard the blast. People said it had come from Ifo 2. His first thought was Billai. She was with her sister that day. Nisho dashed past the new, two-storey school that had been built in the centre of Ifo 2 and down the blocks towards Billai's family's house. When he got to the house, his new wife and his in-laws were safe. They were more concerned about him: 'Hide! Hide!' they said. But Nisho, ever excitable, rushed instead towards the bomb site. He shared a birthday and a destiny with the camp; if something happened here, he needed to see for himself. But as he moved along the road, he met police running towards him. He paused. They were not running for him but chasing two men who disappeared inside one of the galvanized Turkish toilets. Ifo 2 is flat and the buildings thinly spaced. It is not a convenient place to evade the law.

The police caught the men and dragged them onto the road. They laid them on the ground and jumped on the bodies. Then they left them bleeding and unconscious. Nisho watched the beating from the doorway of his sister-in-law's house. 'Hide! Hide!' the women repeated. 'Only God protects,' he told them. Within minutes an ambulance arrived to collect the men and the police left. They didn't enter the compound. Finally, ignoring the protests of Billai and her sister, Nisho was able to go to the site of the explosion itself.

At the road, he saw the bodies of two officers, a male and a female, laid on either side of a tree. There were body parts scattered around, blood and bones. The vehicle itself was a tangled mess. The steering wheel had lodged in the roof, the mine had ripped a jagged hole in the floor like a tin can and the windscreen was gone. The gear-shift hung in space and the bonnet was buckled in half. Looking at it, there was no way the driver survived, Nisho thought. He was right, he didn't. Three others were lucky to escape with major injuries.

There were many people crowded around, staring, come from all over the camp. The police meanwhile were pursuing vengeance, sweeping the new blocks of Ifo 2 from Istanbool north, towards where Isha was hurrying to her new home in block M2 with her husband, Gab.

She saw the police come like a wave down the street chasing someone she knew. It was Bishar, her neighbour from the block. He had been part of their group that had walked out of Somalia the year before. Isha said to Gab 'run!' and he did.

Bishar, too, instinctively (and hopelessly) tried to hide in one of the toilet huts. The police got him. As they beat him he cried for mercy, 'La'illah! La'illah!' but, methodical in their rage, the police carried on. Isha and some other women moved towards the police, to beg on the victim's behalf. But they raised their sticks to the women and screamed, wild with fear, '*Toka!*' – 'go', in Swahili.

Bishar's face was torn and his skin was coming off. The officers dragged his mutilated body into their vehicle and drove away, then, after a few metres, threw it out of the back and roared off. Isha and the other women ran to Bishar and wrapped him a cloth. They carried him back to his house in Isha's block where they revived him with water and milk. One hundred people were indiscriminately arrested following the explosion. No one knows how many more were simply beaten and left for dead. Bishar had a broken rib but it would heal. The damage done to the idea of security in the camp would not.

The police now feared the refugees: just as Tawane predicted, to them, every refugee was a suspected terrorist or, at the very least, complicit in harbouring al-Shabaab. And the people, in turn, shrank from the police. Mistrust festered on both sides. For the agencies it was an impossible bind; they didn't know which way to turn. Travelling with police escorts was a liability, yet moving unprotected in the camps was unthinkable. In rapid succession, two more bombs made the suspension in services permanent. Violence became the new normal and the volunteer model pioneered by Tawane and his youth umbrella began to harden from a temporary solution into a new status quo.

On the morning of 20 December, Guled was complaining about the price of sugar in a shop near Bosnia's Sufi mosque. In explanation, the shopkeeper simply said 'security' and rolled his eyes towards the moody sky. There had been another explosion the day before in Hagadera camp, at the same spot as before. In a row outside women were selling vegetables on the ground. Beyond, another group sat – backs straight, ankles crossed – surrounded by soft pillows of hay: fodder for the goats of the camp.

The shopkeeper poured the sugar into a plastic bag, tied a knot in the top, and placed it on the counter. Guled reached into his pocket to count out the precious notes, too many of which he now laid on the wooden board and then – 'Gow!' The noise. It was a massive sound. New to Guled. He had heard explosions in Mogadishu but never anything so close and so obliterating as this.

Leaving the sugar on the counter, he bolted. A huge cloud of smoke mushroomed into the sky above him and sand showered down. The vegetable-sellers were hurtling in all directions. It was chaos.

The IED appeared to have missed its target. The police car that had so narrowly escaped turned sideways in the road and officers fell to the ground, in shock, already shooting. Guled slipped into an alley towards Lagdera livestock market and cowered there with dozens of others, eyes wide and white as the bullets whistled nearby and more police came running.

Down the street, at the junction where the road goes south to the C blocks or west past the ice factory, Nisho was crouched in a truck among sacks of potatoes. He had been standing on top of a truck in the sun, sweat streaming down his back, unloading bananas and potatoes when he heard the blast.

In the bed of the truck, Nisho was visible. He could hear the police approaching. The thwack of their sticks. The yelp of their victims. He slithered over the tailgate and began to crawl underneath the truck. If he could just get behind the wheels, he thought. Then a hand gripped his foot and he was sliding backwards along the ground. Out into the glare of the sunlight. A shadow loomed above him. Crack! Crack! Crack! The stick came down on his back and legs. And then the hand released him and the shadow moved on down the street.

As Nisho limped home bloody, the police surged on through the narrow alleyways of the market, a tide of nervous violence. Eight of them burst into the restaurant at the end of the street. The manager knew their faces; they were the regular police from the camp: they ate here sometimes. But now they were thrashing people left and right and sending the customers scurrying. The cashier didn't run. He was beaten for a solid three minutes until he lay still on the dirty sand floor. Then the officers took the strong box from under the table next to him, smashed it open and removed the 75,000 shillings ($950) that was inside. When the cashier went, later, to the police station to file a complaint, he came face to face with one of the men who had beaten him. The cashier said nothing and went home, disconsolate.

That morning, the police had broken into one shop after another. Kasim, the bookshop owner, had locked his store and turned away only to watch as several policemen smashed the door of the shop, tossing books into the street. When he returned later in the afternoon, 30,000 shillings was gone.

Guled waited among the goats until the commotion was further off. Then he made a break for it and ran. Out the back of Lagdera, down the alleys behind the mechanics' shops and along the road to Hawa Jube, home. When he got there, Maryam and her mother had been terrified for him: 'Are you okay?' they asked. 'We were calling you, why didn't you answer?' His phone had been on silent, in his pocket. It was hot with missed calls.

'I left the sugar,' was all he could say.

'We don't care about that, just that you are okay,' Maryam said. She had been at the food distribution centre, closer to home. She had just exited the warehouses and two weeks of rations were sitting on the ground as she looked for a porter to carry them for her. When the blast tore open the sky, she thought to herself, 'It's going to be another Mogadishu here!' People were running everywhere, spilling rations on the sand. Maryam left the food and ran. For the next two weeks, the family would have to depend on their neighbours. Soon after she got home, the police had passed through the blocks looking for the men. Mercifully, Guled had missed them.

That evening, Maryam's mother got a call from her brother in the UK. He had heard the news. 'Where you come from there are bombs,' he said. 'And now here there are bombs too. Better the place you know.' Her desire to go home was stronger than ever. She began to make preparations.

The next day the police tore through the camp again. In Hagadera they targeted the newer blocks, where the recent arrivals were concentrated: L, M and N where the huts clung to the end of a gully that had been transformed into a small cliff with the rains. In Ifo they had no plan. Around nine a.m., seven officers charged into a hotel on the edge of Bosnia. 'Go back to Somalia,' they shouted as they beat the watchman to a pulp and loaded him into their truck, along with the hotel's cash box. A worker in a mechanic's shop in Lagdera remembers fifteen officers swarming into the garage, every one of whom put a boot in his belly, he claimed.

Tawane rushed to the UN compound to report the assault to the UN protection team, but they could offer no help. Because of the shutdown, they said, the team was unable to come to 'the field', the phrase they used for the world outside of their secure compounds. 'You must do what we used to do,' they told Tawane. So Tawane's youth umbrella, with no experience of human rights work, went house to house collecting testimonies of rape, beatings and looting. In Hagadera, they compiled a list of 126 victims and passed on the particulars to the UN. The volunteers in Ifo did the same. One of the women they met in the hospital was Fartuun.

Fartuun was outside in her compound when three officers came in, shouting in Swahili, '*Wapi mzee?*' – Where is your husband? – and '*Leté pesa!*' – Bring money. She told them she was a teacher and that her husband was away. Then two of them lifted her into the house. One locked the door from the inside while another gripped her neck with his right hand and unzipped his trousers with his left. She struggled, in vain. 'After a while, I felt sperm rolling over my thighs,' she said. In total, at least seven women were raped and over $300,000 dollars was missing across the camps. No one, of course, was ever held to account.

That same morning that the refugees came under attack, Kenyan F-16s bombed the Somali town of Hosingow, eighty miles over the border. Major ChirChir claimed they had struck an al-Shabaab camp, killing seventeen militants but eyewitnesses in the high street of Hosingow told a different story. 'They dropped bombs and went away without knowing who they have killed,' one told a journalist. In the camp, the Somali radio bulletins spat the news like fat in a pan. To the refugees, it all seemed a crude sort of revenge.

Later in the afternoon, when the F-16s had crossed back into Kenyan airspace and the police were back in their base, drinking beer, Guled returned to the shop in the market. Outside was a huge crater. Soon it would fill with water, deep enough for a man to drown. The shopkeeper had kept the sugar for him. Nisho too had come to the market, looking for his due. But the truck had departed without paying him. With the looting and the destruction, many shops were closed, vehicles stopped coming, and people stayed huddled inside. The economy was hit hard.

Initially, Professor White Eyes considered himself lucky. His vegetable stall was a little further inside the warren of alleys of Bosnia, too narrow for police cars and generally avoided by officers scared of patrolling on foot. As soon as he heard the blast, White Eyes hurriedly closed up and slipped out the other side of the market, towards the section where he lived, opposite Transit, the Ethiopian block, E2. When his grandmother had been billeted to E2 all those years ago, she didn't know the hidden benefits that living in a predominantly Ethiopian neighbourhood would bring. For many years she was offended by the alcohol and the loose goings on among their women. But by 2011 her sinful neighbours were increasingly an asset. The minorities like the Sudanese and the Ethiopians maintained gates at either end of the block to control entry and exit – and when the police cracked down on the refugees, they tended to be safe. It was always the Somalis they were after.

When White Eyes got back, E2 was quiet. There was a new hut in his grandmother's compound – freshly mudded and roofed and equipped with a bed and furniture. It had a new inhabitant too: the illiterate girl Habibo. Although he had done well from the influx, the 50,000 shillings he had saved, while a fortune for him, was not an impressive dowry in the Somali wedding stakes. Fortunately Habibo's family were very poor. White Eyes was frank. He told her he could afford no gold, no camel, no vehicles to escort her from her house to his during the wedding. 'I am a refugee,' he said. But with a downpayment of 25,000 shillings, she had accepted. It was still their official honeymoon and coming home to the new house with the beautiful wife made White Eyes happy and proud. 'I loved her and she loved me so much.' Habibo had never been to school, she was a modest woman, he thought. But for the invasion and the bombs, things might have been so different. The ripples of the war, however, carried far – into homes, upsetting lives, turning everything upside down.

Before the honeymoon period was over, the supplier of White Eyes' vegetables in Garissa called to say he would no longer be sending any to Dadaab. With the insecurity on the roads, he was getting out of the vegetable business. While White Eyes looked for another supplier, he still had to pay the rent on the shop, and, in debt from the wedding, his cash flow was critical; within a week he was bankrupt.

'Togetherness we can do more,' was what marriage meant for

White Eyes, the values he had intended to instil in the illiterate girl. But it was not the life Habibo had imagined. 'Bring, bring!' she commanded. She needed money. She needed things. She seemed contemptuous that her poor husband couldn't provide. And so, as he had done so many times before, White Eyes dragged himself back to Bosnia, to start all over again.

In the aftermath of the bombing spree, there was a flurry of meetings. The UN was frantic. The whole existence of the aid operation was under threat. Refugees were still arriving from Somalia, outriders of the famine, but the registration centres were closed. No one knew the full effect of the suspension of services, but anyone could see that the slums that had been emptied were starting to fill up again, as those without friends or relatives in the blocks found shelter in Bulo Bacte and N Zero. With the rain, measles had licked through the camp, then cholera; with nearly 300 cases by the end of November, MSF set up a separate ward. At a loss, the security heads summoned the refugee leaders to the UN compound.

Tawane and the other refugee representatives in their dusty shoes sat in rows in the big white hall with the air-conditioning and the bougainvillaea framing the windows and the UN staff in their sparkling white T-shirts. Tawane was in the middle, his face pinched and serious. Because of his superior English he had been nominated as interpreter.

'The youth,' the UN security officer said, would need to choose 'which side they were on'. He was an ex-military man and had the military tendency of always looking for targets, of always seeing the faceless enemy dressed in civilian clothing. Tawane was dismayed at the implication that their loyalties might be with al-Shabaab, at the lumping together of the educated older refugees with the troublesome newcomers. He had worked hand in hand with the UN during the famine and now with other UN offices – and still they didn't trust him?

Nonetheless, he saw what was needed. In the early morning mist a few days after the bomb, figures had been seen digging on the road from Hagadera to Dadaab. When approached they had fled into the bush. That main road to Dadaab carried everything – food, fuel, medicine, police – and it needed to be safe. The camps that orbited Dadaab town were only five miles of flooded desert away from the UNHCR compound, but they were at risk of being cut off. And so, when the UN staff in the big white hall asked for ideas from the youth about how to improve security, Tawane was full of contributions. He suggested gating the blocks, tarmacking the roads to the camps, and patrols. Tarmacking was expensive, there was no budget for that. But patrols cost no money, as long as they were carried out by volunteers. The meeting actioned it. Meanwhile, the UN found the money to invest in two miles of blast walls, new steel gates and another line of razor wire around their own compound. The new walls were so high that the agency people could not see out. The separation of helper and victim was complete.

Beyond the walls and wires of the compound, the refugee leaders organised five men and five women per block and took turns patrolling the main roads of the camp. In Hagadera camp that made 675 people altogether, one group from six p.m. to two a.m., another from two a.m. until dawn. Every night, torches traced figures of eight along the roads, one metre at a time, looking for IEDs in the sand. It was dangerous work. The police wouldn't do it. The UN was, in effect, placing the refugees in the firing line. It was an enormous gesture on behalf of Tawane and the youth and one that al-Shabaab would not appreciate.

20

Nomads in the City

The pressure was making Tawane ill. Every day he had meetings with the UN, the police and the agencies in Dadaab, and every night he coordinated fuel, water, food in the blocks. He had bought another phone since the old one was ringing all the time, no one could ever get through, but now the new one rang constantly too. He was not sleeping enough and Apshira was worried about his health: he had gone down with malaria. And she complained that he was endangering the family. Idris, his father, wore a permanent look of 'I told you so.'

The police and the UN security team were pressing the refugees for information about the bombers. Dadaab is a tight knit place, they argued, positively teeming. It is not possible for people to lay bombs without anyone seeing. But none of the refugees talked. They knew that talking didn't pay. When officials arrived, faces drained of all expression and questions bounced off the crowd's silence like water off a leaf. The police were losing patience. A big meeting was called in what people thought was the safest place in Hagadera: the mosque. The host community, the sheikhs, the refugee leaders and the police all came together. It was, Tawane recalled, 'a very serious meeting'. He was taking anti-malarial drugs and sat in the back of the large tin hall carpeted in plastic mats along with his good friend Fish. He wasn't feeling well. The government asked the refugees to be frank. Only one of them spoke up.

Ahmed Mahamoud Mohammed, whom everyone called 'Sanyare' – small nose – was on characteristically outspoken form. Middle-aged with short grey hair, he was the leader of the Community Peace and Security Team (CPST) which was composed of volunteers who liaised between the UN, the police and the refugees; one for every block. A prominent businessman with a taxi business, a small shop and a family of seven, Sanyare was well liked.

'We know who is doing this,' he said. And he located the nub of the problem. 'If we point fingers at those involved, who will protect us? If that man is arrested, his relatives can react and kill us.'

The only recourse for the authorities was another threat. The refugees faced a Catch-22 – even if they did know who was behind the attacks and they spoke out, they were at risk from al-Shabaab reprisals; if they didn't, the government would lose patience and force them back to Somalia. This is our home, Sanyare said, and he urged people to cooperate with the authorities: 'If you have any information about the perpetrators, please share it with the police or the CPST.'

That evening, just as it was getting dark, Sanyare was outside his mud and tin house in block C1 when a man with a covered face shot him in the head. Three days later, in a restaurant in Bosnia market, the CPST leader for Ifo camp was assassinated in similar fashion.

As 2012 arrived, Kenyan forces took the Somali town of Fafadun and al-Shabaab ambushed a vehicle in Afmadow, killing eleven. Airstrikes across the southern part of the country continued. Tawane's family urged him to stop his work. Everyone was telling him to run away from Dadaab. Fish's mother was the same. Years ago, she had seen her husband killed in front of her eyes; on the walk to Dadaab, she had lost three children, including an infant six days old. She had paid a price to keep Fish alive and he was more precious to her as a result. When people said to Fish, 'You and Tawane will be next,' she told him. 'Leave this shit alone!'

Fish didn't wait to find out if the grapevine was right. There were urgent discussions with the UN protection team and the field officer for Hagadera but there were no solutions, and so Fish arranged his own movement pass through contacts at the Department for Refugee Affairs and, in the early dark one morning, boarded the bus to Nairobi. In a plastic sticker across the windscreen was painted in capital letters, the word 'FIASCO'.

Fish had never left the familiar heat and squalor of Dadaab. He was nearly thirty years old. Named in honour of a grandfather who owned a large and famous restaurant on the beach and yet didn't like fish, he had walked to the camps out of the civil war like Tawane, aged nine. He should not have needed a movement pass at all. Having married a Kenyan Somali girl who worked for the UN Refugee Agency, he was, technically, entitled to Kenyan citizenship, but neither of them knew their rights. They thought Fish could not travel to Bhasham's home area of Garissa, so they got married in Hagadera and she came to live with him in the camp, in effect consigning herself – and the two daughters they would have – to refugee status. The curious choice was not unprecedented. Many Kenyan Somalis presented themselves as refugees for the free food and services; North Eastern Province was harsh and the government largely absent. And Dadaab was the largest economy of the region. With similar entrepreneurial panache to Tawane's, Fish used $500 sent by a relative in Norway to set up a small cinema – a TV in a shack – on which he showed international soccer matches. With the income from the cinema plus both of them working – she for the UN and he for the agency CARE – they were among the camp's elite. But Bhasham had died of ulcers the year before and while Tawane hesitated about leaving his family, Fish settled his young daughters with his mother and fled to the city.

Having informed the UN and the NGO camp managers of his plans, Fish thought they might have suggested a safe house or hostel where he might stay, but they only wished him *safari njema* – good journey, in Swahili. This put a lot of pressure on the 9,000 shillings ($110) in his pocket that he had saved from his 6,800 shilling a month incentive salary from CARE. He knew no one in the city and had no idea of the cost of anything, beyond a vague notion that it was more expensive than Dadaab. As his bus approached 'down Kenya', the tall buildings, green hills and huge highways inspired fear rather than awe. Fish spent the whole twelve-hour journey worrying about where he would sleep that night.

He emerged into the filthy streets of Naroibi's Eastleigh just as the sun was setting. For Fish, the night had always been a time of dark. But here, people walked in streets lit with electric lights, shops stayed open and people worked beyond dusk. Suddenly, 'nights were days and days were nights!'

The predominantly Somali neighbourhood of Eastleigh was an incredible mass of life. Thirty per cent of Nairobi's city tax revenues come from here. A hundred thousand shoppers visit the district every day. Goods for sale were piled by the side of the road – oil drums, piles of stones, bags of concrete; cobblers bent over soles, rows of worn shoes arranged on sacks, the sales-girls reclined on one arm, chatting and watching the traffic go by. Large Kikuyu women sweated beneath a tin lean-to, dirty T-shirts pulled tight over multiple straps, their bare arms jousting fires with hot pans of frying cassava. A young pretty girl jumped down from a metallic green minibus that glowed hot white inside from LED lights, a stick of maize in her mouth. She was the conductor and she waved commuters on and off.

The brick skyscrapers tottered overhead and beneath them ruts in the road as deep as cars were filled with stagnant liquid: green, black and stocking blue. And all the time, a constant stream of sassy Kikuyu girls, veiled Somali women, men in white kanzus and street boys with glue bottles jammed between their bottom teeth and lower jaw flowed between them. There were signs in Somali, English, Swahili, Amharic. Children crowded around a video-game shack and a ring of people in the dirt road surrounded a trickster brandishing his three cards.

When the colonial government founded the district in 1921 and assigned the areas of the capital along racial lines, Eastleigh was zoned for Asians. But after independence, Somalis – who saw themselves as akin to Asians in the racial hierarchy, or at least above the Africans – took over and it became known as 'Little Mogadishu'. With the boom in Somali piracy, and an estimated $100m in drug money laundered though Kenya every year, real estate in Eastleigh was expensive. But the rest of Nairobi feared the area, the rich people didn't come. For the poor, though, the separate city that the Somalis had carved for themselves was a dynamic economy supplying the cheapest goods (many of them arriving via the camps, hurried along by Nisho) and they needed it.

Fish was overwhelmed. He was also desperately hungry. On the corner of 12th street was a restaurant called 'Silver Park Hotel'. He ordered food and braced himself for the bill. A plate of rice and meat was 120 shillings ($1.5). In Hagadera it was 80 shillings ($1). Not so bad, he thought. He asked the waiter's advice for a good place to sleep and parted with another 700 shillings ($9) for a bed in the Silver Park. In the morning he bought some phone credit and called home and Tawane. The friends were used to checking up on each other every night, sharing confidences and the latest threats. Tawane missed him, he said. He was more alone and more at risk than ever.

The youth chairman of Dagahaley and the overall coordinator of youth activities in the camps, Abdullahi, had also gone to Nairobi. He had received calls from unknown numbers, warning that he would die. But the final straw came one evening when he was standing on the sandy street outside his house and three men carrying AK-47s asked him, 'Where is Abdullahi?' They had his phone number, but it seemed they didn't know what he looked like.

'I don't know that guy,' he said and stepped quietly down a side alley, his heart rapidly climbing up his throat. He had had more luck than Fish with the UN, who had given him a stipend to survive in the city, but still the voices called him on the phone. He wanted the UN to repatriate him to Somalia. 'The goodness of Somalia,' he said, 'you take your gun and defend yourself.' Not like the camp, where the only protection the UN can really offer is to help people at risk to flee somewhere else. The youth leader for Ifo had run away too. As the only one left, Tawane was now, by default, the youth coordinator for the whole camp. His family's protests had grown to fever pitch. But patiently he carried on with his work; supplying the food, the fuel, the medicines, checking his phones, varying his movements, saying his prayers.

Fish, meanwhile, had exchanged one terror for another. He had only 8,000 shillings left. At this rate, he'd be returning to Dadaab in a week. Without any idea where to get money, where he would sleep, or how he would eat, he did what any refugee who can does in such situations: he called his friends abroad.

Abdikadir had been Fish's dear friend in school but he had got lucky. Eight years earlier he had been resettled to Colorado, USA. When Fish told him of the insidious cold in Nairobi, Abdikadir laughed. 'You should try this place!' Now Abdikadir had completed his masters and he worked as a trader in a stock exchange, winning and losing thousands of dollars every week. 'Gambling is *haram* [sinful] in Islam, actually,' said Fish, 'but I am happy for him.' The $50 Abdikadir sent him was the first American bill Fish had seen in his life. He was to get used to them. The guilt of escaping Dadaab and the custom of helping your age-mates makes for a potent charitable cocktail. Every Somali in the West sends home a huge percentage of whatever they get. During the two months that it took Fish volunteering in a restaurant on 11th street until they trusted him enough to make him a waiter and pay him, Abdikadir kept him going.

Fish stayed only one night in Silver Park. He had always made friends easily and Eastleigh was no different. The second night, a man he met in the hotel offered him a mattress on the floor of his room – in effect one quarter of an apartment that had been divided with plywood – in return for a share of the rent. There were two beds and a mattress in a space two metres by four and in the top corner, crammed against the ceiling, a box of wires like a snake's nest from which emerged seventeen black cables. It was the tenant's internet business. From his single D-Link box, he supplied seventeen homes with ethernet cables for a 1,000 shilling per month fee. For another 2,000 shillings ($25) a month, Fish rented the mattress on the floor. It was a windowless room at ground level near the toilet. The walls were entirely bare, grubby with the routine of men and work. It was a vessel for sleeping, nothing more. Everything spoke of transience. The inhabitants lived in their heads, in the future, elsewhere. In that sense, it was just like the camp.

Opposite Fish's mattress, behind a plywood sheet for a door, the incessant drip of the shower head mingled with the permanent trickle of the adjacent communal urinal and the tap where women and girls filled buckets for transportation up into the building's mysterious higher storeys. Each floor was strung with wires and the courtyard so choked with laundry that little natural light made it down to the concrete floor. There was no privacy and his budget was 140 shillings per day ($2), but it was different. Fish had the refugee's appreciation for solid walls and concrete underfoot and he liked it, even if he wasn't entirely welcome.

There were around 50,000 official urban refugees and who knew how many more illegally from Dadaab in Nairobi, mostly in Eastleigh, but a refugee card is no protection against police harassment. The Somali inhabitants of Eastleigh had grown used to the constant shuffling of ID cards and papers and the regular, reluctant, handing over of notes to grinning police who laugh and joke even as they rob. For the refugee, like the nomad, the city is hostile.

Still, Fish was out of Dadaab. Nobody knew him here. Even with the routine bribes, at 500 shillings a time it was a cheaper freedom than that on sale in the camps. And to Fish, Eastleigh was opening up a whole new world. He liked the 'Obama Studio' hair salon and the 'Big Mack Two' restaurant, and even the shebeen where they brewed *changa'a*, the urban moonshine, its condensing pipes cooling in the toxic ooze of the stinking gully. In the afternoon, the western light caught the yellow walls of the precarious towers with their treacherous balconies stuffed with laundry, jerrycans and sacks of charcoal; it glinted on the roof of the petrol station on the corner of Jogoo ('Cockerel') road (where they diluted the fuel with water) and caught the shifting mass of commuters walking down the hill from town after work, tinting tired faces a shining dusty gold. It sometimes felt as if he were part of some grand urban drama of the twenty-first century, and it spurred his dreams. Soon, he would enrol in college for a diploma in business administration and extend his permission to stay in the city, legitimately.

'When you come, you worry: how will the city treat you?' So far, the city was being kind.

21

We Are Not Here to Impose Solutions from Afar

A sky of perfect blue curved over the city as London enjoyed an eerie spring ten degrees centigrade above average. People muttered about climate change while removing their cardigans to eat sandwiches in Green Park. And in the Long Room of Lancaster House, suited representatives of fifty-five countries assembled to discuss a dusty war in a hotter place; where climate change was not a guilty pleasure but 'one of the drivers of conflict'. The London Conference on Somalia of 23 February 2012 was the twentieth international conference convened in as many years to talk about peace in the country. As is the way with international conferences, this one, too, promised to be different.

White men on horses gazed from the oil paintings depicting colonial adventures as the British Prime Minister, David Cameron, opened the five-hour meeting. He acknowledged that international engagement on Somalia for the last twenty years had been 'sporadic', and outlined what he saw as opportunities and challenges. 'We are not here to impose solutions on a country from afar,' he said. The fact that the final communiqué of the meeting had been leaked to the press ten days earlier somewhat undermined his assertion, and the thrust of its conclusions could be easily deduced from the seating plan. David Cameron was flanked by UN Secretary-General Ban Ki-moon and President Yoweri Museveni of Uganda, the largest troop contributor to AMISOM, the African Union force that controlled Mogadishu. Then came Hillary Clinton representing the USA, and the Turkish foreign minister. Thirdly, the invaders of Somalia, Meles Zenawi of Ethiopia and Mwai Kibaki of Kenya. The Prime Minister of Somalia, Abdiweli Ali, was relegated to the fringe. If the people of Dadaab had been watching, they would have been shocked, and then they would have laughed.

In the run-up to the conference, UK Foreign Office officials acknowledged in private that Ethiopia and Kenya were pursuing their own interests in Somalia and were mostly uninterested in peace. 'But the narrative that Ethiopia and Kenya are helpful on Somalia is accepted as fact at the top,' said one in a moment of honesty. In short, the West needed people to talk to, even if those people had reasons to be opposed to a peaceful, united Somalia. During its brief thirty-year history before the 1991 collapse, Somalia had waged war twice against Ethiopia and Kenya to try and unite with their kinsmen living inside the fictitious borders of those two countries, borders negotiated in that very building. The irony! But such basic questions are not for international occasions; they must remain afternoon fodder for the tea-shops of Dadaab and Mogadishu. A cartoon in a Somali paper had it right: the leaders gripping knives and forks around the Lancaster House conference table and the map of Somalia a steak.

President Mwai Kibaki of Kenya had no need to talk of borders; to him that was history. He reserved his patrician monosyllables for an attack on Dadaab: 'The refugee camps are overcrowded,' he noted, rising in his grey pinstripe suit, probably tailored down the road in Jermyn Street. '[They] have caused huge environmental degradation, have led to growing tensions with host populations and are infiltrated by extremists. Therefore, the humanitarian actors should now take advantage of the areas secured from the al-Shabaab to resettle these populations.' He wanted the refugees to go. It was the Jubaland Initiative in action.

The Kenyan government seems to have an institutional antipathy towards the Somalis. Not at the level of the individual, but a memory inscribed in forgotten dusty files, of Garissa Primary school where hundreds of Somalis were interned and killed in 1980, of blood-soaked tarmac at the Wagalla Airstrip where thousands were executed in 1984, of a litany of collective punishments against whole communities that continues to this day. It is the fear of its own crimes metabolized into hate.

Until very recently, there was no such thing as Somalia, only *Somaliweyn* – the Somali people – and the land belonged to God alone. The journey that the refugees had made across the plain, barely a century ago, would have crossed no borders. But ever since the colonial treaties of the 1890s, made under those same chandeliers in Lancaster House, the Ogaden was now part of Ethiopia and Dadaab was in Kenya. Fully one quarter of Kenya and one quarter of Ethiopia is traditional Somali grazing land. A third of the people of the Somali nation reside outside the borders of the state.

Kenya has always feared the fifth column of people whom it had denied the right to secede. When it watched the desperate people crawling across the desert when the rains failed, the Kenyan government saw not indigenes moving upon their ancestral land but invaders. Invaders, indistinguishable from its own Somali population.

The status quo in Dadaab is dependent upon not recognizing the refugees as humans. Because to do so would be to acknowledge that they have rights. And to recognize those rights would be to occasion a reckoning with history that would be too traumatic. It would see the land that the camps occupy as ancestral Somali land. It would render the border that makes the refugees foreign a sham. And it would make the conditions under which they live a crime. Such a reckoning would tear the very state apart. And so the refugees must, at all costs, be demonized. Kibaki was only stating what was necessary.

Kenya has had its own problems with home-grown terrorism in response to its terrible record, so focusing on al-Shabaab and implicating the refugees was also useful. It was a move the other African leaders present knew well: all of them struggled with marginalized and brutalized insurgent minorities of their own. Domestic uprisings such as the one in northern Uganda or those in the Oromia, Gambella or Ogaden regions of Ethiopia were best addressed, they all agreed, through the lens of the 'war on terror'. And for the Somali President, simplifying the complex and shifting clan alliances with al-Shabaab into a single terrorist threat was an essential part of maintaining international support.

'We are scared,' he said in his remarks; 'today we are looking for security.'

His wish was granted: the key outcomes of the London conference were military. More troops, more training, more guns, more money. The Kenyan, Ugandan and Ethiopian contributors to AMISOM pledged more men while the internationals supplied the weapons and the finance. Some efforts were made to impose a financial management board on the Somali government but it resisted the plan. A UN report that followed the conference explained why: between 2009 and 2011 over 70 per cent of development funds allocated to Somalia had gone missing. A year after the London conference, another report noted that the Central Bank of Somalia had been turned into a 'slush fund' from which most withdrawals were for private purposes. At the same time, the UK would quietly admit that nearly a million dollars of aid had ended up in the hands of al-Shabaab. Just like Afghanistan, Iraq, Libya, Syria and many other wars, the wiles of Somalia resisted the efforts of the West to press guns and money into the 'right' hands. Somali troops trained and armed with foreign cash switched sides all the time, as did the politicians that controlled them. The only ones enforcing any kind of stability in Mogadishu were the Ugandans and Burundians of the AMISOM peacekeeping force. And so, when faced with AMISOM's regular killing of civilians and their casual consumption of women and girls in their fortified airport base, the Western powers felt obliged to politely look away.

The day after the conference, after the black cars had whispered up the grey asphalt and swept the drowsy politicians on to another banquet and Hillary Clinton on to Tunis for another conference, this time about Syria, there was a footnote to the meeting: a US drone strike hit an al-Shabaab convoy thirty-five miles south of Mogadishu. US officials told reporters four people had been killed including one 'international militant'. It later emerged that they were referring to a British man whom the Home Secretary had stripped of his citizenship two years earlier.

To the residents of southern Somalia this was what the London conference was really about. For the next few months, clashes escalated in Lower Jubba near the Kenyan border, and al-Shabaab would gradually retreat from Mogadishu, leaving the ruins to AMISOM. It was the picture David Cameron had prophesied in his speech of a fragile city coming back to life. But in the rest of the country, skirmishes between al-Shabaab and Ethiopia and various other allied militias would intensify. The place to which Kenya's President Kibaki wanted to return the refugees was still a war zone, but a war zone too risky for Western journalists to enter.

22

$Y = al\text{-}Shabaab$

A few days after the London conference, on 29 February, when the secondary school exam results were due to be announced, Kheyro woke dreaming of Canada. It was a feeling, she said, of 'bitter sweet'. She stared at the dead tree thatched around with thorns that separated her compound from the one next door. It would be difficult to leave. She knew everything about her neighbours in A2, their characters, how they walked, laughed, snored even. She had seen the children crawl, totter, walk and marry and give birth to their own. She would be sad to say goodbye. She didn't dare allow her thoughts to dwell on her own family from whom she had never spent a night apart, who were as familiar as her own skin. No. She drew herself up and went through the little gate in the thorns to her neighbours and asked to borrow fifty shillings.

The exam results were not yet pasted on the noticeboard at school but someone had come running saying they were online and, for fifty shillings, a man at the internet cafe would tell you the score. In Bosnia she waited in line outside the cyber shop. On its tin walls, the word 'CYBER' was painted in two-foot-high red letters underlined with a yellow stripe and, above the welded-steel door, also in red, 'BOSNIA INTER' but the 'INTER' was so crammed together it was nearly illegible. 'NET' had been added later, on an adjoining wall. The anxious chatter of the students filled the alley. They talked about the harsh grading of the Kenyan exam board.

Hardly anyone ever got an 'A', but many failed, a 'Y'. Afterwards, some of the students in the camp would stage a demonstration against what they saw as unfair grading, holding signs that read 'Y= al-Shabaab'. They meant that those who failed to graduate high school would have no option but to seek an income working for the extremists. Kheyro thought it was a foolish threat. No one she knew had joined the group and she doubted whether any of her fellow students would even know where to find al-Shabaab in the camp. It was here, somewhere, that much was certain, but no one seemed to know any more than that.

As each student came out of the cyber shop, they discussed, they shouted, they tried not to cry. Kheyro nodded her head and flexed her knees and looked around from side to side, her long face unsmiling. She was terrified.

Inside the cafe, it was roasting hot. The walls were hung with a grey UNHCR tent. A shelf held the precious internet box garlanded with wires high up near the ceiling and on a narrow wooden bench divided with timber screens were five PCs scavenged from somewhere. Above them on the wall was a paper calendar with an image of a waterfall sparkling in a forest and a dusty printer sat on the table. Kheyro took the vacant seat next to the shop owner and gave him her name, her admission number and her school. He looked up the information and wrote her results on a piece of paper and folded it in half. Kheyro took it without looking.

Outside, she walked a distance away from the line and unfolded the paper. She breathed out. It was okay. She knew she wouldn't cry. D+. Not enough for Canada but okay. She headed for home light as air, empty. The stress, the uncertainty, the panic was over. But as she walked she returned to herself, inhabited her limbs again and resolved to go back to school to sit the exam a second time. In the compound, her mother Rukia looked up at her from where she was squatting on her heels. Kheyro told her the score and then explained her plan to return to school to increase her score and go to Canada.

'No,' said Rukia. 'You've spent eleven years in school. Now it's time to get money. It's time to work.' She had had enough of carrying wood. Kheyro didn't argue.

After the KCSE results, the competition for incentive jobs in the camp gets tough. The week after the announcement, a position with the Lutheran World Federation received so much interest, application forms were being auctioned. There was less competition to work as a case worker at Handicap International in the new camp, Ifo 2. Only twenty-seven people applied: eight women and nineteen men. Kheyro got the job.

In the compound, they held a party to celebrate. The incentive salary was 6,500 shillings a month ($75). Kheyro bought Coke and Fanta. Rukia cooked rice, spaghetti, bananas and camel meat. It was the first time the family had ever cooked camel meat for themselves. It tasted 'sweet!' Kheyro said. In Somalia they would have had milk and meat every day, Rukia grumbled, and Kheyro would have been married with children by now. But on the other hand, education would transform her life, she would choose her own husband and she would escape the brutality of circumcision that had caused Rukia to lose so many children in childbirth. She was happy for her daughter, for the life ahead of her.

With her first salary, Kheyro bought new clothes for herself, shoes and lotion. She gave her mum 5,000 shillings. Having money was a new experience. Joining the ranks of female breadwinners gave Kheyro confidence and postponed her relatives' unkind chattering about marriage. With all the men killed or idle or overlooked through the agencies' policies of gender balance, working women were the norm in the camp. The men felt emasculated, but Kheyro with her real job was happy. The concerns of men, she had learned, were not to be entertained. At least, not until she had studied all she wanted.

Each day, she rose at five, prayed, made breakfast, released the goats and walked through Bosnia out across no-man's-land. It was an hour's walk through the scorching heat and choking dust across the barren plain to the Handicap office in Ifo 2, but if she took the bus every day she'd have no money left at all. She took to wearing a niqab veil to protect her face from the dust – at least that was the public reason she gave. It was also a display of status. The poor farmers and pastoralists of southern Somalia didn't veil their faces. Niqabs were an urban thing; favoured by the prosperous, and those with an illicit mission. It made Kheyro feel sophisticated.

Handicap International was a concrete building next to the larger compound of Save the Children on a long wide street that stretched away into the ochre horizon until it simply blurred with the sky. Outside was a square of desert fenced off with rusting equipment: swings, a roundabout and a sign on the fence that said, 'CHILD-FRIENDLY SPACE'.

Kheyro's office was a clean white room with a bench and a steel cupboard. She wore overalls and plastic gloves and massaged patients with impaired mobility. Some were missing hands – the al-Shabaab punishment for stealing – and others had lost legs as a result of shrapnel, gunshots, IEDs, landmines. Many of the disabled had recently come from the war – that was why the clinic was in the new camp, Ifo 2. And then there were the Down's syndrome babies, a surprising number, with a talisman from the Koran sewn around their necks. The ones who were unable to crawl Kheyro stretched over a prickly plastic ball and rolled them in opposite circles, the massage oil dripping from her gloved fingers. The babies usually screamed and went rigid, their eyes adult and wide. Kheyro did about ten cases a day.

Kheyro was giving most of her income to her mum and life in the compound had already changed: her brother's and sisters' diet improved; three months of saving yielded a radio and so, in the mornings when she swept the kitchen and set the kettle to boil, she listened in the dark to the clipped burr of the BBC Somali Service. Kheyro was transformed from virtuous student to commanding professional in hot pink hijab with a matching pink mobile phone; when she spoke now, people in the block listened. And Rukia no longer went to the Horseed Hotel to ask those who could read to see if her name was on the resettlement list. Kheyro, though, still had plans to further her education. She had heard that there were scholarships for teachers to go to college, but first she had to become a teacher. Each month, she was keeping back a little of her salary for what she referred to as her 'ends-meets'.

23

Buufis

Kheyro was not the only one dreaming of Canada. That same February, Tawane heard that his sister and her children had finally been selected for resettlement to Canada. Although he had pushed the idea of resettlement out of his mind to focus on the crisis, the news flooded him like a sickness and he struggled to function. His friends recognized the problem immediately; they smiled at each other and rolled their eyes. '*Buufis!*' they said. It was a common affliction in the camp, but, as Professor White Eyes said, 'Buufis is like HIV, it has no cure!'

Buufis is a word coined in Dadaab; the name given to the longing for resettlement out of the refugee camps. It is a kind of depression rooted in an inextinguishable hope for a life elsewhere that simultaneously casts the present into shadow. There had been thirty-two in Tawane's class at primary school. He was nearly the only one left in Dadaab. Twenty years of waiting and hoping can curdle the spirit. It is hard not to see the process as personal criticism. 'I don't know what kind of mistake I have done,' Tawane lamented. 'Maybe I didn't get picked because UNHCR is very pleased with my leadership system. I have a right to go, I have overstayed here.'

Tawane did not in fact have a right to go, but he did have a right to what the UN calls a 'durable solution' to his displacement. This is supposed to involve return, integration in the host country or resettlement. Since neither integration nor return is possible for the inhabitants of Dadaab, everyone waits for resettlement. But the slots offered by the receiving countries are few, and the criteria, at least on paper, strict. The proper criteria for resettlement abroad for protection purposes under UN rules are a specific threat to life, not a generalized fear of war. Thus, those refugees with stories that involve the targeted killing of a family member or discrimination on the basis of ethnicity are more likely to be selected. This led to what the anthropologist Cindy Horst calls 'identity reconstruction', rewriting a different history for yourself. Before things recently changed, a whole industry had sprung up to help: advising on cases and brokering resettlement slots, which traded at up to $10,000 dollars. The *mukhalis* (brokers) told the refugees what to say, helping them with the paperwork and even buying and selling identities.

The photos on ration cards are often grainy. You assumed the name and the story of someone who looks like you – to the busy officials, just another woman in a hijab – and swapped ration cards. When the embassy folk came to take your particulars, it was the fingerprints of a new person instead. People often take the children of relatives abroad, tearing families apart. And new families are made in a hurry, as marriages are rushed just before resettlement flights since to go abroad is, naturally, to become rich and to become the family's representative (and breadwinner) overseas. Even the UN recognizes the informal benefits of resettlement to the extended family.

'If I can get one person resettled, I have helped five hundred,' said the head of protection for UNHCR in Dadaab, an imposing former Zimbabwean divorce lawyer called Leonard Zulu. For precisely this reason, in the past some refugees had had their resettlement slots traded without their knowledge by a corrupt cartel within the UN and, having had their ration cards cancelled, the refugees were left hungry and abandoned. But since 2001, when UNHCR investigated and sacked dozens of its own staff, that wasn't supposed to happen any more. What remains is simply mistrust: the UN mistrusts every refugee story and the refugees are convinced that the UN is secretly planning to sell their only shot at freedom.

Resettlement is a long process, usually taking years: phase one, interview, phase two, then medical exams and security checks. It is also flawed. Those who have committed human rights abuses are not supposed to be eligible, but that didn't stop Rambo, Tawane's father's old foe, from going to the US ten years ago. Hundreds of minor, and even some major, war criminals are walking freely around Western streets, carrying new passports. But since the UN has never done a comprehensive mapping of abuses committed during the twenty-five years of war, these crimes are recorded only in the trauma of the victims and the oral histories of opposing clans. In any case, since the suspension of services, staff from the embassies were refusing to come to the camps and most of the resettlement cases were on hold. The drawbridge was being pulled up.

Professor White Eyes and his grandmother had been listed to go to the US two years before, but they had heard nothing since then. 'My mind is infected with resettlement,' he said. 'Sometimes I cannot even remember my name. I have to go to the market and do research and ask people who am I?' For those slated to go, life is paused: they cannot plan or dream, they are only waiting. But the numbers leaving are fewer than two thousand a year, while the birthrate for the camps is around one thousand a month. Many young men and women commit suicide when their cases fall through, or simply out of frustration at the waiting.

Still, some people forlornly checked the lists on the noticeboard in Hagadera or the wall of the Horseed Hotel in Bosnia market each week. Tawane did. Nisho did. Guled didn't bother. He had told no one of the circumstances that caused him to flee and so there was little chance his case would even be considered for the lottery. Mahat didn't bother either. 'It's not even in my mind to check,' he said. And in some ways he and Guled were better off not thinking about it. 'The UN is unfair!' Nisho fumed.

Every time one of Tawane's friends left to go abroad he wouldn't sleep the whole night. 'You will be very much stressed and ask why has God left me like this?' When a friend goes away, 'the tears are dripping, actually,' said Fish. They are tears of self-pity as well as loss. In a culture centred on leaving, to remain in Dadaab is seen as a kind of failure. 'Real men are those who go to the USA,' said one young boy. The young people in the camps grow up discussing the relative merits of the few countries that accept Somali refugees – the USA, UK, Canada, Australia, Netherlands, Sweden and Norway – as if they too will soon be going there, as if they know all about it.

'Child benefit is good in the UK,' one young man had heard. 'But there is a problem of wives there. They are too westernized. They can take you to court and redeem all the money in your bank account.'

The pain of buufis was bad before Facebook. Now the youth of Dadaab are tormented by it every time they look at their phones. Some cope by inventing parallel lives online, imagining that they are already there; listing their hometowns as 'Cleveland, OH', or 'Minneapolis, MN', posting photos of cars and urban skylines that they have never seen.

By March 2012, conditions in the camp were sliding back towards emergency levels. The month before, MSF had launched a report titled 'Dadaab: Back to Square One'. The suspension in services was having a serious effect, they said. Health posts were being staffed by volunteers for weeks on end. Malnourished children were filling the outpatients' ward again, joining those who had been saved in the famine who still needed up to a year of supple-mentary feeding. If services didn't resume soon, MSF warned, 'the health of the refugees will continue to deteriorate with life-threatening consequences, with aid organizations helplessly witnessing the situation.'

Several schools had not opened since January as teachers failed to show up for work. Emptying latrines was among the services not classified as 'life-saving activities' and they were overflowing. The rats, and cholera, had moved in. Hagadera was the worst affected and in some parts of the camp a sweet haze hung motionless in the dry-season heat. People defecated in the bush at the edge of the camp among the snakes and the scorpions beyond A1 and A2 block where the bandits often visited. But when the police cars did their rounds there in the outer reaches, the men in long beards gripped their sticks in annoyance and looked down, avoiding the gaze of the Kenya police.

Putting aside his frustration about the lottery, Tawane tried to focus on the urgent practical matters at hand. 'Things are moving well,' Tawane told his friends, but it was more wish than fact. He was, in truth, operating beyond his emotional and physical limit. But instead of quitting or running like the others, he began to perceive the turn of events as a challenge to his sense of duty. He talked to Fish, lost in the flare of the city lights, but Nairobi held no magic for him. Tawane's family was here.

Then, at the beginning of March, there was an attack in Nairobi in which grenades were hurled at a bus station killing ten and injuring sixty. A few days later, Tawane got the text message that he had been expecting. From an unknown Somali number came a promise: 'We know the bad work you have been doing with the infidels. God willing, Islam will catch up with you, wherever you are.'

If ever he had proof of a specific threat to his life, here it was. Others had already been killed; the urgency could not be denied.

Tawane shared the message with UNHCR and asked them to protect him. In the prefab offices humming with air-conditioned cold inside the bomb-proof compound, some emails were dashed off about 'the person of concern', but their efforts soon ran out of momentum. Resettlement slots, the junior UN officials told him, were very limited. But it wasn't even clear that his case had been considered; Tawane knew the process and no one had interviewed him about his experience. Instead, the officials urged him to go to Nairobi, at his own expense. Tawane was so angry he could not speak. The bureaucracy for which he had risked his life had failed him.

'I am emotionally out,' he told a friend on the phone. 'I want to tell the UN: you are an enemy to me. You have not asked me anything. I risked my life. I am updating you day and night. People who have the same title as me have run away, are dead. I am the only one that remains. Do I have a spare life? I should opt to join the ones in the sea, dying inside the ocean on the way to Italy.'

He didn't want to go 'down Kenya', but Apshira pleaded with him and his parents backed her up. So, unhappy and afraid, he boarded a bus to Eastleigh. 'As I left Dadaab, my heart was crying.'

A single night in the cold, cramped room crawling with inter-net cables with Fish and five others was enough. The tenants scrambling for a living in the city had multiplied; there were two or three eager young men to a mattress now. When they made room for him out of respect for their elders – not yet thirty but in Somali terms he was an old man – Tawane felt bad and moved instead to the Maka Karam Hotel on 12th street. But the dingy room with a view over the rubbish-strewn street was no place to spend the day. He missed Apshira and the kids too much. 'A poor man cannot stay in Nairobi,' he told her on the phone. He was worried about the threats and what would happen if he returned to Dadaab too soon, but he had a job to do. 'I thought to myself,

I have not done a wrong to any person. I have tried to live a noble life. If they want to kill me, let them. I will die with a clean heart.' And, after only three days in the city, he took the bus home again.

Going home, though, the threats resumed. On his first day back behind the heavy desk in the whitewashed cube of the youth office, Tawane was having a meeting with his 'legal adviser' in the youth umbrella when his phone rang: the news of his return was already swirling far beyond the camp. The number was from Somalia.

'We know you are back and we can get you any time,' said a voice in Somali. Tawane hung up. The legal adviser called back and put the phone on loudspeaker.

'Who are you?' he barked at the phone. No answer. 'Where are you?'

'Bakaara,' a voice replied.

'Mogadishu?' asked the legal adviser.

The phone went dead.

'Ahh,' said Tawane, desperately clutching at straws from which to thatch a denial, 'if they are far, then they are harmless.' He told a brave story of faith in God, that only He would decide his time and how he'd rather die at home with his wife and children than in the city like a beggar. His faith, though, was not sufficient for him to sleep in his own bed. The chairman of Ifo CPST had been shot back in December. Al-Shabaab had eyes in the camp and they had form. He could have moved along with his family to the so-called safe area of Transit, where Muna was with her family, but whatever trust Tawane once had in the UN's ability to protect him was gone. He took to living door to door, choosing a different friend's house in which to try and sleep each night, but invariably he'd end up lying awake, listening to the dark.

24

Grufor

Insomnia was endemic in Transit too. Those who had opted for the dubious protection of the safe area did not see it as a haven. The family of the murdered chairman of Ifo CPST were now living there, though the broken fence offered no defence against the threatening phone calls that stalked the chairman's surviving children. 'We have killed your father, and we will return to finish you!' said one message. For a son that had seen the body of his father in the market with a bullet wound to the head, it was enough to put an end to sleep. And so the boy joined Muna and her lost-boy husband Monday and the many others in Transit who lay awake in their plastic tents, starting at every shift and creak in the night; imagining masked figures moving, liquid in the dark, scaling the broken fence, silencing the G4S guard sleeping off his liquor, exacting revenge.

As the dry season turned to rain and then the wind of the Hagar, the war moved around Dadaab. Troops and police continued to be blown apart by landmines on the Kenyan border. Grenades and machine guns killed scores in attacks on churches, restaurants and nightclubs in Nairobi, Mombasa and Garissa. In May another landmine claimed a policeman in Dagahaley camp and an IED tore through shops injuring thirty-eight in Nairobi's Central Business District. And each time the President thundered about pushing the refugees into Jubaland. Fish worried about getting on the wrong bus in the city. Nisho asked God to spare him an unlucky day at the market. And Guled feared that al-Shabaab would finally catch up with him.

In June a bomb exploded in Bosnia, targeting Mama Isnino, the chairlady of Ifo. It sent everyone in the food distribution centre running, scrambling on top of each other to get out. Pregnant women fell down, so did Guled, and the stampeding crowd trampled them all. Someone shouted 'The hospital! The hospital!' and Guled joined the crowds racing to escape from the incipient police, but the G4S guards locked the gates of the hospital and beat the desperate crowd back. Avoiding the road he threaded through the blocks but when he reached his hut, his mother-in-law urged him to go and hide in the bush. 'I should not have sent you!' she wailed; Maryam was pregnant again and they were taking it in turns to fetch the food for the family. By the time he returned at dusk, she was rueing her delay in returning to Mogadishu and had redoubled her resolve to quit the camp as soon as her debts were paid and the road was dry.

A few weeks later, armed men attacked a convoy of the Norwegian Refugee Council in Ifo 2 and kidnapped three more foreign aid workers. A few streets away, in Handicap International, Kheyro was safely bundled into a car with her colleagues and taken to the UN compound to wait with the other incentive workers under armed guard.

Through the boom of the landmine and the bomb, and through the panic of the kidnappings, Muna sat in Transit as though the war didn't touch her. She rarely ventured beyond the fence and Monday fetched the rations for her. To her the violence was as distant as news on the radio. Far more interesting were the tragic turns of her own life, whose daily dramas she chewed over with her neighbour Sweetee.

Apart from the lack of space, life in Transit had started off well enough. Soon after Muna and Monday and the children Umaima and Christine had arrived, hundreds of Sudanese moved in – residents of Hagadera who had had a fight with the Somalis there and wanted now to be moved to Kakuma, Kenya's other camp that was majority Sudanese. They served as protection, a buffer against the casual discrimination shown to Monday by the Somali residents, and against any foolish schemes launched on behalf of Muna's inflamed family. The tent behind Muna's was inhabited by a group of Sudanese boys. Impossibly tall, they shared one prized yellow Arsenal T-shirt between them – each one wearing it on alternate days – and on their tent in permanent marker pen was scrawled 'Manchester United'.

Muna and Monday needed the safety of numbers. Moving to Transit had not stopped the phone calls threatening divine vengeance. For the hardliners, miscegenation was not something that they could square with their world view. Even the Dinka in S3 did not condone what Monday had done, but they were less evangelical in their bigotry. As Monday's neighbour Julia explained, 'In our clan it is forbidden to marry outside. But in this place, people are few, so you take whatever you can get.' She was understanding of the Somali wish to eliminate Monday even if she didn't agree with it: 'The Somalis want to kill him,' she said, 'that is their rule.' Clan rules were immutable.

A group of sheikhs tried to make things right. They invited Monday to the compound of the Darfurians – as Sudanese Muslims, their stockade in E block was relatively neutral ground. Four men with long beards, skirts and turbans turned to the young recalcitrant and told him, 'You have married our daughter so now you have to change your religion.' Monday tried to explain that he was stuck: it would be hard for his people to accept him becoming Muslim and yet if he remained Christian, 'You people will harm me.' The sombre sheikhs said nothing, their eyes simply burned. Monday extricated himself by promising to think about converting to Islam. 'Give me time,' he pleaded.

On her side, when Muna talked to her sister in Nairobi on the phone and asked her to send money for sugar, the response was ideological: 'How can I assist someone who has become a Christian?' It was as though she had stepped out of the Somali world entirely.

After the Sudanese were transported to Kakuma in the huge white buses of the International Organization for Migration, the children Umaima and Christine lost their defenders. The other Somali kids began to taunt and beat them. And when Muna confronted the parents in Transit, she got the same uncomprehending response: 'How do you know what my children did? You are a Christian, you don't believe in God, how can we believe you?' So she just kept quiet, stayed at home and told the girls not to go too far. Whatever the neighbours said, she did believe in God. And she prayed to Him to take her away from Ifo.

Whether or not the UN heard her prayers, discrimination on the basis of race or religion was something they easily understood and Muna, Monday and the girls were put on a fast track for resettlement, to Australia. Muna was happy. Her family had been accepted for resettlement once before but her mother, fearing that her daughters would be corrupted in America told UNHCR 'no thanks'. It was a rare and bold move and one that Muna and her sister resented. Now, hope was renewed. Monday had a dream of studying engineering and returning to Abiyei with a big drilling machine to claim the oil of the place for his people. He was pleased that his daughter would have three nationalities. Sudanese, Somali and Australian. 'Maybe she will be an ambassador one day for Australia! ... There is a right there, for everybody,' he said. Muna talked gladly of the fact that 'They say nobody talks bad about anybody there, even a woman with no husband and no children.'

Still, in the meantime, Muna and Monday could not live on

hope alone. Monday went back to work as a plumber for the Red Cross and he found Muna a job as a community health worker for the agency Islamic Relief. Soon, though, she stopped going. One day, she had left Transit at the most dangerous time, the afternoon when the camp's eighteen football pitches were full, and some boys playing football, sweaty and excited, stoned her. Since that day she complained of kidney pain. Tests at the hospital revealed nothing. 'But it is her body,' said Monday. 'You cannot argue with her feeling.'

Monday says that from then on Muna changed. She claims he did. But whatever the truth of it, their relationship began to fall apart.

Sweetee pinpointed the trouble to the visit of her friend Sofia. Sofia came to look after Sweetee when she fell sick and it was Sofia, she said, who taught Muna how to chew *miraa*. Miraa or khat is the narcotic leaf that keeps a large proportion of the male population of the camp intoxicated in the afternoons. Sweetee was a chewer. She admitted to the vice without shame, as though it were simply an unfortunate fact, and she had no choice in the matter at all.

'Stress, that's why,' she said in her forlorn sing-song voice by way of explanation. She drank alcohol too. 'I need to forget, but then in the morning I remember again.'

Born in Mogadishu, Sweetee had fled to Nairobi aged twenty-three after the man she eloped with was killed by the gangster cousin her aunt tried to force her to marry. She was eight months pregnant and the shock made her miscarry. In Nairobi she had caught sight of the gangster again so she came to the camp and threw herself upon the mercies of the UN, who gave her a tent in Transit. She was a beauty, and the Somalis had nicknamed her 'Sweetee' on account of her charms.

'Don't do it,' she warned Muna as Sofia offered her some leaves. But Muna gave a wry smile like a miscreant child and stuffed the green narcotics in her cheek. Soon, the two women were to be seen chewing every afternoon, their tents dirty, food uncooked, clothes unwashed and the children far and wide; Christine was once discovered eating stools by the overflowing communal latrines. One day Monday came home from work slightly early and found the friends sitting outside the tent, chewing and smoking cigarettes. He was no stranger to khat, or to drink; he knew the damage they could cause.

'Is that where the money I brought you has gone?' His 10,000 shillings salary had gone in three days. 'That money is for the kids!'

'Yes,' said Muna, not dissembling. 'I have stress, I need to chew.'

'I forbid you.' Monday chanced his authority but Muna was having none of it.

'You chew. So I can too,' she said.

'I cannot chew when the children are there. I cannot chew the money that is meant for them,' he said.

Monday cautioned her against Sweetee. People said she was a prostitute. It was well known that she drank and smoked – rare, almost unthinkable, activities for a woman. Muna was defensive. 'If I stay alone, I think too much,' she told him.

'That lady will destroy you,' Monday warned.

But Muna ignored him. When he went to work, she did as she pleased. Finding the tent and the children in a mess, Monday would quarrel with Muna and then take his frustrations elsewhere. The Sudanese cooked liquor in S3 and he spent more and more time among his own people, drinking there. Sometimes he brought alcohol from the aid agency compound in Dadaab where he worked. Little bottles with names like 'Hardman', 'Flyhounds', 'Kane Xtra Golden Spirit'. North East Province is officially dry. The only places you can legitimately buy alcohol in Dadaab is inside the UN compound or the police mess. That was where Sweetee got hers.

In some ways the troubles of Muna and Monday could be traced to geography. Transit was metres from Ifo police station and, across a barren triangle of sand, the Ethiopian block E1. The Somalis of the camp called E1 '*Grufor*' – a corruption of the English words 'Group Four', for the security guards who paid for sex and gave the block its reputation for prostitution. It is hard to say whether E1 became corrupted as result of its proximity to the police station or whether it was doomed from the start. The oldest inhabitants claim it wasn't always like that, but over time there developed an unhealthy symbiosis between the two. Grufor was where all the bad girls were. And Sweetee was certainly one of them.

With its ragged line of shops backing onto the windward side of the camp, Grufor was like a lonely outpost in the Wild West. Rickety tin verandas jutted out on poles dug into the sand. Behind green and red scraps of cloth figures moved and eyes flashed in the gloom. Several times a day, across the dusty triangle you could see the officers coming, waddling in their half-uniforms, guns loose, come to buy cigarettes or food or just to look for diversions. 'Burqa hotel' was at one end of the strip and 'Dube restaurant' was at the other behind a huge pile of firewood for the furnaces of the kitchen that never went out. In between was 'Brothers Shop' where the wrapped green stalks of khat lay beneath strips of damp sacking.

Dube was a large man with grey hair and pinched lips who sat on a car tyre behind a broken desk in his restaurant, counting his money into a little wooden box while he waited to join his sons in the US. He had recently wired them $75,000 to purchase a twelve-wheeler truck to save them the ignominy of cleaning toilets or butchering unclean meat. He wanted to go to California, he said, 'just to see it, and to make some money', but then his plan was to return to Ifo to retire. He had set up his restaurant and his myriad other businesses at the beginning of the camp in 1991, with money he had brought from home, as had the Ethiopian Carlos who ran the 'Mini-Shop' next door. Carlos with his soft child's skin and woman's thick lashes, sat in his wooden shop sunk like a coffin buried along with washing powder, sugar, cigarettes, sweets and matches. The shop was a full foot below the surface of the ground. Twenty years of sand blown across the desert had raised the level of the plain making him sink a little every year.

Behind Carlos's, down an alleyway, was Lamma's 'Photo Studio' with its laminated backdrop of unearthly Alpine waterfalls. He had an old Kodak Instamatic and detachable bulbs on stalks which he had purchased through two years of hunger by selling his rations. The films he sent to Nairobi for processing and the finished prints he sold for fifteen shillings a go. His compound was the only green one in the block, perhaps in the whole of the camp. Banana plants, elephant grass and white climbing flowers surrounded a square metre of what could only be described as lawn. He was from the mountains of southern Ethiopia and had recently been reunited with his wife and child whom he had lost, six years earlier, when he fled after being wrongly accused of treasonous political beliefs. Now he spent an hour every morning carrying water so that his child could know what it was like to sit on grass. There was more dignity and resistance in that square metre of green than there was in the whole of the rest of Grufor.

Some people survived the pressure cooker of Dadaab by keeping their eyes on a distant prize: people like Nisho and Kheyro, who worked hard at the narrowest sliver of opportunity that the camp had to offer. But they were few. For every Kheyro who kept their dream alive against the odds, there was a Sweetee for whom the effort of belief in a better life was too much. For whom the evidence of misery and hopelessness was overwhelming and whose only rational option in the circumstances was to pass the time, to dull the pain. It was often the most clear-eyed that slipped through the cracks into the fleshpots of E1. And Muna was no different.

The camp was an introduction to another world. For young Somalis, raised within the strictures of a conservative culture, the exposure to Christians, Ethiopians, Sudanese, Ugandans, Congolese and others was liberating. And this was precisely what the traditionalists and the elders feared. E1, the majority Ethiopian block, for them, represented the worst of Dadaab, the place where Somali culture went to die. Professor White Eyes scrupulously kept to his own compound in E2 next door. Nisho could not bear to hear the name of the place – he would place his hands over his ears whenever anyone mentioned 'Grufor'. Sometimes, young Somali boys from other blocks came to peek at the goings on as though it were a right of passage. The motley inhabitants knew that they were outcasts, 'There are no good people here,' they would laugh. Everyone had a story of how they had fallen foul of the crowd, or their husbands, and they came together, the outcasts, and named themselves 'Survivors'.

Grufor had become an informal refuge for victims of rape and domestic violence, which flourished in a place where men are stripped of their traditional power. The democratic UN camp elections robbed the male-dominated clan of its organizing role in social life. The agencies tried to give the few incentive positions they had to women to encourage what they called 'gender balance' and, apart from those who chose to hustle in the market for a pittance, the remainder of the male population had no ability to provide for their families. They felt emasculated and camouflaged their injured pride in khat and idleness. There was little in their world that they controlled and so the one thing they sought to master, above all else, was their women.

Muna and Sweetee were introduced to Grufor by its chief survivor, Zim Zim, a slender and bewitching Somali girl who, twelve years ago, had fallen for an Ethiopian neighbour, a proprietor of a tin-can TV cinema. Her family had resisted the match and ever since had refused to acknowledge her existence. In an effort to try and change her mind about the Ethiopian, Zim Zim's sisters had kidnapped her and doused her with boiling water, but the rubbery scar on one shoulder simply became a promise that she could not betray. She saw her family every day but said nothing, and they would not cross the threshold of the unkempt compound that she shared with other disgraced single women where Sweetee and Muna now came to chew khat in the afternoons.

'Somali culture should change,' Zim Zim said. 'They are too close-minded.' Something Muna could appreciate. 'Refugee life has opened up new worlds to us,' Zim Zim said in her steady monotone voice, devoid of hope or feeling, as a long-haired, light-skinned child the colour of a hazelnut rolled in the dust at her feet.

As well as Zim Zim, there was Hamdi – a large plump woman with beady black eyes, an enormous muscle of a tongue and a beauty spot in the middle of her uncommonly fair cheek – and many others. There were the sisters whose father had disowned them for their bad habits of drinking and shouting and taking off their clothes in public. And the girl who had grown up in E1 and went about unveiled, her breasts hanging barely concealed beneath a filthy T-shirt, hair uncombed and her two children by different fathers feral in the block. Muna became part of their world.

And so, for Muna and Monday, there began a destructive triangular dance between Grufor, the police post and Transit. Monday would return home to find an empty tent in Transit and the children lodged with the neighbours and lose his cool. 'The lady was driving me crazy!' he said later in guilty explanation. 'There are people who are running Muna, pushing her to a bad life.' When she came back later, drunk, he hit her. And when Sweetee intervened, he hit her too.

Muna would go then to the police post to report the incident. And there, in the little tin-roofed building behind the limp Kenyan flag, she would find Corporal Wanyama ('animals' in Swahili) or his deputy Felix. Wanyama's official title in the Kenyan system was 'Officer Commanding Station', or OCS, but everyone simply referred to him as 'the in-charge'. He was a kindly middle-aged man with a gruff manner and a wide girth who struggled inside standard-issue trousers that were patently too small. Felix was a more slippery individual. In the camp the police enjoy a privileged position among the hordes of the vulnerable. They had long become accustomed to never doing their duty for free. 'I will happily assist you,' Felix reportedly told Muna, 'if you will assist me.' Muna claims she resisted the man and his advances, that she told him 'no'. But over time, alleged Monday, 'That "no" became "yes".'

The police had money. They had khat. And they had the only legal bar in Ifo: a small wooden shack with wooden benches beneath some twisted thorn bushes where off-duty officers soaked in the shade. The mangled carcass of the police Land Cruiser destroyed by the bomb on the road to Dagahaley lay nearby. Sweetee liked to go there and drink and Muna learned to go with her. Both swore that they never did what most of the E1 girls did in return for beer. But there are many people in E1 who'll swear otherwise.

Whenever Muna came back from E1, Monday was usually even more enraged than before. Sweetee was philosophical about their fights, and put the blame firmly on the elemental corruption of violence; she had, after all, had ample experience: 'You know how when someone has started to beat you, he starts enjoying it . . .'

And so the whole cycle would begin again. Monday would take the unattended children to S3 block to stay with the Sudanese and Muna would lodge another complaint in the police station and get to talking with Felix. Muna denied any relationship but she warned Monday that if he continued to abuse her, Felix would put him away for 'a good ten years'. Twice Felix arrested him on suspicion of domestic violence, simply because, Monday thought, he wanted to spend the night with Muna while Monday slept in the single stinking concrete cell in the police compound. Wanyama would hear no criticism of his deputy and dismissed Monday's complaints. 'That man cannot control his woman,' he said of Monday. 'That is the problem with that man.' And he advised Muna to stay in Transit and Monday to go back to S3 with visiting rights for the children only. To avoid trouble, Monday agreed.

Monday longed for their resettlement case to proceed swiftly. When we get to Australia, he told himself, 'everyone has a right; they cannot put you in jail for no reason. Things will be different there.' He planned on staying apart from Muna, but close enough to see the kids. Muna had different ideas: 'If he drinks, he always comes to me, wanting to force me. In Australia I need to be far from him, at least an airport away.'

This made Monday sad. He could not abandon Christine. He drank in the compound of CARE next to the Red Cross where he worked, in the bar the aid workers called 'the Grease Pit' furnished with concrete benches beneath neem trees on ground studded with decades of beer caps. Monday liked to sit there, mix a glass of Guinness with half a bottle of vodka and reminisce.

'The memories of my childhood connect with the present,' he said. 'I cannot allow Christine to be an orphan like me. Something you have witnessed as a child you cannot forget. I grew up swimming and fishing in the Nile. Christine won't have that; here it is dry. The crocodiles are there, in the Nile. You can see them walking outside. There is a small boat made of wood with a paddle. You go, there are very big fish. You take them with a boat. You swim within the water but the crocodile usually comes out in the evening. You take a stick and beat the water and then they run away. But don't dive deeply to their mouth! We usually eat fish. You can't get that here. Unless you have money and then you request it from Nairobi and it comes on the bus. Once I requested fish of 1,000 shillings from Nairobi. It was strange for Muna. She was happy. She liked it. We mixed it with groundnut and okra, like at home.'

Monday struggled with the waiting to go to Australia. He drank, he got depressed, but he tried to be practical and he put his faith in God. 'We are all refugees in this world, and God will decide when it is your time to go.' Muna had a more proactive strategy. She lost patience with the UN process. By September 2012 it had been over a year of waiting, so she took Christine and went to the UNHCR compound in Ifo camp. Behind its big red-steel doors, there is a sandy fenced-off cage, with narrow benches like a makeshift bus shelter where the supplicants wait to petition their masters. The relationship with the UN was medieval. Every day there were hysterics as desperate women hurled themselves against the fence or onto the baking sand. But always to little effect. The men just sat, sullen and angry, as if plotting revenge.

Muna dumped the baby Christine on the desk of Ifo camp's Field Officer, a lightly bearded Egyptian man in a freshly laundered UNHCR T-shirt. Behind his gold-plated Ray-Bans, the Egyptian was unmoved. Indeed, that was his job: like all the well-heeled international staff, he was paid nearly nine thousand dollars a month, tax free, to allow the wheels of bureaucracy to turn at their own pace and to keep the cases of desperate refugees such as Muna from arriving on the desks of his superiors. The camp was full of impatient refugees and, in spite of Muna's desperation, nobody thought to check with the Australians and hurry the case along.

Another time Muna put the two children in the sand in front of the Egyptian's car as he tried to leave the compound. She refused to move. 'I have so many problems and you don't want to assist me!' she screamed. 'You take them!'

And once, she handed the children over to the G4S security guards outside the gate and told them to keep the kids for her while she committed suicide. They called Monday and he came to collect them; by now their case was famous. Muna meanwhile was back at her tent in Transit, busy preparing rat poison in a cup. Sweetee arrived just in time, smelled the cup, and threw it away.

In only a year, Muna's appearance had completely changed. After Christine's birth, she was high on her own audacity, the daring. She had been still full of curves, her skin shone, her gait retained its sassy lilt. But now her cheeks had sunk, her skin was the colour of ash, her eyes had lost their mischievous gleam, and her winning smile rarely surfaced. There was no more swell of a proud bosom, only the careless walk of despair as she flung her body from one day into the next.

Monday desperately tried to hold himself together for the future. Despite the bad luck life had dealt him, he still had faith that tomorrow could indeed bring into being a new world. But for Muna that hopeful future seemed to be still too far away to be worth waiting for. She knew she was powerless to determine her own fate and had lost even the dream that escape might be possible. In that, Muna was perhaps the ultimate child of her generation. Raised in the limbo of the camp, the true daughter of Dadaab, Muna had relinquished responsibility for herself entirely to the testing mercy of events. It had become a way of life.

25

In Bed with the Enemy

Along the hostile road to the coastal city of Kismayo, the Kenyan army slowly, painfully, advanced: 250 miles had taken them twelve months. From the outset, Kenya had claimed that al-Shabaab was its target in Somalia, not any particular city or territory. To admit otherwise would have been to confess that the establishment of the buffer-state, Jubaland, had been the goal all along. But everybody knew that Kismayo – the intended headquarters of Jubaland and the stronghold of al-Shabaab – was the prize Kenya had in its sights, and by the end of September 2012 they were poised to take it.

For weeks, a warship had rained shells on the city sending hundreds of refugees scurrying along the road to Dadaab. There they met the advancing Kenyans, who treated the fleeing civilians as though they were members of al-Shabaab. Traumatized refugees limped into the camps with desperate stories of being stripped, robbed and gang-raped by their supposed liberators, to whom they had come seeking protection.

The shelling was horrendous. The refugees spoke of 'fire that rained from the sky'. One man had shards of orange-coloured shrapnel still lodged in his head: he was the lucky member of the family. He had spent hours collecting the shreds of his two-year-old girl, his wife and their newborn daughter from the rubble of their home in order to give them a proper burial. Another returned home to find a metre-wide crater in the living room and burned corpses scattered all over the house. 'Shells from Kenya,' said one.

'No, French,' said another. Intelligence sources would later confirm that both were correct.

'They say the ships were American, firing at us, but it is all the same to me,' one man ruminated slowly when he arrived in Dadaab. A journey that had taken the Kenyan military one year he had walked in two weeks, barely sleeping. His sandals were wafer thin.

Another of the new arrivals was a lone boy. He had gone to the shops in Kismayo one day only to return and find his home and his entire family turned to rubble. When asked what happened, he said, simply: 'Death came from above.' On his wrist was a beaded bracelet arranged in the word 'Kenya', worn, perhaps, for protection rather than pride. He had buck teeth and dark skin and his head jerked to one side as he talked, as though caught on a fishing line: the tremors of shell-shock. His eyes were bottomless; they were difficult to look into for long. The BBC Somali Service interviewed survivors on the radio, but journalists were too afraid of al-Shabaab to go and verify their claims. If the French and the Kenyan Defence Forces (KDF) were guilty of war crimes in Kismayo, nobody could say.

Just before dawn on 29 September, a woman in a village near Kismayo was cooking breakfast with her mother and grandmother. Outside, she heard shots. It was a moment before she realized that a bullet had passed through the mud wall of her hut, and through the body of her grandmother before lodging itself in her mother's leg. She peered out. She saw 'an airplane, hovering' and troops pouring out of 'black ships'. Later that day, as she buried her grandmother, Kenyan troops preceded by US and European special forces advanced unopposed into the port of Kismayo. The Kenyan army spokesman Major ChirChir was beside himself, tweeting the successful completion of 'Operation Sledgehammer' and declaring 'mission accomplished'.

In Dadaab, Tawane and many of the youth from the Ogadeen clan who hailed from the areas around Kismayo allowed themselves to be transported by the excitement. They dared to believe that the birth of a new state – Jubaland – was at hand. Even if doing so involved ignoring the inconvenient reality that al-Shabaab had merely retreated into the surrounding countryside. Supporting Jubaland – in effect, a breakaway state – was also at odds with a loyalty to Somalia as a whole.

The principal casualty of Somalia's civil war is the very idea of the nation of Somalia. Since the beginning of the fighting in 1991, areas with a settled clan majority have declared themselves states and distanced themselves from the carnage of 'south central', as the rest of the country is called. To inspire loyalty, to call young men to fight for it, the nation must hold some meaning. In the chaos of this fundamentally divided nation, it is no surprise that people have held more fiercely to the solid constants of Somali life: Islam and the clan. And these are the competing political visions for the country now: one based on a patchwork of splintered 'federal' clan-based states like Somaliland, Puntland and Jubaland, and the other the totalizing, unifying religion of al-Shabaab.

Jubaland's supporters overestimated their Kenyan saviours, though. Instead of simply installing a new regime in Kismayo and returning home, the Kenyan Defence Forces (KDF) caught the scent of profit. An earlier UN report had already highlighted what it called a 'pax commercial' between Kenyan criminal business interests and al-Shabaab over the smuggling routes. Now KDF entered the same arena. Although it was only their first war, the

Kenyan military learned fast the game of modern conflict in law-less places. Peace afforded only a generalized prosperity for all. The real money lay in disorder: in the gaps, the margins, the illegal rackets, the opportunities for gaining an edge. Al-Shabaab's main source of revenue in southern Somalia had been charcoal exported through Kismayo to the Middle East. The UN had tried to ban the trade in a bid to cut off funding for al-Shabaab but the char-coal was too lucrative for the Kenyan army to leave alone and the steady burning of Jubaland's once beautiful acacia forests contin-ued, even, in fact, picking up speed; a million bags a month arriving in Kismayo. With the KDF and a local militia called Ras Kamboni controlling the port, soon exports of charcoal were run-ning at 140 per cent of the level under al-Shabaab, jumping in value from $25m to $38m per year. Al-Shabaab still controlled the forested countryside all around Kismayo but logging was only part of the illicit networks that found new life under KDF.

All the sectors in which al-Shabaab had been active in traffick-ing – charcoal, cars, sugar, drugs, weapons and humans – now boomed, confirming suspicions for some that capturing the Kismayo trade had been the goal of the invasion from the start. A Western intelligence agency estimated that 60–70 per cent of the illegal sugar that makes up a third of the Kenyan market comes through Kismayo. Their information suggested that under the new deal, Ras Kamboni and the KDF each took 30 per cent of port duties and al-Shabaab 40 per cent. The Kenyan army was in bed with the enemy.

Criminal networks on such a scale do not pass outside the purview of the state, they usually pass through it – a fact that was demonstrated by the listing of a number of senior Kenyan politi-cians on US watch lists for drug trafficking and other criminal activity. In June 2011 the former assistant minister and current Member of Parliament, John Harun Mwau, was one of two

Kenyans flagged by the US government under the Foreign Narcotics Kingpin Designation Act. But it made no difference to business as usual.

Instead, the politicians in Nairobi eyed the Kismayo trade greedily. In February 2013 elections were coming. They needed cash. Five years earlier, President Mwai Kibaki had fixed the election amid nationwide violence. His godson, Deputy President Uhuru Kenyatta, now stood accused by the International Criminal Court of mobilizing thugs to attack civilians. His political rival and co-accused was former agriculture minister William Ruto, indicted for mobilizing violence against Kenyatta's Kikuyu supporters. This time around, the two erstwhile opponents had decided that their best strategy of avoiding prosecution was to team up and seek election on the same ticket, what they called the 'Jubilee' coalition. Kenyatta was Kenya's richest man. Ruto wasn't far behind him. Both had a reputation for grand corruption. They were running for President and Vice-President respectively and they were willing to spend whatever it took. The kingpins and their illicit flows from Kismayo became more influential than ever. Criminal business – and the price of sugar – rocketed.

With new forces in charge in Kismayo, the supply chain for goods in Bosnia on which Nisho relied, was changing. Al-Shabaab had run a democratic smuggling racket: anyone with money could participate as long as they paid their dues. The KDF, however, allied to one clan, was more partisan and fights over the trade began. In the camps, already expanded beyond the budget capacity of the UN to effectively police them, law and order began to unravel. The refugees who had prayed for the Kenyan army's success, now began to regret it. Instead of making Kenya and the camps safer, the invasion of Somalia was having the opposite effect.

*

The smuggling gangs preyed on the camps and the women began to live in fear. As in the war zone over the border, a breakdown in security is felt first by women: cases of rape rose now by a third. Rape is a violation of Somali custom but the war had long since shattered tradition. As many as one in three women in the camp was being attacked. It was epidemic. Everyone knew someone, many had even witnessed it. Kheyro saw a woman being dragged into the bush not far from her house. Nisho and Billai knew two Rahanweyn women who were raped in Ifo 2, near Billai's family compound. 'The rape of the torch', they called it, because one of the gang of attackers had shone a light in the girls' faces while others pinned them down. Billai had known one of the girls. She was called Selma. After the rape of the torch, Billai's family held a big meeting of all the relatives from Salidley. When the rains came in the new year, they decided, they would go back. But Guled's mother-in-law didn't want to wait.

After the explosions earlier in the year, Maryam's mother had stalled. Water on the roads and the shifting war had prevented her from travelling, and then the debts that the family had run up at the shops; she wanted to return to Mogadishu with a clean sheet. But the rape crisis was too much. Caught between the bullets back home and the probability of being attacked in the camp, she chose the bullets. 'Better to die in dignity,' she said before Guled and Maryam accompanied her to the truck stop in Lagdera market where she boarded a vehicle to Somalia.

The month after her departure, an unprecedented appeal from the NGOs serving the camp further vindicated her decision. 'The current situation in Dadaab is untenable ... Aid programs are failing to reach basic minimum humanitarian standards ... A change in approach to Dadaab is urgently needed,' warned the coalition of agencies. One year after the worst famine in a generation, the world had all but forgotten the victims of twelve months before. The camps were perilously short of money.

The incessant wind of the plain had torn the tents of last year's emergency to shreds. 130,000 needed replacements, or at least permission to build more permanent structures. Many had done like Isha and simply taken the poles and used them for the rafters of a traditional hut and thatched it with grass. And Isha's children were walking long distances to fetch water – they were among the 50,000 in the new camps still without nearby boreholes and tap stands. Health care was also in jeopardy. By year's end, Maryam was worried. She was nearing her term and the hospital was under severe strain as all those without clinics from Ifo 2 crowded the wards in Hawa Jube. More agencies were packing up and leaving.

The absence of the agencies had put years on Tawane. His middle had filled out and a soft halo of grey had settled on his crown. He looked tired. He had plans to hand over power, for his job was becoming impossible. It was hard to see how things could go on as they were: the camps were desperately overcrowded, facing a $100m shortfall, literally overflowing with sewage and sinking into the mud. The situation was, as the NGOs said, untenable.

The approaching election raised the tension further. Although nominally full of aliens, the camp was in fact a key constituency: teeming with Kenyans and people with illegal Kenyan IDs, as well as large volumes of people who could be paid to ink their thumbs in favour of one candidate or another. In Kenyan elections poor people are a commodity and violence is an inexpensive campaign tool. When a woman was injured by an IED planted beneath a voter registration centre in Ifo camp, the camp took it as a sign of things to come. The 2007 elections had seen over 1,500 dead across the country and half a million homeless. At the end of 2012, over 450 had already been killed in political violence and the country seemed on a knife edge. November was the bloodiest month: grenades in Mombasa, Garissa, six dead in an exploded minibus in Eastleigh, forty-two police massacred in Baragoi. If Kenya imploded too, where would the refugees go?

The unseasonal weather was playing its part too. By the end of the year, temperatures were already hitting their dry-season high of 105 degrees Farenheit. There were downpours in December and then suddenly days cooler than anyone could remember. It led to a feeling of unease and the minds of the refugees darted off in strange directions. Maryam and Guled endlessly debated going back to Somalia, she pleading to return so that she could give birth at home in Mogadishu, he still paranoid about reprisals from al-Shabaab. He had kept a low profile, told no one about his past and had had no specific threats so far in the camp, but the memory of that time was vivid and fresh.

Feelings about going home were unrelated to facts on the ground from the war; they were more driven by emotions and the perilous situation in the camp. People were wildly optimistic about peace in Somalia one minute and entirely cynical the next. In the morning Guled bemoaned the bombs and the rape and wondered aloud about walking to Italy or committing suicide. Yet by evening he would be holding forth about how Dadaab was home. Tawane's surreal denial captured the mood perfectly: 'The security situation is exaggerated. We also pray God.'

Nisho's wife Billai clamoured to join her family on their impending trip back to Salidley. Nisho told her to do what she liked. For him, such discussions were moot. Life always seemed to frustrate his best intentions, and experience had left him with a fatalistic outlook, as though his life really was written and there was little point in contesting the matter. Acceptance of fate in Dadaab is perhaps the hardest thing about the refugee existence. Nisho's grace, under such pressure, was uncommon.

In truth, the inhabitants of the camp were trapped; there were no good options, they had nowhere to go. Somalia was racked with violence and the resettlement process remained stalled. In the heat, the fear and the uncertainty, a stable point of view was a rare and precious thing. The refugees' conversation was the dialogue of the prisoner with his own walls.

PART THREE

Guri – Home

26

Crackdown!

In the city, in the one-room bedsit on 12th street, there came a knock on the door. It was not unexpected. For weeks, the whole population of Eastleigh had been living in fear of rape, torture or, if they were lucky, of only being robbed of all the money in their pockets. The three young men inside knew that, one day, it would be their turn for the police to raid their home but there was little they could do to prepare. They looked at each other now and hesitated: their fate would depend on the mood of the officers on the other side of the thin sheet of plywood.

'*Fungua!*' a voice shouted in Swahili. Open!

The men scrambled to their feet. Two police officers stepped through the doorway and, with a glance, took in the scene. Two unmade beds and one mattress on the floor. Three men, apparently ethnically Somali, clean shaven and nicely dressed. Piles of books, open, on the beds, on the floor. It looked as though they'd been disturbed in the middle of a study session.

'*Nyinyi wanafunzi?*' barked the shorter one of the two. You're students?

'*Ndiyo.*' Yes, said Fish.

'*Vitambulisho!*' Identity cards!

Fish and one of the other young men pulled out their student ID cards, which were, thankfully, up to date. The other guy, sleeping on the floor, was a resident of Dadaab and not yet an official student, although he hoped to be. He had no card.

'*Sasa?*' What now? asked the taller officer, who seemed more sympathetic, smiling the cruel greedy smile that Fish had come to dread.

Fish was routinely stopped in Nairobi. The police there detain and extort refugees for sport almost, or at least whenever they need a little extra for beer or school fees. He had learned that the best response was to joke around, pretend that you're Kenyan like them, and to speak Swahili first of all. English aroused their suspicions. And if they asked for ID, Fish always gave them his student card. Police were known to simply tear up refugee alien certificates and say that they didn't count. The transformation from legitimate, protected refugee, to undocumented immigrant at risk of instant deportation was often just as fast as that. It was an effective way of sending some-one scuttling back to Dadaab. And containing all the refugees within the camps was exactly what the Kenyan government intended.

On 13 December 2012 the government's Department for Refugee Affairs (DRA) held a press conference to announce that all assistance for Nairobi's urban refugees would end and that all registered refugees in the country should return to the camps in Dadaab and Kakuma. The acting director of the DRA, Badu Katelo, a shy, bookish man given to outbursts when questioned too closely, said the directive was in response to the recent terror attacks in the country, implying that the refugees were somehow to blame. Since the army had invaded Somalia, there had been over thirty attacks on Kenyan soil against security forces and civilians alike. Seventy-six were dead, and hundreds had been injured. And a few weeks earlier, on 18 November, the capital had suffered the most lethal attack yet. In Eastleigh's section one, a grenade had been tossed inside a minibus – known in Nairobi as a '*matatu*' – killing seven and injuring thirty. Riots broke out. A wave of abuses against the Somali population of Nairobi followed, focusing particularly on 'little Mogadishu', Eastleigh, during which officers shouted at their

Somali prey to 'Go back to the camp!' That was why the officers were in Fish's apartment now. The Kenyan police called it a 'crackdown'. In practice what that meant was just another licensed opportunity for extortion and recreational rape. The city that had been kind to Fish was now baring its teeth.

Kenya has always feared the nomads. It was a fear inherited from the British with their '*kipande*' system – metal dog tags imprinted with the wearer's three names (those of his own, his father and grandfather), location of residence and the white man who was responsible for him. A metal box, like a locket, contained the 'pass' and official information about the individual's rights of movement. Through the idea of lineage and circumscribed reserves, the British sought to tear the nomad from his wandering ways and ground him in a particular place. A 1989 screening exercise headed by Kenyan ethnic Somali government officials sought to do the same thing. Locating people by their genealogy, it tried to distinguish Kenyans from foreigners, ignoring entirely the fluid history of the northern half of the country. Nomadism was not something the southerners were able to understand or accept. Thousands of people from both countries were erroneously deported to a Somalia on the brink of war. Now the government was at it again, trying to keep the outsiders penned in.

Several times a week throughout December and January, Fish was stopped by police and asked to show his papers. He usually made sure to sit at the back of the bus where he stood more chance of the police picking on someone else before they got to him. But one time, returning from class, he had jumped into the front seat without thinking. When he saw the large policewoman flag the bus to a halt at the entrance to Eastleigh where the traffic bunches as it leaves the highway, his heart sank.

She laughed when he offered her his student ID, and told him to alight from the bus.

'We are not in an examination room, I am not your teacher! Do you have any other document?'

Fish spluttered, and fumbled for his other papers. But before he could show them, the policewoman lost interest.

'What do you have?' she asked. Fish knew what she meant.

'Two hundred and thirty shillings,' he said. (It was true. 'Sometimes the police will put their hands in your pockets, so you'd better tell the truth!' he explained.) The woman was busy with another passenger by then and she took the money he pressed into her hand and waved him off.

Another time, stopped while walking down his own street, he handed over his money and walked on, only to be stopped again at the corner. Fearful of incriminating the man who had just shaken him down to his colleague, he made a run for it, back to the first policeman and begged him to come to the end of the street to explain to the second that he should be allowed to pass. Each time an officer lazily waved a truncheon in his general direction Fish stopped and sighed and reached into his pocket for the money that would allow him to get home: they usually didn't like less than 2,000 shillings ($22). It was expensive. He took to studying in the bedsit and avoiding class, only venturing out for food and essentials; his world shrank.

Fish was lucky: he had friends willing to send him what the Somalis in Nairobi called 'caution money'. Those without were locked up until relatives came to post what was called 'bail', but since the cases never went anywhere and the charges were fiction, it could only properly be described as 'ransom'.

For ten weeks, the wave of round-ups continued, mostly at night. Thousands were arbitrarily detained and had to pay $100, $200, $300 or more for release. Hundreds were beaten up. And rape stories piled up on the desks of social workers, too many to enumerate. 'This is Kenya, we can rape you if we want to,' a policeman told one woman stopped on 2nd street and detained in a police truck. 'You are all al-Shabaab and you are all terrorists,' a female police officer told another Somali woman.

On top of the 55,000 refugees in Nairobi with UNHCR mandates – asylum, permission to stay – Kenya reckoned there were at least another 100,000 undocumented aliens, mostly Somalis, in Nairobi too. And it wanted them all in Dadaab. The urban relocation effort, Mr Katelo said at his government press conference, would be 'closely followed by repatriation of Somali refugees back to Somalia'. The Kenyan government seemed to think that the arrival of the army in Kismayo signified that southern Somalia was now safe for refugees to return. But peace is not so easily built.

Kenya was flying into dangerous territory. *Refoulement*, the forcible return of asylum seekers and refugees, is illegal under Kenyan and international law. On such a scale it would be unprecedented in modern times. Keeping refugees in camps and restricting their freedom of movement is also illegal, but Kenya had been doing it for so long it was a way of life that was no longer questioned. By the end of 2012, UNHCR had no money even to look after the existing refugees, let alone 55,000 more. At the beginning of 2013, the budget was one third of what it had been in 2011 during the emergency. The needs were around $130m. The budget was $35m. All UNHCR's spare funds were being eaten by the Syrian crisis.

The crackdown provoked an outcry from Somali ministers and human rights groups as well as a court case. On 23 January the Kenyan High Court ordered the government to suspend the relocation plan while the court considered its legality. It didn't matter: the beatings and the extortion were already having an effect. The crackdown had shifted the odds. Faced with the inevitability of beatings, imprisonment and extortion, thousands of Somalis in Nairobi chose instead the random dangers of the war and headed across the border or on to aeroplanes. The Somali embassy in Nairobi reported issuing 'go home' permits – basically a temporary passport for people who had fled the country without one – at the rate of a hundred a day during December and January. The UN noted 8,000 crossing overland into Somalia during January and February, but that was just the official figure. The movements were clandestine, so no one knew the real total.

If the Kenyan government believed that the only way to get the refugees moving was with a kick, it worked with Fish. In the bedsit in Little Mogadishu, the tense back-and-forth with the officers was eventually resolved without bloodshed for the surrender of 500 shillings. As the door closed on the officers, Fish and his room-mates breathed a deep sigh of relief, but it was the last straw. Staying in Nairobi was getting too expensive. At least for a little while, he decided, it was time to go back to the camp.

27

The Stain of Sugar

After two seasons in Ifo 2, Billai's family were recovered from the famine. The rape and the declared intentions of the government of Kenya to return the refugees had primed the air. When the rains arrived in February, it was their cue.

Along the lines of the blocks in Ifo 2, the bare patches on the sand and every second tent gone spoke of a mass movement. The established refugees estimated that 50–80,000 of those who had come to Dadaab in 2011 had gone back by April 2013. The UN though could only guess at the numbers, since almost no one ever handed in their ration card. The card was currency: entitling the bearer to food every two weeks. Departing refugees entrusted their cards to family members or, if they were confident that they wouldn't be back, sold them in the market for a tidy sum: 10,000 shillings for a family size 10 ration card, 5,000 for a family size 7. Tents were selling for 1,500 or 1,000 if they were damaged and old. Billai's family gave her their card of family size 8 and they agreed that Nisho would send cash back to Salidley every two weeks.

One damp afternoon in February, Billai and Nisho walked with the family across the scrub to the stage in Dagahaley camp where trucks departed for Somalia. Billai's family climbed on top of the cargo of a rusty ten-wheeler and people passed the younger children and their belongings up. Perching on top were two parents, eight children and one large mattress that Nisho had bought for them at a cost, he reminded people, of 1,800 shillings. At five p.m., under a rain-cleansed sky, they began the long journey back to Salidley. With the rains it would take a while.

As she waved them off, Billai was sad. Her world was being torn in half. She had come to Dadaab with one family and now they were leaving her in the hands of another. She wasn't sure she'd made the right decision to stay. Despite advances by Kenya and AMISOM in southern Somalia throughout January and February, al-Shabaab was still in control in her small hometown, but the family was poor, and with little to give the insurgents, they had little to fear. In some sense they looked forward to the security of a stable government. At least back in Salidley a woman could sleep without fear of being raped.

Shortly after Billai's family had gone, the sheikhs called everyone to the football field beside the thorny graveyard for mass prayers to end the rape epidemic. Nisho and Billai went. For them it was a personal matter; Billai's friend Selma, who had undergone the ordeal with the torch, would be there too. For two days residents of Ifo 1 and 2 had been fasting. By ten o'clock in the morning, thousands filled the plain, spilling among the graves, onto the road and into the fringes of the bush. The turnout was impressive, mobilizing far more than the Kenyan general election campaign that was nearing its climax. People had had enough: families had nowhere else to turn. God was their last resort.

Selma had been taken to the hospital by her family, but, after a brief examination, she was discharged. There is a rape survivors' clinic at the Hawa Jube hospital and a well-funded counselling office although few women avail themselves of their services. After two months, the family brought her back. Selma was pregnant. When interviewed, she said she had conceived from the rape. The elders called another meeting and decided that to mitigate the shame, Selma must be married to the boy that had previously tried to seduce her. Since the rape he had shown no interest, but on the day of the mass prayer he was also present on the football field. He was now her husband.

Up to the temporary loudspeaker system stepped Sheikh Mohammed, the leading moderate cleric of the camps. He wore a red-checked head-dress in the Saudi style and a white jellaba over black socks and shoes. In his hand he clutched the tools of his trade: a wooden staff, a Koran and a mobile phone. The crowd bent their heads and murmured in response, 'Aleykum Salaam.' In a commanding voice, he led the prayer and then he called down a curse on all those perpetrating the crimes against the women of the camps: 'May God punish them and take them to hellfire. Let them die soon and may their flesh be torn to pieces. May they surrender!'

As the prayers ended and Nisho walked back to B block, there was a commotion by the little makeshift shops on the road from Hawa Jube to Bosnia, where the drivers usually bought their damp bundles of khat wrapped in banana leaves. Kenyan Police Reservists (basically volunteers with guns) had discovered two men with five-litre jerrycans filled with ammunition. The oncoming crowd was unforgiving. Armed gangs were blamed for the rape scourge and the men were severely beaten before real police arrived and took the wounded bodies to hospital and then to jail. Some days later, groups of vigilante refugees turned over several suspected gangsters to police. Prayers of thanks were given in the mosques for what was taken as a sign of God's providence, but was more probably due to the traditional fear of a sheikh's curse that still carried weight in the camps. In any case, the episode seemed to bring the rape crisis to a close and the number of attacks fell after that. For Billai's family though, and for Selma, it was too late. A few days after the prayer, Selma and her new husband went back to Somalia, too, preferring the uncertainty of the war to the shame and the memories that were ever present in the camp.

*

A month passed. The rains stopped. The Hagar came again. Billai's mood would not lift. She hated the dust storms brought by the wind. From the unceasing struggle in either mud or dust, there seemed no respite. Without her family, Ifo was empty. Staying in the camp seemed harder when considered against the alternative of a life back home, even one under the authority of al-Shabaab. To accept the limitations of Dadaab one needed to imagine that the alternative was worse. And as conditions in the camp deteriorated further, the demands placed on the imagination stretched credulity. For a young girl with an independent mind, it was almost impossible.

But for Nisho, joining the in-laws back in Somalia was not an option. He had no income there, and no hope of one. He earned something in Ifo, even though inflation and insecurity were rapidly depleting its value. One day in April, Nisho brought the 200 shillings profit he had made in the market back to their home in block B: the humble compound, the small mud house with its tarpaulin roof, bivouac kitchen covered in sacks, cardboard boxes and plastic bags and the laundry drying on the sparse thorn fence. Billai flew into a rage. With her green polyester veil trembling about her, she threw the money back in his face.

'How much do things cost?' she screamed. 'Milk? Sugar? Shall I cook my own body?'

Nisho tried to explain that it was the market that made the prices go up and not him. But Billai did not want a lesson in economics. She wanted money.

When he fought with Billai, Nisho usually went next door into the little lean-to made of sticks and a plastic sheet, to mull over his troubles with his sidekick, Mahat. Mahat had problems of his own. His mother had found a new man, a 'turnboy', working on the refugee minibuses that connected the camps, whom Mahat had hoped might fund a uniform and exercise books so that he could return to school. But when he approached the man for money, he told Mahat he had none to spare. It pained Mahat to see the man spending money on other things and so he had taken again to sleeping at Nisho's place.

On an old and sunken mattress in the lean-to, the two boys lounged and chatted late into the night. 'She may divorce me because of poverty, if it continues like this. I know she will ask for it,' Nisho worried. 'I was married by the grace of Turkey last time. So if she runs away where will I get another one from?' If he took the long view, and placed all his troubles and his poverty in context, Nisho might have discerned a grim pattern; one that had no relief. Hope lived withih a shorter time frame: it was less depressing to find cause and effect in current events. And so Nisho's life was a routine lament about the mysterious secret machinations of the economy that affected the ebb and flow of trucks into Bosnia, and thus the relative harmony of his domestic situation. This time he placed the blame for his marital tensions squarely on the election.

The northern counties had voted as one for 'Jubilee', as the new Kenyan government was being called, although 'voted' is not the right word. Business and politics in Kenya are inseparable. People said that the sugar trade, control of the northern smuggling routes, had been mortgaged to buy the election. Now the cartels had to make their investments pay. And this was Nisho's problem. The sugar trade was haywire. Competition didn't take place on the terrain of products and pricing, or even through the ballot box. Instead, gunmen came to town. Fifteen attacks hit Garissa and North Eastern Province in the first five months of 2013. Masked assailants opened fire in restaurants, threw grenades at police cars, shot public officials in broad daylight, and machine-gunned ten at the Holiday Inn in the middle of Garissa town.

Nisho didn't care who was President. He paid little attention when the vastly expensive computerized voting system collapsed amid accusations of corruption, nor when the final result was announced several days later, against a backdrop of a large electronic screen displaying numbers that did not add up and about which none of the attendant journalists asked any questions. It mattered little to him that the Jubilee coalition had won. The rest of Kenya was divided between those who believed the poll was genuine and those who agreed with leading anti-corruption campaigner, John Githongo, that, 'It was stolen massively, and stolen well.' But Nisho was less bothered about corruption than its consequences. And he drew connections that the analysts in Nairobi didn't see.

The stain of sugar was all over the election. The new mayor of Nairobi, Evans Kidero, was a former managing director of Kenya's largest sugar producer, Mumias. A newspaper report that nervous editors refused to publish claimed that the one billion shillings he used to purchase the nomination and the election had been acquired by slowing production at Mumias as part of an orchestrated cornering of the market. Aden Duale, the first-time MP and sugar scion from Garissa, emerged as the House Majority Leader in parliament, his inexperience apparently no bar to the role. The refugees nicknamed Duale 'Aden Bomb', since they blamed him for the insecurity in the camps. Whatever sugar deals had been done in order to pay for the election, it was not good for the economy of Bosnia.

'Before Uhuru came to power, I used to unload seven vehicles a day,' Nisho complained. 'Sugar, rice, pasta, milk, shoes, mostly from Somalia. Now it is only one.' Nisho sensed a plot. Indeed price fixing between the cartels was common. Since the Kenyans took control of Kismayo, the cost of a fifty-kilo sack of sugar soared from 4,000 shillings ($50) to 6,000 ($70). In the market, a kilo had jumped from 90 shillings to 130, and from there inflation galloped ahead. The price of a sack of maize had doubled too, from 3,000 shillings to 6,000. That was why Billai stomped around amid the blackened pots in the compound of B block and why Nisho feared going home at the end of a long day.

The day after Billai threw money at him, Nisho told his fellow market porters of his wife's attitude. It turned out he was not alone. Everyone was suffering from the fall in income. Among themselves, in their porters' association, they agreed to raise the price of their labour. That day they unloaded a vehicle but, afterwards, the money in Nisho's hand was the same. He was nostalgic for the old days, 'when Ifo was Ifo', he said. In the evening, when he went back to the compound and tried to explain to Billai, she exploded before he had even finished, hurling the money at his chest.

'If you throw money at me again, I will report you to your relatives!' he said, but his threat failed to interrupt the torrent of her words. Nisho raised his voice instead.

'If you don't shut up I will divorce you!' he shouted. And then he was out of the house and in the lean-to with Mahat. Mahat was struggling for work too, but he tried to console his friend and mentor. He put it down to the windy season. When the monsoon blew north, it was always bad for business, he said.

'Maybe the population of the camps is decreasing too,' Mahat speculated. 'I've seen so many going home from Ifo 2.' He had been spending more and more time there, pushing wheelbarrows a sweaty mile across the scrub to earn twenty shillings ($0.25) a time. At a tap stand in Hawa Jube, he had met a very pale girl, 'whiter than a white person', he told Nisho. Amina was fourteen, her breasts had just started to show. He wanted to marry her when he grew up. Nisho promised to help him with the dowry, even as he cautioned his young friend against the terrorism of womankind.

*

What Nisho attributed to the irrational vagaries of the female species was in fact a problem familiar to many married couples in the camp. Romance places heavy demands on the future. Making the intolerable situation of the camp into a tolerable domestic reality for the present was a gymnastic trick that broke many marriages and tested reserves of patience. Frustration found a ready outlet in domestic violence: quarrels (and bruises) were for some a regular part of daily life.

Monday and Muna were suffering from the tyranny of an uncertain horizon and their strategies for coping with the wait were not complementary. The delay was slowly destroying them.

Guled and Maryam were also struggling. In January, during the hottest period of the year shortly after Maryam's mother had gone back to Mogadishu, a baby boy had arrived. That birth too had been by Caesarean and this time the doctor advised Maryam not to carry anything on her head for two years. The necessary daily jobs of the camp such as fetching water were beyond her, and she no longer had her mother there to help out with housework and with money. Without work and unable to assist, Guled lived under a cloud of shame, a shame for which Maryam appeared to have little sympathy. Going home became the only topic of conversation and when he tried to explain his fears about al-Shabaab in Mogadishu she told him he was exaggerating. To Guled, it just seemed that Maryam was becoming more difficult. What Nisho had in mind, though, in his warning to Mahat was the famous story of Professor White Eyes. It was a tale that the men of the camp repeated with glee for it seemed to confirm, from the perspective of a humiliated male, the essential wickedness of women.

At first things between him and Habibo seemed good. White Eyes had eventually found a job well insulated from the climatic and political ups and downs of the economy: running a grinding mill in Bosnia that turned the surplus yellow maize of America's Midwest into cornflour from which refugees of every community – the Sudanese, the Congolese, the Ethiopians – could make their traditional dishes. The tall Anuak from Gambella in Ethiopia with their hair braided into electric patterns were the most demanding customers: they liked the mill to be spotlessly clean. So he cleaned, and he oiled and maintained the machine, earning himself another new nickname: *kawaingris*, meaning 'spanner'. It was in honour of his ability to open anything, to adapt to any kind of life.

Early on, he nearly lost a hand in the mill but soon he got the hang of it and every day he brought 200 shillings home to block E2. His wife Habibo wasn't happy but she said nothing. White Eyes thought he had a partner who would help him in solving life's problems, perhaps in saving a little to start another business, to provide for the coming family that he longed for so deeply. But Habibo had other plans. For nearly a year he wondered why his wife was not with child. He knew that the problem could be with either of them, so he kept quiet and persisted in his hope, until one day he overhead a fight. Habibo was quarrelling with their neighbour over a pair of shoes. Habibo had borrowed the shoes but not returned them and now, it seemed, they had found their way into the communal pit latrine. Habibo was pleading innocence.

'You cannot be trusted!' screamed the neighbour. 'You are a liar and a cheat. You even injected yourself and cheated your husband!' White Eyes's heart missed a beat. He pretended he hadn't heard. Later, he sought out the neighbour, apologized on behalf of his headstrong wife and promised to buy her new shoes. Then he broached the real issue: 'In the name of God, what were you talking about injections, tell me the reality?' he begged. The neighbour was only too happy to oblige.

Habibo had been going to the hospital in secret to have contraceptive injections, without telling her husband. The neighbour had seen her more than once, while White Eyes had been at work; she even offered to introduce him to the doctor who had injected her. He was furious. He vowed to take a knife and slit the throat of the doctor. But then he calmed down and took the bus to Hagadera camp to stay with a friend. After a week, he returned to confront Habibo. At sunset, when she laid down to sleep next to him, White Eyes asked her for an explanation. She didn't try and lie.

'I am not going to give birth in this fucking refugee camp!' she said. It was, of course, an entirely rational choice. But although many women might have agreed with Habibo's attitude, few had the temerity to insist on it. She had turned out to be not at all the pliant young girl of White Eyes' imagining.

In the morning he told Habibo to pack her clothes and marched her back to the house of her family. When he met her father in the compound he took a pen and paper out of his pocket, asked the father to call two witnesses and signed three times that he divorced her.

'But why, what happened?' the father asked when they were done.

'Ask her,' he said. And with that, he rushed back to work at the grinding mill. For weeks he was, he said, 'out of service', like a mobile phone switched off, his battery empty, his heart most thoroughly broken. Confined to the endless stony present, another marriage had bit the desert dust.

28

Becoming a Leader

Next to the youth centre in Hagadera is an octagonal building built half of brick and half of timber, roofed with tin sheets and with steel mesh for windows. Stepping inside out of the glare of the sun, in the momentary black before your eyes adjust, it seems like a cage. It is called the CARE social hall, named for the agency that built it. Outside, a line of young boys sat on a low wall, the ruins of a previous humanitarian venture. One wore a Gabon football shirt, one was dressed in Real Madrid, completing his outfit with a pair of shorts and women's platform sandals with little plastic heels. Another was more ragged: no shoes, dirty shorts and a green T-shirt whose faded message was no longer legible. Their eyes flicked from side to side as an electric piano, speakers, table and chairs were carried in and set up. There was going to be a rare show and the boys were not going to miss it.

It was nine a.m. A gang of birds occupying two low trees next to the hall made a loud chorus of 'boo-wop, boo-wop'. Tawane was inside the office, making last-minute changes to his speech. Two girls and two boys sat at the controls of the computers in the centre, delicately, reverentially, stroking the mouse back and forth, while members of the youth umbrella bustled about organizing. From the hall came the squeal of a distorted electric piano and then the clash of a drum machine and the screech of feedback. The musicians were warming up. After another hour and a half all was ready.

In the hall, about forty well-dressed young people, earnest and freshly barbered, sat on a circle of chairs facing a high table upon which lay the piano and a microphone. A large woman in a blue hijab got up to open the meeting and beside her a tall handsome man in a shiny brown shirt prepared to translate. It was Fish. Back from Nairobi, he had immediately returned to the fold of the '92 group while he considered what to do next: whether to stay with his daughters and his mother in the camp, or whether to try and continue with his studies. As the best English speaker, he was central to the youth umbrella's internationalist ambition to conduct the proceedings in English. As the meeting's opening remarks slipped into a soporific rhythm, a boy in a sparkling white kanzu with pomaded hair made eyes at a slim girl in a yellow polka-dot dress and a brown veil. She looked down first and smiled later.

'The open and transparent election is a good example to the youth of other camps,' Fish translated. 'I acknowledge the former regime of Mr Tawane and I call upon the incoming chairman to warm up.' The youth umbrella had held elections for a new leadership and today, 4 May 2013, Tawane was formally handing over. His effort was finally at an end. He had considered running for re-election but after glancing at the national political landscape he had withdrawn himself as a candidate. He had felt a shift in the attitude towards refugees among the incoming Jubilee government and he had turned his attention instead to another venture. His political sixth sense could not have been more acute. And his timing could not have been more adroit.

The day before Tawane's handing-over ceremony, on 3 May, the new President Kenyatta had delivered his first foreign policy speech, on Somalia. The controversy over the results of the national election had been settled after a court case that conveniently ruled out the need for a recount and Kenyatta had been sworn in three weeks earlier, on 9 April. He was addressing the twenty-first Extra-Ordinary Summit of the Heads of State and Government of the Inter-governmental Authority for Development (IGAD) in Addis Ababa, Ethiopia, a regional cooperation forum of governments in the Horn of Africa. In a gloomy, panelled conference room, under a cross-hatched gold ceiling and seated at a table covered in green velour, the President eschewed the bluster of his predecessor, the slurs on the refugees and the promises about Somalia being safe. Kenyatta instead offered substance. 'Kenya will embark on consultations with the Somali government and other players, especially the UNHCR,' he announced, 'to develop modalities for the safe and orderly return and resettlement of Somali refugees. This will culminate in the organization of an international conference on the safe return of Somali refugees co-chaired by Kenya and Somalia.'

In the camps, the detonation of this bombshell was bigger than anything planted by al-Shabaab. This was not the urban refugees being moved to the camps, this was a plan for the camps themselves to be dismantled. On the radio talk shows and in the tea-shops there was outrage. Under international and Kenyan law, refugees are supposed to return home voluntarily at a time of their choosing. Refugee leaders repeated the mantra that peace was not yet there in Somalia. Kenyatta's speech came five days before the second London Conference on Somalia, and although the communique following the London conference was careful to use different language, talking instead about 'creating the conditions for voluntary return', the refugees had heard Kenyatta's message loud and clear.

It was as Tawane had forseen. He joined in the anger even as he adjusted to the change in policy. To his friends, Tawane talked of setting an example like Nelson Mandela of an African leader willingly relinquishing power. But he had actually decided not to seek re-election as chairman of the youth umbrella because he had another idea, 'downloaded,' he liked to boast, 'straight from the fresh mind of Tawane'. He had set up his own organization to do projects back in Somalia to promote peace, and to facilitate the return of refugees. With a good reputation among the UN and the agencies, he could become, in the language of the humanitarian industry, an 'implementing partner', running projects that the UN could not do. That was where the dollars would be now that Kenyatta was so keen to get the refugees back over the border. It might enable him to move the family to Kismayo – if the fledgling Jubaland administration held firm, or maybe it would just allow him to visit his homeland and do some good while earning real money and still living in Hagadera. The plan was, at least, a vehicle for his imagination that had more mileage than the eternal cul-de-sac of the camp.

While the speeches in the hall went on, Tawane slipped outside, talking on the phone, sweating in a reflective purple shirt with black buttons and new trousers, threads still clinging to the fiercely pressed creases. Around him the grubby onlookers poked their noses through the mesh, to watch events in the hall. Several of them wore free T-shirts from some NGO with the message: 'Together We Can Make Change'. Peering in, Tawane smiled a self-satisfied grin as a succession of speakers trooped up to pay tribute to his brave and extraordinary leadership. The last three years had been a heyday for the youth of the camp but the future loomed, uncertain. President Kenyatta's words hung over proceedings and undermined their confidence.

The manager of Hagadera camp stood to speak. Kiai was a short Kenyan man from Central Province. 'This is the happiest day of my life in Hagadera,' he told the meeting. He welcomed the 'incoming regime' with its new 'cabinet' of officers. The language of government was part of the youth umbrella's game of pretend. And he said nice things about Tawane, even though they had quarrelled in the past: 'If he wanted something he would not rest. When he got what he wanted, that is when he would sleep.' The deputy youth chairman from Ifo camp praised Tawane's example: 'Through him, we have learned what accountability means.'

The youth of the camps saw themselves as leaders-in-waiting; indeed they had been encouraged in that vision by the rhetoric of countless NGO workshops and trainings. They adopted the political correctness, the bureaucratic habits and even the dress of the NGOs, and they spoke in clichés. Words like 'democracy', 'transparency', and 'accountability' were to them like new outfits. Having marinated in the UN vocabulary their whole life, they had a naive idea of the outside world: that there was a standard, a normality that existed somewhere, in America, in Europe, in the United Nations, for which they were practising. For a democratic future that they would inherit and make real. As though what was missing from the current motley crew of criminals and warlords governing Somalia was simply a proper grounding in liberal principles.

The next generation was embodied by the new chairman. Several years younger than Tawane, Garad had precision hair and his soft skin was unlined. He wore a shiny black shirt with a white fringed collar, and when he rose to speak he left a black backpack with the NGO logo 'IRC' of the International Rescue Committee by his chair. Tawane returned to the hall in time to catch his words.

'I thank the outgoing chairman, his excellency Noor Tawane ...' said Garad. 'My fellow Hagadera youth, today we celebrate democracy, peace and brotherhood. Let justice be our shield and our defender ... May we go forward in unity!' His co-chair was a young woman perspiring in heavy black dress and veil. Many men were after her, she claimed, and she appeared to compensate for this with extremely demure outfits. 'We are the future,' she told the gathering, quietly.

When it was his turn to speak, Tawane stood up, sweating still, his hands shaking slightly, and buried his audience in statistics: 2,478 members of the youth groups, 516 of them female, 78 disabled and 40 minorities; 112 football teams, 16 volleyball teams. 'These are the groups and individuals that are under my fingertips,' he announced. He handed over a list of the assets of the youth umbrella and enumerated them: 'The computer centre has one toilet, one tap stand, three staff, two trainers and one cleaner. Stand up, that I may handover.' The mentioned staff shyly stood up. 'I will not disclose their payment, it is a close-door issue,' he said, emulating NGO-speak. The audience tinkled with laughter. Various other sensitive issues, like the state of the finances, he promised to share 'in close-door'.

The second half of the speech was motivational: 'We are refugees by status but not by choice,' Tawane said. 'We are not vulnerable people, we are super humans. Refugee is a state of mind. Look at the examples of Madeleine Albright, of K'naan.' It was a valiant effort, but it was more an expression of faith than experience. And that was the contradiction of Dadaab. To many of the educated young people coming up behind Tawane and trapped in the camp, Tawane's vision might have seemed like a distant dream. To the tens of thousands denied a place at primary or even secondary school, to the grinning boys pressed up against the mesh windows, it was in practice almost meaningless. And yet, the defining characteristic of the young people in the camp was a surfeit of brimming optimism: a conviction that life for them had not yet begun; even Fish, the wrong side of thirty, spoke in the future tense. Among the rowdy kids outside was a budding teacher, a doctor and a premier league football player.

When Tawane finished, Garad solemnly received the accounts, recommendations for the staff and the three stamps of the organization. 'I want to say 'bye to all, and I will be in the White House,' said Tawane with a smile. America was still the lodestar in the refugee firmament, the model, for better or worse.

The new regime stood and introduced themselves and after that, finally, what the little boys assembled at the windows had been waiting for: the music. The sound of live instruments and singing was not common in Dadaab. The calendar of traditional cultural festivals had been forgotten and the religious ones, once a carnival of song, were now tuneless. The few weddings that did take place were, increasingly, silent, either as a result of a lack of money to pay the musicians or out of fear of the mullahs. The position of artists in the conservative milieu of the camp was desperate. They crept out and appeared at occasions such as this one more to affirm their own memory of who they had been than for the meagre amount of money people offered. It was only recently that the agencies had stopped compensating musicians in surplus cooking utensils instead of cash; the musicians had complained. They considered it an insult.

A tall man wearing the flowery shirt of the artist over a wiry frame topped with a heart-shaped face and a receding hairline stood up. Madar had small dancing eyes and a warm smile that revealed tobacco-stained teeth. During the speeches, he had been smoking outside, squashing the cigarette between his long fingers with the definite motions of an experienced smoker. In Somalia in the early nineties, he had just been getting famous but the arrival of the war had ruined his chances at establishing a reputation. He played the piano robustly and sang into the microphone which a woman alternately lifted to his mouth and pointed at the speaker of the Casio keyboard. The kids outside were delirious, reeling in circles.

Next was Sid Ali, in jeans, sunglasses perched on his crown, a novelist and 'event poet' in his own terminology. On the spot, he composed a poem, more of a rap, in the traditional Somali style, to express and commemorate the spirit of the event in song. If it was good, others would memorize and recite it and it would live on, although here in the camp the chances of that were remote. Sid had fled Mogadishu after he was hunted by al-Shabaab for writing a novel about love. His wife's parents had forbidden her from leaving the capital with him and so now he missed his children terribly and spent his freedom in exile writing more novels in thin-lined exercise books about the same subject: love, heartbreak and longing.

Jowahir drew the largest crowd. While some of the kids had wandered off during the poetry, they raced back when the tall gap-toothed singer in her flowing orange dress and casually draped veil picked up the microphone and began to sing of home. The sound seemed to freeze the air and calm the birds. Jowahir had grown up next to a barracks for military bands in Kismayo. When she was fourteen she joined them and had never known another profession. 'If you give me money and tell me to go to the market I cannot do it,' she says. When war arrived, she sang and earned good money as a member of a musicians' co-op in Kismayo where people who wanted a band for a wedding or a celebration would call, but when al-Shabaab took over in 2007, people stopped coming. The rise of the militants coincided with her husband's taking of a second wife. Unemployed and consumed with jealousy, she fled to Dadaab with her five children. She was thirty.

As she sang, she tapped her hennaed toes in their beaded flip-flops and touched her bangled wrists with long painted fingertips, one finger carrying a fat gold ring. Jowahir lived to sing. In the camp though, her spirit was fading. 'If I thought there was peace in Kismayo, I would not wait for the night to come. I would go,' she said. 'Here people don't understand the importance of poetry. Here people have problems, collecting food, firewood. There are no parties now. They have forgotten their culture. I don't understand it.'

The music stopped. The earnest young people carried the chairs back into the computer centre and Tawane and Garad and other cabinet members of the new regime put on their serious faces as they squeezed into the chairman's office for the 'close-door' part of the handover. The ragged boys poured into the hall and gathered up all the plastic water bottles discarded by the delegates. Then they perched on the wall in the midday sun and, one by one, sucked them dry.

A week later, a group of women were sitting on the floor of the CARE social hall watching DVDs called 'sensitizations' on how to wash vegetables, HIV/AIDS and 'harmful cultural practices', a nice way of referring to female genital mutilation. Outside, in the shade of a tree, Tawane sat squinting at a laptop. He was impervious to the background noise of constant FGM campaigns. That week, his eldest daughter, Jehanne, had been circumcised. 'Not mutilated,' Tawane insisted, only a small cut, what medics refer to as a cliterodectomy. Tawane faced the future but he still had one foot in the past. Apshira had sourced someone from the hospital to do it, he said approvingly, not just any old lady with a rusty knife. 'The ones who have been cut in the sunna way can feel the same as men. The girls themselves want to be cut, otherwise they refer to you as a Christian. Who will marry her?'

Following the announcements on repatriation from Kenyatta and the London conference, the NGOs, like Tawane, anticipated a shift in donor policy and rushed in with unseemly announcements of programmes supporting refugees to return. Tawane was energized, eager for a slice of the new funds. On the plastic chair in the shade of a bush he tried to ignore the ritual droning of the television as he drew up a mission statement for his new NGO on a borrowed laptop.

An old man in a skull cap, his hands resting on a knobbled worn stick peered at him, this vision of modernity with his computer, through the chain-link fence. Under another tree, the new chairman Garad was also bent over a laptop, sweating and rubbing his forehead in concentration over spreadsheets of the youth umbrella's finances.

'How are you doing?' a friend came over and asked.

'I think I am becoming a leader,' Garad replied.

29

Too Much Football

With President Kenyatta's speech, it seemed that Somalia was being treated to the same brand of hubris that had seen declarations of peace foisted on other countries still at war like Iraq and Afghanistan. Instead of a settlement, a bargain, and at least a patchy attempt at reconstruction and victor's justice, these conflicts were being declared over with an election and a timeline for troop withdrawal. Peace became not an objective standard to be reached but a slippery, elastic concept: a matter of opinion. And Guled and Maryam could not agree.

Ever since Maryam's mother had gone back to Somalia at the end of the year, her phone calls brought a steady drip of cynicism about Dadaab contrasted with expansive stories of fresh fish, fruit and the rebuilding of Mogadishu. For Maryam, a young woman with two small children, the rosy stories of Mogadishu coupled with the promise of childcare were hard to resist. And with a husband hooked on football and unable to bring home an income, there was little about camp life to hold Maryam. Most of all, she wanted milk.

Like many poor communities the world over, the camp was gripped by the insidious myth that a newborn needs powdered milk, or formula, and it was expensive. Many nursing mothers sold valuable food to buy it. Guled had no money for such things, and little idea how to find any. He had asked about driving jobs but there were few cars around. There was shoe-shining or portering but the competition for new entrants made it almost pointless. Anyway, from his point of view, apart from the lack of money for incidentals and better food, life in the camp was good. There was no rent to pay, there were rations and he had plenty of free time to indulge in his twin hobbies: 'Playing and watching football is my ideal life, I am addicted to football,' he readily admitted. He had begun to harbour a new dream, to play for the junior team of Manchester United. In Ifo he was famous for his skill and he considered himself one of the best in the leagues in the camp. Of the two teams in Guled's block, he played for Leopards FC and wore No.9, striker. His team shared the football pitch with sticks for goalposts with four other teams and played on alternate days. On the off days, he sometimes helped out 'Auntie' with her stall selling khat but it wasn't enough to make up the shortfall between Maryam's demands and the UN rations.

'Children need milk, will they get that from the UN?' she asked him. 'Do they know that their father cannot work? That it is not his fault?' Maryam had little sympathy for his excuses. She wanted him to provide. 'Too much football!' she grumbled. She wanted to go back home. Guled's sister advised him on the phone not to come, that the threat of al-Shabaab discovering or press-ganging him was still there, but Maryam disagreed. She thought that the militants had more important things to do than hunt him down and that Mogadishu was full of young men in the same position. There was nothing special about him, she said. He thought she was playing down the risk to suit her own agenda of going back. They were stuck.

With walls made of sticks and roofs of plastic, little in the camp is private. When they discussed al-Shabaab, Guled urged Maryam to keep her voice down, but when the argument moved on to football, she gave full volume to her frustrations. The neighbours of course overheard their discussions and they joined in. 'What is it with your idle man? Only playing football? He doesn't care about you,' they told her, and sometimes even to his face.

Kenyatta's declaration on returns had made people insecure; it created a frame of borrowed time. But it was the accretion of little details that tipped the scales in every household; with every security incident in Dadaab, Guled's case for staying was eroding. Two suspected suicide bombers had accidentally blown themselves up in Hagadera camp a few days before his and Maryam's little boy was born, and another IED hit a police car in Dagahaley some days after. Now, in May, attacks on incoming trucks along the road to Somalia were a weekly occurrence. Policemen kept getting killed. No one knew the precise details of the sugar smugglers' conflicts. One theory had it that the cartels were paying off the police and groups within the police were taking sides. Another rumour claimed the slowdown in trade was making the police chief in Dadaab greedy and the cartels were picking off his officers as a bargaining tactic. Either way, the sugar wars were far from over, and the refugees grew to expect violence.

On Friday 10 May, Kheyro went looking for a goat that had somehow escaped from the little thorn hut in which she kept them penned. Her wandering took her to Bosnia and she was walking down the main street when a man rushed out of a tin-walled restaurant holding a pistol. By the side of the road, a police reservist in uniform was sitting on a stool clutching the fresh bundle of khat he had just bought. Kheyro heard a shot, then she saw the policeman falling down, his AK-47 clattering to the ground that was already pooling red. Blood pumped down in hot spurts from three bullet wounds in the man's head and neck. Everybody ran. Kheyro bolted for home. She was shocked that the face of the young gunman – not more than twenty-three or -four, she thought – was open, not covered. Back at the restaurant, another man appeared and snatched the policeman's rifle from the ground. When the crowd turned on the men, he levelled the weapon at them and the attackers managed to run away.

They didn't get far. The wave of shootings was affecting business and a crowd from the market chased after them. As they tore down the street towards Lagdera the attackers split up, one aiming for the playing fields and the other heading straight ahead. By the car wash, one of the boys was grabbed. The other one had a trail of pursuers. A man working at the car wash watched as a ring rapidly formed around the killer. People came with rocks, another with a *panga*, a machete.

'He's the one!' somebody shouted to a woman brandishing a metal bar. 'He's the one that shot your relative!' Men were holding the attacker and she brought the metal bar down on his head. Blood came. The crowd started roaring. Then another man aimed at his neck with a panga. Within fifteen minutes, the man was dying on the ground. The crowd got hold of his two legs and dragged him through the streets, some shouting and cheering. Thirty minutes later the body was discarded, lifeless and sandy in the road. Somewhere on the playing field, the mob caught up with the other kid too.

The camp was shocked but jubilant. People smiled with the news of the twin lynchings and looked a little drunk, sated, perhaps, with revenge. But not Maryam. She had been looking for a final straw. Now she had it.

The cinema where Guled watched football in the evenings was a wooden structure with a UNHCR relief tarpaulin for walls and steel sheets for a roof. Inside was a huge flat screen TV and narrow benches dug into the sand. The football team charged the young men of the area a few shillings to come and watch the games to raise money for their strip. The block leader had promised a 'uniform' if they campaigned for her in the elections but she hadn't kept her word. The cinema was on the corner of the main street in Hawa Jube and tacked above the door was a sign in black paint: 'MAN UNITED'.

Later that evening, Guled was outside chatting to his friends in the team. They were excited. Manchester United was unreachable at the top of the English Premier League, and at the penultimate game of the season against Swansea that weekend, they were expected to lift the trophy. Sir Alex Ferguson had announced his retirement two days earlier. 'I don't think Man U will ever have another like Sir Alex, we are expecting a big loss,' Guled was saying when in bowled Maryam.

'I am going. You'd better come to the house,' she said. Guled looked at her in surprise; their previous discussions had never concluded in a decision. Embarrassed, he left his friends and followed his wife the short distance home, with each step the inevitable quarrel getting closer. There, the kids were asleep on the bed in the one-room mud hut. All her possessions were packed as well as some of his: the family's cooking utensils, blankets and the children's clothes. In the single remaining sheet and the mosquito net above the bed, Guled could read that she was serious.

'I've had enough!' she said. His argument centred on the children; that it would be unfair to separate them from their father.

'Life will be better for them in Mogadishu,' she said. 'You see what happened today?' she added referring to the lynching. 'There's no security here.'

'If you want to go, go alone,' said Guled. 'Just leave the kids.'

'No!'

'If I go there, my life is at risk,' he pleaded. Their voices rose. They stepped outside so as not to wake the kids, but they woke up anyway. So did the neighbours. They came now, through the dark with smoky kerosene lamps and the roving beam of a torch; their nose for drama alerted. Guled stopped shouting; he sensed the danger in numbers. Stools were brought, a meeting called to order, cases were made for and against but Guled's trump card, the true reason he feared returning to Mogadishu, he could not play in public. He had managed to keep his past with al-Shabaab a secret; if he revealed it now, he'd be ostracized by his neighbours and at risk from al-Shabaab. With only half the picture, the neighbours made their ruling.

'Let her go with the kids,' they said. 'She's tired of life here.' Guled had been outnumbered.

There was no vehicle traveling to Mogadishu the next day, so Maryam had to sleep another night in the hated camp. But on the Sunday, the day of the match against Swansea, Guled shouldered children and luggage to the truck stage in Lagdera. All along the main sandy road from Hawa Jube, the silence sat cold and hard between them; they had not spoken since Friday night. Guled wanted to break it, but then his pride boiled up. 'She disobeyed me!' he said to himself, 'why should I talk to her?' The next minute, he thought of jumping on the truck with her, but then he remembered the men in black who were at the other end, waiting for him.

The truck was an ancient, once yellow, Fiat. It was what the refugees called '*anda meeley*' – the long bottom. It had no brakes and no windscreen and the shell of the engine was open to the sky. The cab was upholstered in plastic linoleum and the steering wheel had rags tied around the inner steel core. To travel up there was expensive; Maryam had no money for that. She was travelling economy class, in the bed of the truck in the back with about 80 others, women and children mostly, huddled among the cargo – hundred-gallon plastic water tanks, mattresses and suitcases piled up. Jerrycans were tied to the back. The fare for her and the kids was 5,000 shillings ($45) of which, to his shame, Guled had not contributed one shilling. The family had outstanding credit of 2,000 shillings ($22) at the shop in their block; they had survived on borrowed milk and sugar for too long and so the neighbours had rallied round. To get a higher credit rating they would have needed remittances from the West, and with Maryam's mother's departure, they had lost their connection there. 'Lack of economics' was the reason he was losing his family; that was what Guled told himself as he passed the luggage wordlessly up into the back of the truck and the little girl, Sadr, crying.

Guled's daughter, who had arrived in the camp in Maryam's womb, was three days past her second birthday and with the few words she had, she made her protest. 'Abo, Abo, Abo,' she cried, 'Dada, Dada, Dada.' She didn't want to leave him. Her voice tore a hole in Guled's chest. He felt like crying but the crowded stage of other families bidding people farewell inspired some self-control until the truck departed. The first half of the match at Old Trafford was already under way; all his friends would be in the cinema for this historic moment: Manchester United's twentieth league title and Sir Alex Ferguson's thirteenth. Guled was wearing his plastic Manchester United wristband along with jeans and his favourite button-down shirt in preparation for the match but the game was far from his mind.

When the engine finally roared into life at four p.m. and the carcass of a lorry gave a jolt as it went into gear, Maryam leaned over the side of the truck bed and spoke to him at last. 'Keep on playing football,' she said. 'We have gone.' Beside her, standing on her little legs, tiny fists beating the rusted steel, Sadr howled, 'Abo Abo Abo,' until the truck bounced away over the dusty maidan, turning left at the telecoms tower, and he could hear her no more.

*

Guled walked back down the sandy street towards Hawa Jube and the cinema, his brain barely functioning, turbid with thoughts, his feet almost walking themselves. 'If we had money,' he thought to himself. 'If I get money, she might enjoy life with me again . . . even in Mogadishu she cannot work, because of the C-sections.' He tried to deflect the blame for their situation where she had placed it: on his shoulders. It was also a way of directing his thoughts away from where they naturally went: to worrying about her. It was three days on the truck to Mogadishu, open to the elements and to the random sparks of the war. If she was here with the kids, at least he knew how she was doing. 'We shared the same plate,' he said in his mind, over and over. If she had a problem now she was on her own.

The cinema was crammed with bodies. Guled made it in time for the second half but the problem with the family 'overwhelmed the love' he had for Manchester United. Three minutes from time, Rio Ferdinand smashed home a corner from Van Persie to win the match and Guled smiled shyly as his friends rubbed his head – he was known in the team as 'Van Persie', for they were both the striker and top goalscorer for their respective teams. When Sir Alex lifted the Premier League trophy, 200 young men in the cinema went wild, jumping on the chairs and screaming at the tin roof but Guled just sat there, a ghost in the maelstrom. Two of his friends, noticing, asked him what was wrong and he told them. They tried to be kind: 'This is part of the world,' said one.

Normally, Guled stayed up til midnight chatting with his friends at the cinema but tonight, on what was supposed to be the climax of the season, he went home to bed, early.

'Has Maryam gone?' the neighbours called through the fence. He ignored them. He knew they knew. It was, he thought, just female *fitna*, ill will. As he lay down in the hut now stripped bare of their family things, his mind turned over. They had only one phone, and it was with him, encased in a plastic Manchester United cover. He could not call her. In any case he had no money to call; phoning Somalia was expensive. He wondered where they were. The territory was treacherous: the frontline through Afmadow, Jilib, Barawe and Merka crisscrossed the road north.

Wednesday was his turn at the food distribution. Still he had not heard from them. He was getting more and more anxious. Through the warehouses he went with his single ration card and the family one with the photos of Maryam and the children for a family size 3. At each window and each cup of extra rice, flour and oil, his heart ached a little more. He kept looking at the chubby black-and-white photos on the ration card of his little boy and girl.

On the fourth day, Thursday, a Somali number flashed on his phone. He begged money from his friends and called back. Maryam had borrowed the phone from the driver of the truck.

'Why are you not yet there? What happened?' Guled's voice was full of crisis.

'We are on the way from Bu'ale,' Maryam said before the phone went dead. He kept trying to call back but nothing. One time the driver answered and said, 'I am busy driving, stop calling.' Bu'ale was only just beyond Afmadow, still far from Mogadishu. His mind and heart raced ahead of each other and the fragile calm he had worked hard to construct collapsed.

Auntie was kind. She knew he needed money to call and she gave him more and more work on the khat stall, selling the drug. The stall was a low bivouac made of sticks and sacking, next to the cinema. Although a convenient and lucrative spot, trade was slow. The sugar wars meant the loaders and the drivers and even the police, the people whose income depended on the smuggling, had no cash.

A week after Maryam had gone and worried sick, he was minding the khat stall during a break from watching the final match of the season, Manchester United against West Bromwich Albion. A crowd of about thirty men dressed in white turbans with tails and white jellabas approached. He knew who they were, he had seen the '*tabliq*', the religious messengers who evangelized in the camp, before: they were peaceful, spiritual people, conservative but not violent like al-Shabaab. But they had never spoken to him directly.

'What you are doing is wrong,' they said, referring to the selling of the khat. 'Come, let us pray together.' Guled got up and followed them. They went then into the cinema and repeated their message. 'It's time for prayer,' they told the soccer fans. But the rows of eager boys on the wooden benches, eyes glued to the screen, didn't move. Football was the only thing they were fanatical about: the match was nearing the close and West Brom were about to be relegated. When the tabliq gave up and left, Guled mingled with the fans inside the cinema and then returned to selling khat.

The next day Maryam finally called. The journey had been longer than expected but they were fine, at home, living back with her mother. Maryam did not apologize. When Guled asked her why she had left, she just said, 'Life there is hard. Here there are relatives to assist.' It was true. 'And here you can work, not like in Dadaab. Why don't you come and work and look after your children?'

'The security there is not good for me, you know that.' Guled was angry.

'The security here is adequate,' she said. But Guled didn't trust her assessment. He had been spending the little proceeds from khat on calling the friends he used to drive with in Mogadishu: was it like people said, improving? The reports from his friends were not conclusive; people said different things on different days. There were still regular explosions and suicide attacks by al-Shabaab. But it was little better in Dadaab, and this was Maryam's point. The

night before, there had been a major attack, although he didn't
mention it. 'Mogadishu has come to Ifo,' people said. Guled was
torn, in turmoil. Or, as he put it, 'I was stuck in fifty-fifty'. The
decision to make the journey back again was, like the one to flee,
an uncertain leap of faith; like letting go of one leaky life raft to
reach for another.

He had one photo of Maryam on the ration card and one other
with her holding the baby boy, taken on his phone a month before
they left. It was a blurry image but among the pixels you could
make out Maryam's unsmiling impassive face. Guled looked at it
often. And at the others on his phone: the screensaver of Wayne
Rooney doing a reverse kick, a bedroom furnished in Man U
decor (bedspread, pillow and counterpane) and the whole team of
Manchester United in action shots, with extra photos of Van
Persie. He added some new ones too, copied from his friends: soft
porn pictures of Arab women in alluring poses and some of female
underwear models, all white.

Some weeks later, Maryam sent fresh photographs with an
acquaintance on a vehicle from Mogadishu. Guled thought it
might have been a kind of blackmail, tempting him back. With
them gone, Ifo became again temporary, a transitional place. His
mind began to wander: where could he be free to work? Maybe
Tanzania, South Africa, across the sea even? But every journey
began with money. And in Ifo there was no prospect of that.

The photos showed the baby boy in a new outfit, eyes rimmed
with pencil, and the girl, Sadr, against a background of multi-
coloured Parisian streets in a pink head-dress with a curly wig and
blue and white frilly dress holding a golden ball: he kept both on
the packing case next to his bed. They were the only personal
touch apart from the bare orange mud walls, the blue mosquito
net and the single square of foam for a mattress on the floor.
Without Maryam's things and the children's clothes, and without

the hope of money to oil his dreams of escape, the mud hut that had been their family home now resembled a cell. At night, when he went to sleep, Guled put the photos of his children on the pillow next to his head. He slept a little better that way.

30

The Night Watchmen

In a way, Guled thought, it was lucky Maryam left when she did. The sugar wars were coming to a head. The tempo of the attacks in the camp was increasing and the climax came on 23 May with an attack on the night watchmen of Bosnia.

That night, Kheyro and her sisters woke with a jump. The noise seemed to be right outside their hut. They held their breath. Kheyro counted the shots. Ten. Afterwards, the sisters lay awake on their mat together listening to every little night-time scratch until morning. Even the whine of an insect triggered fear.

At dawn, Kheyro's mother took the goats to the herder at the corner of their block. The camp was fresh with the news of the shooting. Rukia returned breathless. 'The gunshots we were hearing last night, three people were killed and one injured,' she reported. 'Two of them are our relatives, Ero and his son!' The news crushed the household. The boy had just come from Ethiopia and Ero was a kind and gentle man whom the family knew well. Kheyro phoned Handicap International to inform them that she would not be coming to work that day, a day off for which she would not be paid, and accompanied her mother to the hospital.

The green-and-white buildings of the hospital rang with the commotion of neighbours, relatives, onlookers and police. Several women wailed in a courtyard. Ero, the cousin of Rukia and Kheyro's sort-of-uncle, was in the ward with a doctor; he had been shot in the shoulder. His son was in a different room – the morgue – and they were not allowed to see the body. Kheyro remembered his face, a bright boy of twenty, come from the Somali region of Ethiopia, Ogaden, to study in Dadaab. 'He had a nice character,' she said. The doctors were preparing to take Ero to Garissa for an X-ray but Rukia and Kheyro managed to reach his bedside through the throng before he left and he told them what had happened.

Ero was a handsome man with white hair and a strong face built around clear steady eyes that sparkled as if with secrets. He had come to Dadaab from Ogaden three years previously. Rukia's people had a history there. There are around forty thousand registered refugees from Ogaden in the camps. But leaders of the Ogaden community estimate that a similar number have registered as coming from Somalia because it's easier. Despite a low-level insurgency in Ogaden and stories of the most brutal repression imaginable, Ethiopia is not classified as 'at war' like Somalia, and so its refugees do not enjoy the same prima facie recognition. Nationality in the camp is less a fact than a game.

For twenty years Ethiopia has been fighting a brutal counter-insurgency campaign against a rebel group called the Ogaden National Liberation Front (ONLF) that wants to secede. Ero had been imprisoned in a military camp in a dusty desert town for collaborating with the ONLF before he escaped and walked five hundred miles to Dadaab. Now he ran a small stall in the market cooking cosmopolitan food for the traders in the morning – a mash of beans and maize that Kikuyus call *githere*, the Somalis call *ambulo* and the Swahilis know as *mseto* – and worked as a watchman at night.

His clients were a group of twenty-five shopkeepers who contributed 300 shillings each a month for him to guard their shops in the poorer section of the market. The beat was a mixture of food and clothes outlets in a tinned alleyway behind the main sugar warehouses of Bosnia. When his son, Weli, came from Ethiopia seeking education he joined Ero in the guarding business in the evenings. Yesterday though, Ero had been worried. Some people he thought were linked to Ethiopian intelligence had come by his stall in the morning. He recognized their accents. 'Why did you leave Ethiopia? How come you ended up here?' they asked. He ignored them and they went away. But that evening, as a precaution, he told his son to stay in the mosquito net where he was sleeping on the ground in front of a lock-up shop while he did the rounds of the other shops himself. The alley was narrow and sloped into a gutter down the middle. Awnings were stretched overhead nearly touching in the centre with colourful scraps of cloth tied to the uprights.

At about three a.m., as Ero came round the corner of the alley, he saw two men leaning over the mosquito net speaking to Weli.

'Where is Ero?' they asked him. 'Where is your father?' The boy was silent as far as Ero could make out. The moonless night was murky black. Pressing into the shadows, Ero moved towards them. As he was preparing to walk forward and say, 'Here I am,' the gun fired. He ran. More bullets followed him into the dark, loosed in the direction of the sound of his feet pounding on the sand. The third shot hit his shoulder, he fell down and crawled under some thorns. Footsteps hurried after him and he saw a torch, scouring the alley. Around another corner, as quietly as he could, he slid away on his belly. From a distance he heard the attackers retreating towards the junction of the alleyway with the main road of Bosnia where other watchmen had gathered together in numbers.

'Where is Ero?' the gunmen shouted.

'We don't know Ero,' the watchmen responded.

'You're lying, where is he?' But the men stayed quiet, a beat, then four of them bolted. That set the gunmen shooting. Three others were injured as they ran away, shot in the back. And two more died there. The last bullet, number ten that Kheyro counted, hit *Atai* – it was a nickname meaning thin. He was Nisho's friend and skinny 'like a branch', he remembered. For six months Atai had worked in the market, calling Nisho when there was a deal to be had. They had unloaded a truck together three days before.

Around the corner, Ero found people stirring from the noise and begged them to come and assist his son. Out of the warm patch of sand where the boy was soaking in his own blood, twenty people lifted him onto a donkey cart that took him to Ifo police station. They feared the killers were still on the loose in the market and so the caravan passed through Corporal Wanyama's office before reaching Hawa Jube hospital, by which time Ero was also laid on the donkey cart, unconscious from his bleeding shoulder, and the boy was dead.

The following day, Friday, the camp turned out in force for the funeral of Weli, Atai and the other man. They took the bodies to the sandy plain in Hawa Jube where the famine victims of N Zero had camped, where the MSF women had been kidnapped and where so many now lay beneath mounds of thorns, buried far from home. Nisho pushed his way to the front of the thousands of mourners and seized his turn with the spade to dig Atai's grave. 'He was my friend. I had an obligation,' he said. Guled was there – it was near his home on the outskirts of the camp. He was amazed at the crowd. 'They cannot all be related,' he reasoned to himself, 'they just felt the pain of humanity for the deaths of those inno-cent people.' Professor White Eyes was there too. It felt like almost all the refugees had come. The killings were a shock and people felt a need to register solidarity and disapproval, sharing their fears and seeking comfort in rumours.

Ero was not there to bury his son. He was in hospital in Garissa. That same day, while the mourners hid behind each other to shelter from a wind that snapped and pulled at the crowd, he got a phone call. 'Are you still alive?' someone asked before hanging up. During the two months it took for his shoulder to heal, Ero slept badly, in different houses, on the run. The threats on his phone continued. He wrote a letter to UNHCR and lined up in the hot sun for an interview in the UN field office, twice. A fat lady with short hair told him to change his SIM card to avoid the threats and referred him to the police. He laughed. No one in Dadaab had any confidence in the police to protect them, and especially not from the efficient and deadly Ethiopian intelligence services. But if the Ethiopian spooks really were that serious about targeting him, who was he? Either his story was an elaborate attempt at being fast-tracked to America or else there was more hidden behind Ero's sparkling eyes than Kheyro would ever know.

Later reports would confirm Ethiopian covert action inside Kenya including assassinations of ONLF leaders, but the only certain thing was there were many strands to the violence in the camps. Untangling fact from fiction was often impossible in Dadaab. And even then, people usually preferred a story based not on its relationship to truth but on its ability to make sense of the confusion of their own lives.

Everyone had a different theory about the shootings. Nisho said it had been attempted robbery; the shops were full of sugar and clothes: this was the story he got from the loaders. They needed an explanation that was random; if it was a turf war then they too could be in the firing line. Professor White Eyes had heard a different version: it was a sugar clash, gangs had not been paid. A policeman claimed with authority that Mr Tall, the main

smuggler in Ifo, had lost patience with the watchmen whom he
had warned before not to leak information to the police about
when his trucks were being offloaded at night. A UN official had
it 'from a reliable source' that a new gang was trying to muscle in
on Mr Tall's patch. Meanwhile the Nairobi news media, without
a single correspondent in Dadaab between them and without a
second thought, were perfectly happy to attribute the killings to
al-Shabaab. Further evidence, some journalists claimed, of the
threat to Kenya, of the need to close the camps. So the prejudice
against the refugees was built, one misconception at a time.

31

Sugar Daddy

On Saturday 25 May, the day after the funeral, most of the young men of the camp sought distraction from their fears in the consolations of soccer. Boys without money were begging everyone they knew for the fifty-shilling entrance into one of the camp's many cinemas. It was the UEFA Champions League final, and Bayern Munich were playing Borussia Dortmund at Wembley stadium in London. Nisho was disdainful: 'I am not a fan of football, I don't have time for that.' But he was in a minority. Guled desperately wanted to watch, but Auntie warned him that she had heard there was going to be a police operation in the camps that night; crackdowns – the house-to house-looting and random beatings – usually followed security incidents as the moon followed the sun. It pained him to miss the match but he followed her advice and stayed inside, calling his friends for updates about the score.

In fact, the police had no such plans. The chief of police in Dadaab was called Sharif, a tall, wide barrel of a man, with a clipped moustache and the habit of wearing both a pistol and an iPhone in his waist belt. That weekend he had other things on his mind. The sugar wars had exploded on his watch and he was deeply involved.

As the sun approached the horizon, painting the plain with streaks of shimmering copper and bronze, the cinemas were packed for kick-off. In the police camp by the chicane road block at the entrance to the main street in Dadaab, the mess was noisy and full. A small television was perched on top of a double fridge covered in stickers advertising Guinness; the picture was bad and the jagged wire that poked out of the top had only a passing relationship with the nearby satellite dish corroding in the sand. The off-duty officers were more interested in their game of pool. Sitting on the wall, a collection of Kenyan women from Dadaab town – economic migrants from 'down Kenya' in jeans and tight T-shirts – monitored proceedings with a lazy eye. Tomorrow they'd be back again, dressed in their Sunday best for church. Both the weekend pastimes of the Bantu migrants from the real Kenya, drinking beer and church-going, of necessity took place within the protective cordon of the police camp.

A little way off, under a very old, very twisted, thorn tree, the Muslim police officers distanced themselves from what they saw as the grubby goings-on of their Christian colleagues and concentrated instead on an enormous plastic bag of khat, several flasks of tea and half a dozen packets of cigarettes. Mohammed the CID, usually a staple of the khat table, was not there today. Perhaps something was going on.

On a rough wooden table nearby, the Corporal took a commanding slug of his bottle of Tusker lager. He lifted his chin towards the sandy driveway that traced a wide circle in front of the entrance to the station itself. A Toyota Land Cruiser 'Prado' with blacked-out windows and Kenyan plates was parked before the faded-blue front door dusty with rot, its screen crammed full of desiccated insects. Sharif had visitors.

'They're even there now,' he said to the Sergeant opposite him. The Sergeant, a thin man with small eyes beneath a pinched brow, narrow mouth and brown teeth turned his head to look.

'Don't stare!' said the Corporal. Then, muttering under his breath, 'Smugglers.'

'We don't need this man,' said the Sergeant. And there were murmurings of drunken approval from around the table. The tit-for-tat killings had got out of hand and the rank-and-file had had enough. Around the table, the junior officers were discussing their favourite topic: how much the boss was making from the sugar trade and, by implication, how much they were missing out on.

They reckoned that Sharif was collecting around 100,000 ($1,400) shillings per sugar truck that came into the country illegally. Now he was branching out to other sectors as well. Trucks full of flour stolen from the UN were heading back into Kenya with fake papers saying that they were imports that had been inspected. Some of the officers had been asked to draw up the papers. They thought something else was probably mixed in with the flour, but they had not been allowed to inspect the vehicle. They were angry. For months now, they'd been sent on patrol in one direction while trucks full of contraband passed by in the other. The bush surrounding Dadaab was full of unofficial tracks, but it was possible to predict which one the sugar trucks would take simply by going in the opposite direction to their orders. And their colleagues were getting killed.

'Even the locals are pissed off,' said the Corporal. At that time there were three to four trucks a day coming through, but it had been as high as twenty. Many weren't even stopping off in Dadaab, but going straight to Nairobi, with the blessing of high-ups in the government: that was why Nisho had seen his income drop. Twice the Corporal had been sent in the wrong direction to avoid incoming trucks. And once, by accident, he had come across 200 bags of sugar hidden in the bush that were being transported by donkey cart to avoid the road. Several of those around the table had complained to headquarters in Nairobi about Sharif, but nothing had been done. For his staff, paid a pittance and risking their lives while he drove around Dadaab with a private escort of five armed men (not police officers), Sharif's wealth was a terrible insult.

His business was such an open secret that even the UN staff referred to him as 'sugar daddy'. But he talked a good game and he cooperated with the US-funded community policing programme. And every morning his corpulent frame in its patent shoes and pressed uniform could be seen taking breakfast in the UN canteen. Perhaps it was a way of keeping the UN sweet, or maybe he just felt safer there than in the barracks. Not for him the rickety shack with 'Hilton Hotel' painted on it, surrounded by broken beer crates, bottles poking out of the sand and the wooden chicken hutch – a failed attempt to improve the policemen's diet – slowly decomposing. The mess was also haunted by a terrible smell, as though somewhere a septic tank had gone horribly wrong.

Darkness settled over the little tables under the thorn trees between the kitchen and the bar. The Corporal ordered some boiled goat and the talk moved on to other things: the Woolwich beheading in London. Three days earlier two British men of Nigerian descent had murdered a soldier outside an army barracks in south London. The weekend Kenyan newspapers carried a photo of one of the attackers, Michael Adebolajo, arraigned in a Kenyan court in 2010. Now the world wanted to know, what had he been up to in Kenya? Was he, the officers wondered, among the foreigners on their way to join al-Shabaab in Somalia that they had intercepted and arrested around that time? No, said one: 'Those ones were Indian British, not Nigerian.' And the paper said he had tried to enter Somalia by boat not by road.

Adebolajo's relatives claimed he had been tortured in Kenyan detention and then pressed by MI5 to work for them afterwards. It was probably not what Jonathan Evans, chief of MI5, had meant when he had said it was 'only a matter of time' before people trained in Somalia committed an atrocity on the streets of Britain, but it seems likely the three events were connected. As a later study found: more than half of recruits to al-Shabaab were motivated by police brutality. To the Kenyan police, the allegations were neither surprising nor avoidable and the conversation alighted on a more diverting topic: their women.

Heavy, lubricated eyes slid along the wall to where the local women were by now draped over various officers younger and stronger than those nursing their beers under the tree. One girl danced alone on the sand, gyrating her behind to an imaginary tune. There were few female officers and they were in such demand they avoided the mess at weekends – it only caused trouble. The Sergeant passed round his phone glowing with photos of an overweight girl in her underpants, smiling shyly at the camera. The Corporal had married one of his colleagues posted to Dadaab but now she had been transferred to the other side of the country. Their children were at boarding school. He broke off from drinking to wish them good night on the phone.

'Did you pray for me?' he asked each one in turn, then he plugged his phone in to charge at the bar and returned with another round of drinks.

Some minutes later, a flustered senior officer marched up to the table with a glare that brought the Corporal scrambling to his feet.

'Didn't you hear your phone? I've been calling you!'

'It was charging inside . . .' he began.

'Are you sober?'

'Yes, sir,' the Corporal lied.

'Come,' said the senior officer turning on his heel in the soft sand.

The table tried to resume its conversation but they had been disturbed. With the sixth sense of security men, they knew something was wrong. Soon, other officers were rising from their chairs, phones pressed to their ears, eyes suddenly alert, watchful, blinking back the booze. Then the Corporal was back, moving among the revellers lit by the weak yellow light of the bar, tapping people on the shoulder, speaking in their ear and dispatching them to the station. He was selecting the least intoxicated officers to send into the night to go to the relief of Damajale police station forty miles away near the Somali border. It had been attacked by al-Shabaab. There was a shortage of drivers even on a weekday, and now they were nearly all drunk. The rapidly sobering-up policemen threw on guns and uniforms and climbed into the large police trucks waiting with their glassy-eyed drivers, engines running, lights blazing, and headed off towards the border, into the insurgent dark.

The militants had picked their moment, a major soccer game on a Saturday night. They knew their enemy. In Damajale six were killed, including policemen, local government employees and a teacher beheaded. Two policemen were kidnapped and taken back inside Somalia. Forty-eight hours later, the assistant chief of the village appeared dazed and wounded after fleeing into the desert and wandering, lost. The al-Shabaab spokesman in Mogadishu gleefully accepted responsibility on the radio the next morning. But there was a sub-plot.

'With al-Shabaab, we always get warnings,' said a security officer at the United Nations. And the attack on Damajale, he said, had been no different. Disgruntled police later claimed that Sharif had been told by the NSIS, Kenya's National Security and Intelligence Service, about an impending attack, but he had done nothing to reinforce Damajale. He was annoyed with the police there, the story went. They had stopped four sugar trucks on which he had given his word and for which he was expecting to be paid. The Corporal said by the time the relief party reached

Damajale late in the night, the trucks had already been sprung.

Of course, no one could say for sure. In his office in the Department for Refugee Affairs with its oversize conference table that left little room to squeeze around it, Mr Lukingi wouldn't comment on the role of the police: 'That's a hot one!' he said. Opposite, in the District Commissioner's office, Albert, the DC, smiled and shook his head. 'That man [Sharif] is operating on a very independent line.' Whatever was going on, it didn't look good.

After Damajale, the mutterings about Sharif were difficult to control. The police felt they were dying for the sake of his business deals. And the UN was unhappy with the impact on the refugees. People were supposed to go home because they felt safe to return to Somalia, not because they felt too unsafe to stay in Kenya. Something had to change.

Those who control things that really matter in Dadaab do not live there. Somewhere in a State House hallway or by a manicured pool in Nairobi, a conversation was had, orders were issued. And, within a month, a new Assistant Commissioner of Police for Dadaab was appointed and Sharif was transferred to Western Kenya. He left without a party and without a farewell. One day he simply called a meeting, introduced his successor, a local Somali man from the neighbouring Fafi district called Hassan, and left. A rumour went round that his bank account had been frozen with a balance of 38 million shillings ($500,000).

The central government in Nairobi has a habit of putting non-Somalis in charge in North East Province, perhaps a lingering doubt from the days of the irredentist Shifta wars. But whenever Somalis have been appointed to positions of power, to Provincial Commissioner or as now, Assistant Commissioner of Police, the improvements are immediate. Hassan knew the local leaders personally. He went to work. He walked around the camps without security guards and he spoke to the refugees as an equal. Very soon the sugar smuggling was almost entirely stopped and the fighting with it. A notorious gang was captured and their leader killed in a shoot-out with police. The refugees were happy.

But prices in the market stayed high. The restaurateur Dube from E1 explained the problem: 'Smuggling contributes to insecurity – but the smuggling keeps the cost of living down for the refugees. People don't see the link between the insecurity, police and smuggling, they just care about the prices in the market. Bribery is part of the problem, but it is the culture of Kenya and you can't go against the culture of the country.'

Nisho still grumbled about the cost of living. In the poorer parts of the camp, people stopped drinking tea, since tea without sugar was unthinkable for Somalis. They ate boiled kidney beans in the morning instead. Sugar became a luxury item, nearly doubling in price since the election. The situation was unsustainable for the refugees and, it turned out, for the government too. The problem was a curious one: Hassan was too efficient. The smugglers were complaining to the higher-ups. Two weeks into his new post, rumours circulated that the new police chief was a marked man. Somewhere in Nairobi more discreet conversations were had and, after a month in the job, Hassan too was sacked.

In July, during Ramadan, a new boss would arrive, Roba, a tough man from the Borana tribe, clearly under different instructions. He would pin a 'Dadaab Command Crime Clock' and a hand-drawn map of the border areas in biro to the wall above the huge black lacquered desk in the corner office where he hid from the sun with the curtains drawn most days. And slowly the trucks would start coming again and the price of sugar would fall back to historic levels, 90 or 100 shillings a kilo instead of 130 or 140. Nisho would be relieved; the tense state of the camp would ease. People would superstitiously attribute the change to the virtue of fasting during the holy month, to God. But Ahmed, the new Somali head of UNHCR, fresh from duty in Peshawar, Pakistan, knew better. 'When things are quiet, the smugglers are happy,' he said.

32

Italy, or Die Trying

On the Sunday morning after the Damajale attack, uncertainty flooded the camp. Fear that had been set aside for the UEFA Cup final returned, with interest; the concatenation of events was so rapid it seemed as if Dadaab would be swallowed whole by the war. People sought reassurance in numbers.

Around Guled's khat stall, they congregated. The boys talked together while Auntie, her beady eyes dancing and her flesh shaking with laughter, anchored the scene, joking and doing business. Among the ten young men, all beneath the age of twenty-five, there were no unfamiliar faces, the atmosphere was intimate, as though among family; indeed for many of them it was the only family they had. Groups in the camp had code words to police their conversations and to warn against strangers whom they didn't know. Some developed hand signals for use in crowded spaces like the tea-shops of the market. 'Be quiet. Turn Around. Watch your back,' or 'He's with me. It's okay.' Loose talk was dangerous. Informers from al-Shabaab, or the governments of Kenya or Ethiopia could be listening at any point. In other settings, with people he didn't know, Guled was wary and said little, but here, sitting on mats behind the stall with his friends, he felt free. They were joking about khat.

One of them told the story of the goat in his block that cried out at dawn prayer, like a cockerel, an ungodly sound that woke him up when he had a khat hangover. The drug, like other narcotics, does not allow the chewer to sleep or have sex until the effects begin to wear off. Another boy told Auntie the price of her khat was too cheap.

'I eat too much! It's bringing problems. I haven't been to the toilet for three days – only urine. And my wife is complaining that I haven't slept with her for a month. She claims I have another woman, that's why I don't want her. Look at me now! I start chewing at ten a.m. and I continue to midnight every day!' The other boys laughed and Auntie smiled. Then somebody's phone rang.

It was one of the group, their friend, a boy that Guled had known when he had first arrived who had left the camp about a year ago. Now he was calling with news: he was in Italy. The boys couldn't believe it. He had gone overland, through the smuggling routes from Kenya into Sudan, to Khartoum, across the Sahara desert through Darfur into Libya and over the Mediterranean sea to the island off southern Italy called Lampedusa. The phone was passed around and the boys took it in turns to feel envious and ashamed. To get to Europe was a success and they had failed to leave Dadaab.

When it was Guled's turn the boy told him, 'Life is cool here. I am working. I am happy. There are opportunities.' He said he missed the friendship of his old team-mates but that you cannot compare the life of here and there. He was supporting his family in Somalia now, and he was ready to help his friends, he said, when his income improved. The boys in Hawa Jube felt helpless and diminished. There were other friends who called sometimes from Europe, taking about where they lived and what they ate. As always, these phone calls from another planet provoked fierce debate.

'We have to go to Italy, immediately!' said one. They were energized, caught with the idea. A boy who was awaiting resettlement, and who had been waiting for some time, said, 'I am in a process, I have to wait for UNHCR.' Another was dismissive: 'We cannot wait for UNHCR, it takes too long!' They shared their stories from the phone call.

To one of them, the boy in Italy had described his difficult journey through the Sahara to Libya and over the sea. When the listener had expressed doubt, he had been encouraging: 'You are a man, you can manage.' The boys knew it was dangerous and expensive. But they all wished they could afford to try; it was a dream for which they were only too willing to die.

'It all depends on the traffickers. If you get a good one, you can reach quickly and safely,' said one of the boys, keener than the others. A month later, having slipped out of the camp without a goodbye, he would find out for himself.

But there were plenty of stories of bad ones. Of kidnappings, of migrants held to ransom at each stage of the journey: in Sudan, in Libya. And of whole truckloads dying of dehydration. Survivors recounted begging their fellow travellers for their urine, and, on one occasion, resorting to drinking Benzene. A few months later, ninety-two would die in the desert from lack of water when their vehicle broke down. And police were only too happy to lock up migrating Africans until they phoned their families for a ransom delivered via Western Union or the Somali money wires. The ransoms were creeping up into the thousands of dollars with the flood of people taking advantage of the collapse of the Libyan government and the blocking of the eastern routes.

The cheapest way to prosperity, over the sea to Yemen and then up the baking Tihama coast of the Red Sea to Saudi Arabia, was closed. Around 100,000 people a year had been going that way, one quarter of them Somalis, the rest Ethiopians and Eritreans. But Saudi Arabia had built a fence and in 2013 had begun deporting thousands of Ethiopians and Somalis home.

The other way, to Europe up through Egypt and Sinai, to Israel and then through Turkey and Greece or the Caucasus and Ukraine had been shut by an Israeli fence, a disturbing succession of shoot-to-kill incidents and a 10,000-capacity detention facility in the Negev desert with a new law permitting indefinite detention. Bedouin and Rashaida tribes had made an industry out of kidnapping and harvesting the organs of stranded Eritreans using the Sinai route. Sometimes people paid as much as $30,000 to secure the release of relatives.

'You need $2,500,' someone in the group around the khat stall said, 'to pay the police or the bribes along the way.' Although Somalis interviewed in the Netherlands said on average that their journeys overland had cost them $11,000. Each migrant has a whole extended family who has invested in their trip and who expects a return on that investment.

'If I had that money, I would either die or get to Italy,' said Guled.

'The biggest expense is the boat, another $1,000,' said another.

In fact, often it was more. In the low season, during the winter, you could pay that, but in the summer, when the weather conditions were more favourable, berths on an overcrowded boat could go for as much as $2,000. The unscrupulous traffickers usually nominated a passenger to drive the vessel and left the migrants to navigate by the GPS of their mobile phones and what little they knew of the stars. Many people had to buy a place on the boats more than once. A pair of Somali girls famously tried nine times. 45,000 people crossed the sea in 2012. More in 2013. More still in 2014.

'You are paying $1,000 to purchase death; they are death boats, that is what they are,' said one man who made it after a terrifying ordeal at sea. Thousands died in the Mediterranean. It became a familiar story: survivors recounting the haunting screams of the drowned, being given babies to keep afloat and corpses, even pregnant ones, bobbing on the water.

'Why are you still there?' the boy had asked on the phone.

'If we get money we can go today,' the friends at the khat stall agreed.

Italy was not their preferred destination. But the young men chewing in the wind of Hawa Jube had little concept of Italy other than as a staging post, a gateway to riches and the good life. They had no idea of the overcrowded detention centres in which people were often held for months, nor of the cold reception they might face: in December 2013 a video appeared on Italian TV of male and female migrants being stripped naked together and hosed down upon arrival in Lampedusa.

This outlying island, Italy's southern-most point, had a capacity to receive 850 migrants, but regularly holds double. Unable to process them all, and in violation of European standards, without a policy of providing for them, Italy often simply released the migrants to fend for themselves, sleeping in railways stations, camping in olive groves, surviving on stolen lemons and pizza dough cast out from the tourist restaurants. All along the ancient coast of southern Sicily, church soup kitchens and hostels in picturesque Roman squares lined with palm trees swelled with foreign visitors dressed in donated clothes who wandered the streets wary and wide-eyed. From Nigeria, Mali, Niger and Chad, they came; from Cameroon, Burkina Faso, Ivory Coast, Senegal and Congo; from Ethiopia, Eritrea and Somalia, and even from Syria, Iraq and Afghanistan. In the future, this period in the history of the Mediterranean will have a name of its own, 'the great migration' or some such. In the present, though, it is simply a crisis.

From Italy it is a long way to the gilded cities of northern Europe of which everyone dreamed: Paris, Amsterdam, London and the welfare state paradises of Scandinavia. The European Union has a rule, called the Dublin II Convention, that requires all refugees to claim asylum, and to stay, in their country of first arrival. The ambitions of many were cut short by police and border guards at the Euro Tunnel terminal in Calais or on the trains and buses through Germany and France who, after checking fingerprints, returned the asylum seekers again to Rome. Italy, though, thinks the Dublin rule is unfair and so doesn't bother to fingerprint many of those it releases onto its streets. And the refugees too, often mutilate their fingers to avoid being returned to one of Europe's more depressed economies. To work, above all, was what the young men wanted.

'If I get money, I can make that difficult journey,' Guled said quietly to himself. He felt impotent; he could not look after his family. It was the most common complaint of men in the camp. And a man who cannot look after his family has no voice in the collective decisions of the clan; he is not, in essence, a man at all. Even if, despite the insecurity, Guled went back to Somalia and he was unable to find work, if the kids asked him for things he would be embarrassed. It was thoughts of his children that made him ready to risk his life to escape Dadaab.

Twelve days later, there was another explosion in the night. The whole camp had heard the blast; Kheyro, Nisho, even Muna far away in Transit had woken up, but Guled had been closest. A grenade had been thrown into the base of the telecoms tower between Lagdera and Hawa Jube. There would be no phone network in Ifo camp for ten days. People said it was part of the Kenyan plan again: to make life harder, to encourage the refugees back to Somalia. In those days the government's campaign was never far from the conversations in the camp; it was a latent threat, suspended in the air like electricity in a storm waiting to be conducted. In the terror and confusion of such attacks, the brain involuntarily reached for dots to join together.

Guled's friends sat again on the mats behind the khat stall, huddled out of the unrelenting wind, to discuss the bomb. One wore a Barcelona strip and one a new design: a black tracksuit emblazoned with the brand name 'Al-Shabaab'. Guled's face was drawn with worry. The boys talked about a 'deep fear' that was now leeching through the camp: Somalia was unsafe and so was Dadaab. The explosion had chased everyone back inside their houses; waiting to see what would happen. All across the thorny compounds on that windy Sunday morning, urgent conversations were taking pace, turning over events.

'The drama started again,' said Ilyas. The boys nodded wearily.

'Where can we run to, if we fled Somalia because of war and here the problem is still the same?' asked Guled.

'We better fly to the sky,' said Yusuf.

'No,' Ilyas warned. 'In the sky is also trouble, because I hear people are claiming the sky.'

Without any prospect of riches on the horizon, and to protect himself from the apparent march of war towards the camps, Guled decided to fast. Ramadan was coming. Devout people in need of a little extra of God's love had a habit of fasting on Monday and Thursday before the holy month. It saved money, enabling him to send the little he got from Auntie to Maryam, and it made him feel good.

33

Waiting for the Moon

The fasting seemed to work. And as the rest of the camp joined in for the holy month, blessings multiplied. When a strange unseasonal breeze brought a cool spell in the middle of the Hagar, the refugees praised God. They didn't believe in climate change. There was a breakthrough for the hostages too. Ramadan is traditionally the season of suicide bombings by al-Shabaab but this year brought good news from Mogadishu. The kidnapped Spanish women working for MSF were finally freed on 19 July, after long negotiations and strenuous denials in the media about any ransom being paid. Their release presaged no change in security procedures for the agencies; the damage, in that respect, had been done. But for the refugees, a circle had been closed, a wrong had been righted. MSF was popular in Dadaab and people had felt bad for the women and the organization.

At the beginning of August, as Ramadan drew to a close, Guled felt able to say: 'Life is becoming normal again now.' His Leopards FC team had even managed a friendly football match against a team from Ethiopia in Ifo 2. They had impressed Guled with their organization: contributing money for nets behind the goalposts and lining up to shake the hands of the visiting team. He still missed Maryam and the kids and his fantasies of escape remained, but they had been subordinated to the quotidian demands of pushing khat that was, contrary to expectation and custom, selling especially well during the holy month.

'When there is peace,' said Nisho, 'the first thing you notice is people building things.' It was true: along the wide roads of Ifo 2 women stood on chairs binding branches together, erecting huts to replace the shredded tents. Carts loaded with grass for roofs creaked across the no-man's-land from Ifo 1. At Billai's request, Nisho was constructing a new house next to the old one that they had been renting. He had even been able to afford to take his mother to see the witchdoctor again.

Like everyone else, Guled and Nisho attributed the improvements in the situation to the miraculous power of fasting and the devotions of Ramadan. They thought He was rewarding them for their virtue, giving them a break after an exceptionally hard year. They were happy to ignore the economic link with the resumption of the smuggling and the departure of the corrupt police chief, and the effect of the other main event that season: the new UN biometric procedures for the food distribution.

Although the official population in July 2013 was 402,455, tens of thousands of those on the food distribution list did not live in Dadaab. They were the people who preferred the city life, dodging the police in Nairobi and Garissa, but who were unwilling to relinquish what they saw as their 'right' to free UN food. Then there were the ones who had returned to Somalia and left their cards with relatives like the family of Billai and Maryam. Together with the habit of not reporting deaths in the camp, the general distribution manifest was hardly ever adjusted downwards. And so every few years the UN conducted what it called a 'verification' of cards – every holder had to appear and match a face to a card. With the suspensions in services, it had not been done for five years. Now the camps were teeming with people come in a rush to 'verify' their ration cards.

Before, people had been accustomed to travelling to the camps and staying with relatives for a week, re-registering their cards and then returning to their farms in Somalia or to the city with their fake ID or their Kenyan resident's permit bought with a bribe. But now the UN was getting wise and had planned a new system, the 'biometric'. A crack team of consultants for the World Food Programme flew in to oversee the rollout of the new biometric system. WFP was also facing a funding crunch (something they kept to themselves at that point); it needed to cut costs and that meant reducing the number of people it was feeding.

For months, hundreds of temporary workers had bent over hot computers from six a.m. to five p.m., as noisy crowds filed through another set of enormous warehouses, wire stays squeaking in the wind and loudspeakers popping and crackling at the long lines of people baking and waiting in the dust. They took fingerprints as well as photographs and only holders of the new machine-readable cards would be allowed to collect the rations. The established refugees didn't like it: they considered collecting food a waste of their time. Many among the middle classes hadn't been to the food distribution warehouses in years, decades even, they simply rented out their card to a shopkeeper who paid them a percentage of the value of the food. And then there were the brokers who had bought up the cards of people leaving the camp and ran a business collecting and wholesaling relief food far and wide; some had as many as a thousand cards each. The biometric, the UN hoped, was going to put an end to all the cheating. The refugees, however, saw it as part of the same overarching plot: to relentlessly squeeze them until they went back to Somalia.

On 18 July the verification process for Hagadera had been completed and 21,991 who hadn't shown up were struck off the register. A similar number had been removed from the lists in Dagahaley, Ifo 1 and Ifo 2. UNHCR staff were confidently predicting that they would reduce the official size of Dadaab by 20 per cent. When the UN announced that by 1 September the old cards would not function at all, the non-resident refugees had panicked and the camp was full. Every bus arriving from down Kenya and each shack and tent was bulging with visitors trying to get their cards reinstated. 'If we simply stopped all the buses arriving from Garissa and Nairobi, we could reduce the population of the camps by half!' laughed one UN staff member.

They came from all corners, from as far away as Mogadishu even. Dadaab is a major part of the coping mechanisms for the vulnerable across a whole region. Guled wished that Maryam would come so she could sign over her card to him. He thought about asking the block leader to vouch for him saying that his wife had had an operation and that he must collect the food for her, but the man had a habit of discriminating against people not from his clan. 'The soil belongs to us,' he was known to have said; like most of the block leaders, he was a member of the dominant Aulihan, a powerful influence in the camp. It was the block leaders that had threatened some refugees not to use the new system and had stymied cooperation with the UN. They represented the vested interests, the brokers holding all the fake cards. But the UN was standing firm.

'We are men of steel!' the UN staff joked over beers in their Pumzika bar. The authorities were braced for trouble.

From Salidley, six months after he had taken his remaining family north, Nisho's father-in-law returned to secure his card. He looked older and greyer, but he was happy and well. He stayed a week, sleeping in the house with Billai and Nisho and talking in the evenings: stories of freedom, of cultivating your own food, milking your own animals, and of tragedy. The village had pooled their resources for their first season back but all their collective crops had been eaten by a plague of birds. Nisho had had to send his father-in-law the fare for the vehicle to come back to the camp.

To allow a family member to collect food on your behalf – and to maintain the expatriate posture of one foot in Dadaab and a life elsewhere – you needed an excuse. The most popular one was to claim that you were looking after elderly relatives and so were unable to attend the distribution. This was the story that Billai's father adopted and it worked. To Nisho's relief, Billai's aunt who was still in Ifo was now mandated to haul the sacks of food for a family size 8 to the market instead.

After a week, the old man returned to Somalia leaving behind him a potent legacy of imaginings. There was peace, he said, under al-Shabaab. 'Somalia is better than anywhere,' he said and encouraged his daughter and her new husband to return too. Billai had wanted to return with her father, 'just to visit,' she said. 'Do what you like,' Nisho had told her. In his view, peace under al-Shabaab was a mirage. It may look like that to you, he told his father-in-law, but not to me. He pretended no power to compel his wife, but he was saved instead by the aunt who, divining something, advised Billai not to travel. Her father went back to Salidley alone but soon he was blessed with news instead: Billai was finally pregnant.

It had taken ten anxious months for her to conceive. They had both worried that something might have been wrong, but now Nisho's natural bravado was unchecked: 'I have shown my manhood!' he announced to Mahat. The happy news had emerged when Nisho, curious that Billai had gone from using one lemon to three or four with dinner, had discreetly approached the aunt. A single glance from the older woman had confirmed it.

'This is a normal thing, don't worry,' the aunt advised Billai. 'Let it not bring a change in your behaviour, continue with your life. Everybody goes through this.'

But Billai had insisted on some changes all the same. If Ifo was going to be her home and she was going to raise a family, she wanted a proper house, not something rented. So that was why Nisho now spent his afternoons digging in poles and mudding walls, laying rafters and nailing down tin sheets for a roof. The site of the new house was a semi-circle of ground right next to the old one. As families have grown up and multiplied in the older camps, compounds have been subdivided many times. The UN long ago ceased trying to police construction. Nisho had grumbled about it but he was happy, he paid no mind to the talk of return. Until the UN bulldozed his house and dragged him from the wreckage, he was going nowhere. Pride shone in his face as he bounced around the building site in his dirty LA Lakers T-shirt scavenged from a friend. '5 is better than 1,' it read.

Next door, Mahat was building too. When he had heard that Nisho was moving he had begged some poles and dug a barrow of mud with a friend and together they had made a bedroom for him in Nisho's new compound to replace the lean-to. There was a gap in the mud, a kind of window, so the breeze would still whisper through the sticks. Since he had resigned his latest job, he spent a lot of time there lying hungry in the shade.

For a while he had joined the mill working for Professor White Eyes and it had seemed that the upswing in the economy would benefit him too. At six a.m. he would start in the small tin room of the grinding mill on the back alley in Bosnia, clean the ancient green metal of the machine and then spend the whole day gradually becoming coated in the dust of maize until five p.m. Before Ramadan there was one break, for lunch. The food was *muwfo*, a mixture of maize and wheat flour ground in the machine, like a chapati but bigger and fatter, eaten with vegetables but never meat. One plate between three people. Not enough, Nisho advised Mahat.

If he had been paid more, Mahat might have persevered; 100 shillings ($1.25) a day he could have accepted. But often he only got 50 shillings ($0.65) after White Eyes had deducted petrol, lunch and the other expenses of running the mill. White Eyes claimed Mahat earned 150 shillings ($1.8) a day, but Mahat says he never saw that kind of cash. One day during Ramadan, sitting in his new room, he discussed the situation with Nisho. He told him the hours and the pay and the food, and said he felt discouraged.

'Just leave it,' said Nisho. And the following day, without a word to White Eyes, Mahat stayed at home instead. That had been a few weeks ago. Eid – the end of Ramadan – was coming, people in the camp were weak now, after a month of fasting during daylight hours and praying through the night, at two a.m. and five a.m. For Mahat, accustomed to skipping lunch, to have his hunger sanctified by God was a relief. Towards the end of the food cycle, even the evening meal was hard to come by: Mahat's stepfather had been laid off from the vehicle and his mother did not work, so the rations never lasted the full two weeks. Another reason why he found himself increasingly at Nisho's.

Ramadan was also a time when the militias came calling, trying to tempt people with the promise of food and a noble cause to fight for back home. But their presence in the camp made people feel uneasy. The refugees spoke disapprovingly of 'the children', as al-Shabaab had come to be called. So the outlaws spread their message surreptiously, on the fringes of the mosques and madrasas; they didn't have enough support in the camp to attempt to take recruits by force: there would have been uproar. Nisho took a strong stand against the extremists. Mahat, too, was unimpressed. He was tired of sitting idle, but the camp had instilled something in him, a sense of ballast perhaps, a value for his own life, or just a sufficient dose of cynicism to vaccinate him against the glamour and the lies of war. None of his friends was inclined to join either; they were more interested in going back to Somalia to farm. When some of them boasted to others of their plans, Mahat's girlfriend, the pale child from Hawa Jube, came to him flushed with anxiety.

'Are you going to Somalia?' she pressed him. 'If you do, will you marry there?'

She was in primary school and fourteen years old, but they had already been spending time together hidden in the lean-to or in the compounds of friends, and she was worried that people might have begun to notice. For their generation, there were no restrictions among themselves on what they could do in private, but once a relationship was public, a young person's virtue was on the line. He reassured her that he was going nowhere, he had no plans to flee; his remaining family were here and he had neither land nor contacts back in Somalia. Even though he was jobless, there was nowhere he could imagine being better off.

On 4 August, at a conference of countries contributing troops to AMISOM – the African Union peacekeepers in Somalia – President Kenyatta once again spoke of the need for the refugees to go home. But in the dusty north that the president had never visited, the words struggled to find meaning. For Mahat, Ifo was home. If anything, he felt more fatalistic, less motivated to shape his own destiny since the Kenyan government appeared to be intent on shaping it for him.

Without work, he was hungrier but happier. 'I was getting money but my body was dying,' he said of his time at the mill. The dirty jobs in the market had made him black, he said, because the sun was cooking him. Now he was improving his lifestyle, becoming healthier. 'I am coming back to normal, my skin is getting lighter, when people see me they say, "You are shining, what have you eaten?"' Away from the struggle of the market, his brain was more settled and he was, strangely, putting on weight. Idleness suited him.

What he really wanted was to go back to school, but he still hadn't found a way to pay for exercise books and a uniform, the hidden costs behind the rhetoric of 'free education'. The religious schools were cheaper; there was no uniform and you wrote on a slate. And that had given rise to a new idea for Mahat: to become a sheikh.

His family were not particularly religious but, when he was younger, a dedicated uncle had taught him to recite the Koran and the practice had sharpened his memory. In the quiet, hungry days of Ramadan he had begun again and by the end of July he could recite 40 suras of the 114. That was around three hours of chanting. Nothing compared to the five or six needed to sing the whole book. There were legions of boys younger than him who would be competing with each other soon at Eid but if Mahat stuck at it and avoided getting the pale girl pregnant and being forced back to the market to look after her, he might be in with a chance next year. Meanwhile, the annual dilemma of Eid-el-Fitr approached.

In the new hut, Mahat and Nisho wondered where they could find meat to celebrate. In a few days' time, God willing, a sickle of a moon would appear to signify the end of Ramadan and those with means in the camp would feast and those without would try and get themselves invited to the house of someone who did. All Nisho's resources had been taken up with the construction. Mahat had nothing but the oversized clothes and decaying pink flip-flops that he wore; even if he had a few coins, the priority would be a gift for his sweetheart. The Turkish Eid of the camel when Nisho and Billai were married was now two years ago; the memory had calcified into legend. There would certainly not be another feast like it for them this year.

Nisho and Mahat were not alone. Many, if not most, in the camp would not be feasting. The annual drive to raise money for the unfortunates in the new camps of Ifo 2 and Kambi Os had begun. In the mosques, the sheikhs told stories of people breaking their fasts with bark from trees, or soup made from stones. And the wealthier refugees, moved and ashamed at this time of almsgiving, donated over 200 sacks of rice. The madrasa teachers in every block were charged with the task of identifying the vulnerable ones. The really desperate had nothing to hide, they were known. If one could afford to dissemble, to maintain a public pride despite a howling belly, then one was not considered needy. Mahat was hungry but he would never consider himself worthy of charity; hunger was normal. Nisho, too, was a master at keeping up appearances. When asked where he would be feasting for Eid, his reply glittered with multiple truths: 'We are only waiting for the moon,' he said.

34

Eid el-Fitr

The night of Wednesday 7 August was murky and black. A crisp wind transported a curtain of perpetual cloud across the sky, veiling the drama of the crepuscular moon and creating a problem for the mullahs whose job it was to spot it. A breeze at night was a superstitious thing; the dark desert became huge and frightening, full of the possibility of criminals, monsters and magic. Just after nine the news went around that the new moon had been sighted in Garissa, and in other parts of northern Kenya. But an hour later, the radio struck a note of doubt. The Chief Kadhi of Kenya said on air that there had been no confirmed sighting of the moon and asked Kenyans to defer their prayers until Friday. In Dadaab and elsewhere though, the faithful did not wait. That year, in Kenya, Ramadan ended in confusion.

The morning of Eid, in Dadaab town, rang with excitement. By nine o'clock the street was a parade of women in finery, men in pressed and shining kanzus and children in box-fresh outfits and shiny new shoes. Shops were flung open to the milky sky as sweaty hands exchanged dirty notes for all the last-minute preparations for the festivities. The town was quivering with commerce. Children raced across the road shooting each other with that year's toy of choice: plastic guns that emitted a sound and flashed red when fired. No one commented on the irony apart from the town madman who pointed his finger and pulled an imaginary trigger at the kids. He was enjoying himself.

A man of bottle-green eyes and ageless features, with grey-brown hair that seemed matted with tar and wrapped in a rag headband of a matching hue, he wore tyre sandals and a tin can attached with string to his shorts which he held to his ear and chattered into as if it were a mobile phone. Leaning on his knotted stick, he wandered down the thoroughfare gathering soft drinks from every shop. On this day, no one could refuse. Outside one of the shops a disabled man in a wheelchair was sipping a gift of Fanta too. The businessmen and shop-owners themselves were shaved and oiled and dressed in expensive silk, dispensing largesse and gleefully pressing hands and praising God. Feast days were a time for politics too. The businessmen, forgetting their sins and whatever ugly compromises underwrote their fortunes, went with the crowd to Ifo, where the mass prayer was being held.

On most days of the year, the Kenyans from Dadaab town disdained the camps and restricted their contact to essential business. But on Eid, a festival whose unique power and excitement lay in the huge numbers of people praying together in one place, the well-dressed host community piled into minibuses and trucks and joined the refugees on the plain at the edge of the camp where the sheikhs had hoisted a loudspeaker into a tree.

Nisho had heard a rumour in the market in the days before that the Wahabis were planning to usurp the location of the mass prayer. That, this year, they would have more adherents than the traditional Sufi majority. But while the rate of converts joining their sect was picking up, Sufi dominance was still total.

At ten o'clock, lines of men facing the north rippled into the distance as far as the eye could see. Mats covered the ground. A bare patch of sand separated the men from the women who lined up in an equally uncountable mass. Tens of thousands of people, arms by their sides, standing, silent. An army of glittering, shimmering colour in the weak morning light. In the expectant silence, the birds sounded like a riot over the rhythmic cough of the generator that powered the speaker. Then it crackled into piercing life with the call to prayer and the incantation from the sheikh. The response from the massed umma was a soft wave of sound breaking over the heads of the worshippers as the lines knelt, folding like fabric, five times.

The sheikh uttered the ritual blessing giving thanks for the end of Ramadan, and then it was done. The vehicles that had been parked randomly to one side in the bush started up and the moving crowd looked, from a height, like water, spilling and breaking on the plain. Dust rose gently in a powdered mist and hung, shifting in the breeze. The lucky ones moved off to compounds rich with the smells of roasting meat and the chalky tang of sacrificial blood drying to a crust on the sand.

Nisho was tired, he hadn't slept. He had been offloading sugar and potatoes all night, but he was happy. There had been many trucks and now he had 700 shillings ($9) in his pocket for the big day. From the prayer Nisho walked through the bustle of Bosnia in his best clothes: a T-shirt with buttons at the neck, clean grey pin-stripe trousers and big red-leather sandals. Beside him, Mahat was smiling in a new shirt that a friend had given him over his dirty vest, trousers with no button that flew open at the waist, held together with a webbing belt in rainbow colours borrowed from Nisho and dusty espadrilles that were his new footwear of the moment, until they too disintegrated and he begged something else.

There were beeping horns, a flood of men dressed in white and down the alleyways boys and girls jostled around the juice- and sweet-sellers, eager to spend the festive coins they had been given by parents, neighbours and relatives. In the thick of an alley was White Eyes, passing out little plastic bags of juice fist over fist from a huge blue cool-box. Ever the opportunist, he had bought a vat of concentrate for 500 shillings and was selling the bags at 20 shillings a piece; he was making a killing. The children tittered and pressed around like birds pecking at seeds. Within twenty minutes, he had sold the lot.

An hour later, Professor White Eyes joined the crowd of men drinking tea with Aden, a businessman from the market who had a low hut in block E2 near the police station with wire windows and a USAID tin door. In a stroke of eleventh-hour luck, Nisho and Mahat had been invited to come and feast. But it was also an awkward coincidence. Mahat had not seen White Eyes since he had failed to show up at the grinding mill for work. But the ebullient professor made no comment on the incident and Mahat maintained a shy quiet sitting on a rush mat in the corner as White Eyes regaled the guests with a parable about Ifo while they waited for the women of the household to prepare the food.

He told a story of a woman who demanded gold for her wedding but when the parcels of gifts arrived on the day, there were fine clothes and other things, but no jewellery. Outside, drums were playing, people were waiting for the bride to show her face. She called the husband-to-be on the phone and asked, 'What happened?'

'I couldn't afford it,' he said. 'I am a poor man!'

'Then I am not leaving the house!' she said and switched off her phone. Her mother tried to persuade her, others came, but the lady would not budge. The groom was in a fever of embarrassment.

'There's a saying,' White Eyes said. 'Bring gold or leave my ass alone.' His male audience collapsed with laughter and knowing.

He told how, while the stubborn bride remained inside, the family debated what to do. The clan was expecting a marriage. They decided that the groom must marry the lady-in-waiting; the bride's best friend, and so the next day there was another wedding, another camel was slaughtered and the best friend and the man were married. When the jilted bride heard what had happened, she left her house in a rage and went to the police, paid a bribe and had the man arrested. But his family paid another bribe to have the man released. Later, the man and the best friend were resettled to America and the proud woman married someone else, a cook, who slaughtered not a camel but two goats at her wedding.

Everyone laughed. It was a familiar theme, the vindication of a poor man's worth, and an example of a universal myth essential for social harmony: that social mobility is possible, even in Dadaab. White Eyes' choice of story was telling. He had marriage on the brain. He was dressed in stonewashed jeans of a crazy pattern with the word 'fashion' embroidered in velour along the leg. His love of vivid colour had resulted in a multi-coloured shirt of exploding starbursts and large puffy trainers with the name 'OAT' printed to look like 'CAT' pasted a brilliant white. Such finery on Eid could pass without suspicion. But he was in fact dressed for a wedding, a secret one, in Hagadera, later that day. He had already phoned his friend and told him to prepare the mullah. This time, he later explained, the girl called Fatuma was not hazardously beautiful and she was partially educated, sufficient to tame any natural anarchy although not enough to encourage independent thinking: 'She failed Standard 8 and she wants Mr White Eyes!' he laughed. The catastrophe with Habibo had not dented his optimism.

Outside the hut the clatter of pans announced the presence of the women preparing the food for Aden's guests. The compound of a relatively rich man in Dadaab differed little from that of a poor one. The walls of the huts were still made of mud and the roof tin, although there was a satellite dish and a television. The codes of wealth in the camp are more evident in electronics, clothes and food. Aden had a wide range of outfits and, on that day, he wore bright-blue Adidas slippers.

Aden served more tea and the conversation turned, as it invariably did when Somali men were gathered together, to politics and tribe. White Eyes was forceful again: 'I don't believe in Somaliland, in Puntland ... these federal states. I believe in one country!' Nisho meanwhile sang Rahanweyn traditional songs to himself in the corner as a kind of theatrical protest at the topic, but he got animated at the mention of federalism.

'I need Ahmed Madobe!' he said. Nisho was not from the Ogadeen clan of Madobe, the new President of Jubaland. His enthusiasm was based on sugar: Madobe was Kenya's proxy and he was a kingpin of the sugar trade. Jubaland was good for trade and for Bosnia market, he said. It was the perspective of someone with no intention of going anywhere else. While the others talked about what was good for Somalia – an inexhaustible subject – Nisho's point of view was firmly rooted in Dadaab. Having made his point, he lost interest and went back to singing once again. Mahat pressed himself into the corner, smiling and saying nothing.

White Eyes droned on, heedless of his own proverb, 'speaking without thought is like shooting without aim,' until the turgid political talk was broken by the arrival of food. A woman's voice called from outside the hut and Aden rose to ferry in the dishes: the women would not enter the men's house. They would feast separately, in the kitchen, on the poorer cuts of meat or the leftovers. Aden laid out a thermos of soup, two huge platters of chips and spaghetti, a bowl of pilau rice with roasted meat mixed in and a stew of goat, juice with ice in a glass jug and bananas piled high.

White Eyes continued trying to make his points as the talking unravelled and concentration settled firmly on the food. Nisho zeroed in on the meat, helped himself to a large joint and set to work. Quiet descended and two circles of hands made a blur of the food scooping it up and away. Ten minutes later, all the guests were reclining, flecks of rice scattered on faces and the floor while Nisho, back hunched, steadily chewed through the pile of meat remaining. Someone made a comment.

'I am a porter! I need to eat a lot,' Nisho snapped and then let out a long burp for effect.

White Eyes though was quiet; he was late. His phone rang and a female voice could be heard on the other end. Soon after, he made his excuses and scuttled out. Nisho was still eating. When he finally finished, the others rose and soon the party was over. Aden was expecting a female visitor and most of the others had girlfriends to go and see too. Nisho had begun to fall asleep amid the empty plates but he dragged himself up and went home to Billai who had shared a more simple meal with her aunt. Mahat went to visit the pale girl at Hawa Jube.

Also in Hawa Jube, Guled was visiting too. 'My wife is away,' he told himself. 'A man cannot stay alone' – a common saying among the boys of the camps to justify things that religion forbade. On this most sacred day in the calendar, the camp was at its most profane, crawling with furtive couplings.

Across the camp in Hagadera, White Eyes' friend had failed to arrange a sympathetic sheikh. The mullah refused to do a secret marriage without the girl's father present and, 'because I was feeling hot,' White Eyes said, he had to scramble an alternative back in Ifo, a sheikh called Hibil. Hibil was well liked by the youth for his willingness to perform ceremonies in a rush for a fee and in a simple hut he sat the couple down: a man nearing thirty in a multi-colour outfit and a girl of eighteen covered in a hijab of dark cloth.

'Name?' said Hibil. They told him.

'Block?' They answered.

'Do you need this woman?'

'Yes,' said White Eyes.

'Do you need this man?' the sheikh asked Fatuma.

'Yes.'

Then, *Nincah*, the practice of reciting verses over the couple's joined hands, and they were man and wife.

One block away, in E1, Muna wasn't eating anything. She was spending Eid with a group of her friends but their feast consisted of khat and brandy. They were sitting in a house that was a cross between a hut and a tent, with a mud wall and partial roof of tin but bordered on two sides with the remains of an antique UN tent. Thorns poked through the roof where a single yellow bulb burned. On the canvas in pen someone had written 'L.R.G.' and, beneath, an explanation of the initials: 'Life Research Group'. On the ground against one wall was a foam mattress, a plastic chair with broken legs jammed into the dirt and a sack of potatoes. Scattered around were jerrycans that served as chairs. On a charcoal stove in the corner was balanced a kettle full of tea from which the toddler Christine could now pour herself a cup. The ground was covered with the shredded stalks of khat and empty bottles of spirits as well as a child's bottle. The air was thick with conversation and cigarette smoke.

The house belonged to Muna's new boyfriend, an Ethiopian called Gemekis, a raggedy-looking guy with few teeth, a straggly beard and a pot belly. He was a veteran of Dadaab since 2001 and spoke Somali, Swahili and English as well as his native Oromo and Amharic. He wore a baseball cap and a T-shirt with the word 'DAWGZ' in large letters on the back. He was one of the chief members of the Life Research Group who spent their days in khat- and alcohol-fuelled analysis. Another was Sweetee and another Amina, a Somali woman with an enormous afro that she refused to cover who lived next door and who now poked her head into the hut. She was dressed in a tight-fitting patterned green jump-suit and she wanted to know if anyone had seen her child. No one had. Muna wore a red skirt and a figure-hugging black T-shirt. When Umaima and Christine whined that they were hungry, she handed them some of the money that Monday had given her for Eid and sent them to the restaurant at the edge of the block. Then she got back to chewing.

She had been staying in the house a month, ever since Monday broke the door and Gemekis's teeth searching in a rage for Muna. 'You are taking my wife!' Monday shouted at him. But that day she had been somewhere else chewing khat with Sweetee.

'You say I am friends with all these men!' Muna screamed at Monday. 'Felix, Gemekis, who else? You broke his teeth so it must be true. Now, I will make it true!'

Gemekis wanted to report the assault but her friends in the police station warned Muna, 'If we arrest Monday, your case for Australia will be destroyed, better you sort it out among your-selves.' So, reluctantly, Gemekis dropped it and Muna went to live with him, a move that enabled her to sell her tent in Transit for 1,500 shillings, a useful amount of khat. She sat there most days, on the mattress, and her survivor friends would join her. Sweetee would come mincing and delicate and Hamdi would bounce down on her huge haunches and cackle with her burnt voice about how she had slept with 'him, him, him', and lament that she didn't know the name of the father of the black child that she roughly clutched in her pale hands like a handbag. 'I call him Obama, but who will pay for him? If I knew!' It was the same rou-tine every time.

Next to the sitting area was a bedroom with a lock on the door. Inside were two beds, a shelf held up with wire and clothes on a string. On the one solid wall above the bed was a Bob Marley calendar, a drawing of a heart inside which were the words 'Gemekis and Muna' and a photo of a Mongolian boy in an oversized suit beneath the legend: 'Happiness is a thing to be practised like the violin.' Muna was feeling high that day, but not just from the khat and alcohol: this Ramadan, her prayers for release from Dadaab finally seemed to have been answered.

A few weeks earlier, Gemekis had accompanied Muna and the children to the UN compound in Dadaab when she had been called, along with Monday, to the Ban Ki-moon hall for their predeparture interview with the Australian immigration officials. Muna always liked going to the UN compound: 'the UN is good for the eyes,' she said. After the unrelenting brown and dust, its trees and flowers were pretty to look at and a welcome relief. Gemekis had a job there as a handyman and he went to work while Muna joined Monday outside the hall and Monday looked away refusing to meet Gemekis's gaze.

The interview was conducted via video conference. A young blond man asked Muna and Monday questions about their problems in the presence of their children and two interpreters and they told him their story just as they had told it countless times before. They made a kiss for the Australian even though they had spent the whole morning waiting in silence not talking to each other and had already come to a private arrangement that when they got to Australia they would live in separate houses. Monday had recently taken his complaint about Felix arresting him for personal reasons to the police chief in Dadaab and, after examination, Felix had been transferred. The couple were on bad terms but they managed to smile at the Australian man while he told them, Muna recalls, that 'everything is freedom' in his country; that the lady President had no religion and that you can be Christian or

Muslim, without problems. He said they would call, that the family would be leaving soon.

One week later, the family had a medical. Monday worried that Muna had HIV/AIDS from the men she had been sleeping with. Her mother was worried too. 'She looks like her father,' she said, 'only bones moving, too thin.' The old lady was unmoved about her going so far away. 'Let her go,' she said. She would have preferred her sons to have been taken since they could be relied upon to send her some money, but of Muna she had no such expectation. 'A man has spoiled her,' she said.

The doctors vindicated Muna: she didn't have AIDS. They only told her not to get pregnant, since that would invalidate the resettlement process and they'd have to begin again with the new family member. Muna smirked: there was little danger of that, she thought. But when Eid came, she still tried it on.

'I need money for Eid, the kids need clothes,' she told Monday on the phone.

'I'll send something,' said Monday.

'And what about me?' she asked.

'Are you my wife?' said Monday. She laughed. So did he.

Afterwards, though, Muna regretted his generosity. She knew that khat was bad, that it was compromising her ability to care for the children. Monday had even suggested that she let him look after them. She vowed that after Eid she would go and stay with her sister in Nairobi, get herself clean before she went to Australia.

'If I stay here, I will not stop khat, my body will finish,' she said. Everyone in E1 chewed and they were generous with their leaves. She needed distance from Dadaab. 'No chewing, no smoking, no drinking,' she said as she lit a cigarette and watched the smoke drift upwards into the shadows of the tent lit by the single grubby bulb in the middle of the day. And then she remembered something.

'I heard in Australia there is khat too. Oh no!'

35

Solar Mamas

It was the third Eid that Isha and her family had celebrated in the camp, since their long, desperate walk from Baidoa. They were stronger now. The children were in school. Isha had managed to start a business reselling snacks for small change and life in the camp had stabilized, but she spent Eid alternately gripped by feelings of excitement and worry. A few days before the end of Ramadan, she, too, had been touched by the season's blessings. Her block had chosen her for what she called 'My chance . . . my golden opportunity.' While a few people in her block had returned to Somalia, driven by the insecurity and the squalor of the camp, Isha had stuck it out, and now she and her neighbour Hawo were going in another direction: to India.

A tall, brown-skinned man with white hair and steel-rimmed glasses had come and given a speech. His name was Bunker. He informed the people of M2 that because their block, isolated as it was on the corner of the camp, bordered by hyenas on two sides, had suffered disproportionately during the rape crisis, they had been selected for a programme to provide them with solar street lights. Not the ubiquitous portable lamps that leaked out a kind of weak bottled daylight but large, solar-powered lights lining the street. There were a few such lights in the camps, but the UN could not afford to install them everywhere. The day before the tall Indian man came, a UN staff member visited to explain the idea to the block leaders. The Indian needed women, he said.

They should be illiterate grandmothers willing to go abroad for six months to be trained as solar engineers. When they returned, the community would contribute money to a solar fund to pay them to install and maintain solar power in the block.

The project was the brainchild of Indian philanthropist Bunker Roy who ran an institution called 'Barefoot College' in Rajasthan, India. Inspired by the teachings of Mahatma Gandhi, Barefoot believed that the village should be the site of technology and innovation and that literacy was not a prerequisite for learning. Several generations of 'solar mamas' had already been trained using limited language, hand gestures and visual copying from Peru to Pakistan; there was even a Hollywood documentary about them. Isha thought it sounded neat but many of the other women in her block were suspicious and weren't interested. Heedless of the Indian's selection criteria, the elders simply chose two women, neither of them grandmothers: Isha, because she was the only woman who could read and write in the block. And her neighbour, Hawo, who was truly illiterate and only spoke Mai Mai, Nisho's native Rahanweyn dialect, because her husband had four wives and he could spare her.

When Bunker showed up with his UN entourage to conduct the formal briefing and selection the following day, he decided it would not be appropriate to go back on the community's decision. Isha never got the chance to tell him that her children were too young to make her a grandmother and she could read and write perfectly well. In block D2, which was famous for crime, and in M2, renowned for rape, Bunker gave two rousing speeches to hundreds of residents and answered questions from the community. He was brusque.

The women worried about their security in India: would they be raped without their husbands to protect them? 'No, don't worry,' he said. Could they practise their religion there? 'Yes.' Can't we do the training in three months instead of six? 'No.' Can we come back during that time? 'No.' The men wanted to know if they were allowed to communicate with the women while they were in India. 'Yes.' The women didn't ask that. There were many more questions than Bunker had time for but he was a visionary and, like most visionaries, he only had eyes for his vision. Later, when explaining the plan to the consternation of UN staff in the Pumzika bar, someone asked if the women could change their minds about being selected for the programme; he replied, 'They cannot!' And what if their husbands divorce them while they are away?

'As soon as they install their first solar panel, their husbands want them back again,' he assured the UN workers with a brutal confidence totally opposed to all their trainings and policies on participatory approaches to development. One of the UN staff was horrified at the abrupt transformation of the lives of the four women within twenty-four hours. 'It's completely mad ... There's an accountability problem if they can't speak the language. How can they complain? There is no preparation, no real consultation.'

Regardless of the pace and the lack of information, Isha ended Ramadan believing what the loud Indian man said, that, within two months, she would be issued with a passport and a visa and be on her way to India. She had no idea of the place; she had only seen Indian movies once, when she was younger, in Somalia. 'Is India near Turkey?' she asked. Before she had come to Dadaab, Hawo had never even seen a white person before, let alone an Indian. She regarded the world through eyes huge with wonder and a mouth that smiled a lot but said little. She was excited by the plan because, as Isha said on her behalf, 'She will return a civilized person. She has never been to a city, because she is a pastoralist.'

*

On the Friday after Eid, Isha and her fellow solar mamas were called to the UN compound in Dadaab; there were forms to fill for their travel documents. The place was a building site. For all the talk of return, the UN appeared to be investing in infrastructure for the long term. Privately, senior staff admitted that they still expected the camp to exist in ten years' time, whatever the Kenyan government might wish. Men covered in white dust resembling spirit dancers trudged up and down pushing wheelbarrows of rubble. The offices were being refurbished, flowerbeds were being relaid and a massive network of new pathways were being constructed ahead of the coming rainy season, so UN workers would be able to walk from their quarters to their offices to the bar without getting muddy shoes. Meanwhile some in the camp, like Isha's children, slept in puddles in their tents. UNHCR had a surplus administration budget that had to be spent before the year's end and which was, alas, non-transferable.

On that Friday there were two planes laid on to Nairobi because of a surge of employees requesting leave over the weekend. Hungover after what had been an intoxicating week with parties and films every night in the compound – part of the refugee film festival that comprised one morning of short films out in the camp, and a week of feature films in the agency compound – the UN staff members barely noticed the four Somali women who sat there, dressed in their best clothes, waiting.

Isha had a headache. The hammering of the builders made it worse. The lunchtime prayer approached and she wanted to pray. Dhabo, one of the women who had been selected from block D2, unwrapped her head scarf and gave it to Isha to use as a prayer mat. She went behind a low shrub, placed the scarf on the sand and knelt. Hawo went with her, and then Dhabo and Fatuma took their turn. Dhabo had come from Mogadishu in July 2011 and Fatuma from Gedo region at about the same time. Dhabo was a commanding figure, tall and dark. Fatuma was round and jolly, her sharp sense of humour soon revealed. She wore a name-badge with the logo of 'Save the Children': she was a cleaner in the compound in Ifo 2, earning 5,500 shillings ($60) a month, without which she was concerned her family would struggle if she went to India.

A kind, careful man from the UN called Sam appeared with the passport forms and slowly filled them in one at a time, writing the answers for the women. Instead of measuring their height, he asked them to stand up so that he could estimate it. While the process inched forward, Isha sat like Cleopatra in a blue-and-red dress and grey hijab, her fingers curled around the arm of a black swivel office chair that rocked on the uneven concrete, as if it were a throne. Her feet tapped on the floor, impatient, and she stared around, her eyes roaming the ceiling and tracking the cleaners advancing down the walkway towards them. Along with the builders' banging, birds gargled in the courtyard. A cleaner came and plugged her mobile phone to charge inside the low wall of the hut. As soon as she was out of sight, Dhabo unplugged it and connected her own phone, quick to spot an opportunity for free power: phone-charging cost money in the camp.

When he had finished filling the forms Sam gave the women a pen to sign them with. There was laughter all round. They explained that they could not write, that was why they were there, although Isha proudly plucked the pen from his hand and signed her name in a flourish. For the others, Sam fetched an ink pad and pressed their thumbs to the paper. When he tried to explain what would happen next, it didn't work.

'Passporta? Somali?' Dhabo asked.

'UN,' replied Sam.

In principle, refugees have the right to a UN passport, what is called a 'Convention Travel Document' that allows them freedom of movement from their country of asylum. In practice, in Kenya there is a committee made up of members from the UNHCR and the Department for Refugee Affairs that issues them. But they issue very few. The women didn't understand. They motioned for a translator.

'Somali! Somali!' they shouted, laughing. Sam called someone to come.

A short plump boy with slick hair, a staff translator with the UN, arrived and explained. Relieved, Sam decided to share his personal experience of visiting. He was a Kenyan but he had somehow acquired a Pakistani passport.

'Make sure you visit the Taj Mahal,' he told them.

'Yes,' they nodded.

'In Rajasthan there are very good flowers in winter, make sure you take pictures . . . photos!'

The women looked blank. But they smiled at the mention of elephants.

'You can ride them like camels,' said Sam.

'No, no, no,' they laughed and shook their heads.

'The holy animal for them is the cow. So when you see the cow, don't beat it. The cows there are very friendly, they even walk in the street like human beings. The Indians worship the cow like a god.'

Dhabo looked shocked.

'There are over nine hundred gods.' The translator heard 'goats' and there followed some confusion. Then the cleaner returned and frowned to see her telephone set to one side and her charger commandeered. She replaced it.

'And the ladies in India have different ways of dressing,' said Sam. 'Traditional women wear a sari wrapped like this, with the belly open.' The women shrieked and laughed.

'Modern women wear like this,' he said, pointing to a white woman in slacks and T-shirt walking in the compound.

'We will dress like this,' said Dhabo, smiling but defiant, indicating her current costume.

'You can buy that there,' said Sam. 'Don't carry a lot of stuff.'

'With what money!?'

There were too many unknown variables. The experience was too big to fully describe, the disconnect between the worlds too great. Sam sensibly retreated.

'We'll discuss more when we get near to the date of travel,' he said.

Fatuma, worried about her cleaning job, began to talk, but Sam had changed the subject.

'The visa is only valid for one month. You have to report to the police, it is the police that extend the visa.' The women looked confused. There came a flurry of words and jabbed fingers. The four female faces frowned, their eyes pinned on the translator as he delivered their message.

'They say they need someone to look after them, and a Somali translator,' explained the plump boy.

'Yes,' said Sam, slowly, 'it is our responsibility to sensitize them. We will coordinate with Barefoot College to help them.'

'Okay,' said the translator, 'I have a meeting at three p.m. – I've got to go. He'll contact you before you go to discuss more . . .' he said to the women, backing away. And then he was gone, the women left adrift, a forest of questions sprouting in their minds and no way to communicate them.

Sam tried to find a UN vehicle to take the women back to their homes but failed and in the end simply pulled out notes from his pocket until the women seemed happy. Being managed by aid agencies through mysterious procedures half-understood was a common experience and they accepted the confusion good-naturedly: they trusted the UN and they surrendered themselves to its knowledge. When they said their goodbyes they were all smiles, Isha's gap tooth appeared and the women slipped out of the huge steel security gates, their veils snapping in the wind like wings. They were going to India!

'This thing is not real,' people said in the block. They were suspicious of the motives of foreigners.

'Your blood will be removed.'

'They will sell your organs.'

'Why are they taking the uneducated ones? Because they want to cheat you.'

Hawo got worried and came into Isha's hut for reassurance.

'Don't listen, they're only jealous,' Isha explained.

'Don't go, Mum!' Isha's children cried. 'There are lots of Somalis abroad, and they are fine.' She told them not to believe the stories.

Isha was worried not about being exploited but about money: how would the family survive without her income? Gab said he would manage and supported her in her opportunity. Now the family had something to look forward to. Their life had a horizon. The programme meant her family would be confined to the camp for at least a year: the six months of the training and then some time afterwards setting up the solar panels. Isha set about winding down her commitments in readiness for departure. She stopped the small business and she resigned her position as a governor of the local primary school for which she had been paid a small stipend. It made her nervous, this relinquishing of her survival mechanisms, but she felt an obligation to be honest with people and she had been inspired by the magnetic words spoken with conviction by the strange Indian man. She trusted him.

36

Knowledge Never Expires

Kheyro, too, for the first time in her life, was planning on leaving the camp. It wasn't quite Canada, as she had dreamed, but it was an adventure – further into Kenya – and it felt like a divine reward. In block A2 the family had had the best Eid ever. 'Now we are one of the wealthy,' Kheyro said. With her wages she had bought new clothes for the family, they had fed ten people in their home and even given meat to the neighbours.

Ever since she could remember, Kheyro had wanted to visit Garissa, the capital of North Eastern Province, the nearest large town to Dadaab. But, without a legitimate reason for travel and without the money for a bribe, a movement pass had been out of reach. In a way, it was the bombings that made Kheyro's dream come true. The shortage of Kenyan teachers willing to work in the camp due to the insecurity had led to a drive to recruit more, less-qualified, incentive-refugee instructors. So now she would be going for training in Garissa.

She liked the people at Handicap International but giving massages was not furthering her knowledge, and she had come to dislike the job. When an advertisement for teachers appeared on the tin wall of the Abu Woreda Hotel in Bosnia, Kheyro had bought foolscap, made copies of her certificates at the copy shack in the market and written an application letter that she took by hand to the education officer in the compound of the agency CARE in Ifo camp. Four days later, she found herself in an interview room facing three men: two Somalis and one Kenyan.

'Teaching has its problems,' one of the men said, 'What do you do if a boy that you are teaching says, "I love you"? How do you deal with that?'

'I think I should tell him that I am like his sister, his mother,' Kheyro said. They seemed to like that answer, she thought.

The next day, Friday, they offered her a job at Equator primary school in Ifo 2. She called her friends: 'I am going to be a teacher!' On Saturday morning there was a meeting of all the new staff. Everyone said their name and they were asked which subjects they could teach. Kheyro said she liked science, social studies and religion. She had never stood in front of a class before. But on Monday morning she started her new job. There was even a minibus to ferry the teachers from Ifo 1 to Ifo 2: no more walking two hours back and forth to work!

Equator primary consisted of two long lines of classrooms made of concrete walls either side of a compound dotted with young trees too short to offer shade for the current generation, perhaps the next. To one side of the compound was a door with 'Staff Room' written in chalk. On the wall inside was a hand-drawn crest with the school motto, 'Knowledge never expires' and a list of the class sizes. Total: 2,154 pupils. And these were the lucky ones, part of the 43 per cent of the children enrolled in primary school. It made for a ratio of around one teacher to eighty pupils. The mandated maximum was supposed to be forty-five.

Every morning, Kheyro wrote her name in the attendance book. If you forgot, you missed your wages. Then she would greet her colleagues, take her chalk and her notebook and go to class. The headmaster was a Ugandan who had fled his homeland in the 1980s with the warrior priestess and spiritual forerunner of Joseph Kony, Alice Lakwenna. He had been

Kheyro's teacher at Ifo secondary only a few years ago. His deputy was a stocky Somali nicknamed 'the belly' whom Kheyro liked to tease.

The day before Eid, she had given the results of an exam on Islamic Religious Education to Standard 5. The children were mostly below fifteen, the youngest, nine. School years did not follow biological age because of the random effect of the war; children simply continued where they had left off, where they could. Kheyro held the precious test papers in a bundle tied with string beneath her arm. Early light poured through the mesh windows lighting up the Roman alphabet and the annotated diagram of a bird on the wall. Kheyro flashed back and forth in her blue and gold dress and an ochre veil, up and down the freshly sawn desks distributing the papers. The boys had shaved heads for lice, dusty faces and sandy feet. The girls were cleaner, all dressed in the uniform of green skirts and magenta shirts – each school had its own unique colour. Eagerly, they snatched the papers to study the verdict on their work. The girls sat scowling to one side while a mass of boys crowded together in the middle, all leaning over each other to read what Kheyro had written.

She had one textbook, in English, for each subject, and in the evenings she sat at home and prepared her lesson plans, trying to remember how her teachers had done it. Science was her favourite topic; she still had an idea that she might become a doctor one day. The poor pupils of Ifo 2 were disciplined and eager to learn. But they were embarrassed learning about the human body and its reproductive systems. 'Madam, you cannot teach about this, it is very difficult,' one of the boys said. 'In our religion girls cannot talk about men's bodies.' She told them she could, that it was not haram, and they got used to it.

Teaching three subjects was hard work. The salaried Kenyan teachers taught only one specialism and for that they were paid

40,000 shillings ($490) a month. The pay for incentive teachers was 6,800 ($82), slightly better than the 6500 ($80) she had been getting at Handicap International but the difference with the Kenyan teachers caused resentment. There were two at Equator. One of them, called David, was a special needs teacher with a class of deaf and dumb kids. 'David is a nice man,' Kheyro said, 'but the system is not good.'

The new job opened Kheyro's eyes to something the pioneers of the '92 group had already confronted: the iniquities of the incentive system. A few years earlier, Fish and Tawane had joined others in protesting the unfair burdens of work placed on incentive workers. In a letter to the media they had called the incentive system a violation of national and international labour laws, which it probably was. Kheyro had no paid vacation and if she fell sick she would not be paid by her employer. But Kenyan teachers had a contract with the Ministry of Education that included generous terms for vacation and sick pay, even a pension.

That incentive workers were allowed to work at all was a compromise between the UN and the Kenyan government. But what had started out as a charitable idea had degenerated into a kind of slave labour. Incentive workers are the backbone of the humanitarian operations in the camps, often working harder than the paid staff. Of two people working side by side doing similar jobs, one can be paid $90 a month and the other $9,000.

There were occasional strikes and protests about pay but in a decade little had changed. The incentive system had only become more entrenched: since the kidnappings and the scaling back of services, there were more incentive workers and more need for them than ever. And the refugees needed the jobs. Without her wages, Kheyro's family would be reliant solely on the rations which had recently switched from rice to sorghum. Sorghum was unknown to them, they didn't know how to cook it, but luckily with Kheyro's wages they did not need to learn: they fed it instead to the goats.

Soon after Eid, Kheyro took the bus to Garissa from the CARE compound along with eighty teachers from the other camps who were also going for the training. With neither ID nor a movement pass, she dreaded the police. The road to Garissa that runs dead-straight west for seventy miles through the barren scrub had several checkpoints. At the first the teachers' supervisor showed a list of their names. At the second, at a place called Modigari, the police refused to allow the refugee teachers into Garissa. They demanded to see work badges and alien cards. Refugees have a right to an 'alien card' like an ID card, but at that time refugees said the standard bribe to get one from the DRA was 5,000 shillings. For thirty minutes, Kheyro and the others waited in the bus while negotiations proceeded on the phone. In the end the camp chairman of CARE phoned the police headquarters in Dadaab and the bus was released. From the window, Kheyro saw beautiful houses and compounds, 'well-planted and green'.

The teachers were hosted at Garissa Teachers' College. It was the first time Kheyro had slept in her own room made of concrete and on an elevated bed with a mattress, bedsheets and blankets. The staff of the college had prepared chicken, spaghetti and rice, mixed fruit and even tea. Kheyro ate a lot. 'My whole life I have had two meals a day,' she said. Although she had the means now to eat three times, the family often didn't bother; their bodies were trained. In Garissa she ate all three meals, and at four in the afternoon there was tea and cake. 'I was getting fat!' she said. 'Happy!'

Lacking documents, the student-teachers feared the police and so stayed in the college, not venturing into town. One boy with a Kenyan ID who went to the market, Kheyro gave money to bring back lotion for her. She was amazed at how clean Garissa was, no dust. She took one bath in the morning and by the evening she was still clean while in Ifo she sometimes had to bathe three times. She loved it. With an ID card she would have come often, she would have even seen Nairobi. In a way it made her sad, all those years of not seeing.

At the end of the three weeks, the trainees were expecting a cash handout, a stipend, but the supervisor told them they would get it when they returned to Ifo. Wise to such tricks by NGO workers, the teachers refused to board the bus home until their allowance was paid. The stand-off escalated until late in the day when eventually the District Officer from Garissa was called to referee. He ordered the supervisor to pay the teachers their due but by the time the money arrived, they had to sleep another night in the college and travel in the morning. The contract was expired, the staff said, and so the trainees went to bed hungry.

Back in Ifo, Rukia was delighted to see her daughter. The good food, rest and hot water had had an effect. 'You have become beautiful!' she said. 'If you leave this refugee life, you will become a beauty, my daughter!' The trip had whetted her appetite for exactly that. Kheyro dreamed now of university, diplomas, of Nairobi, Canada and even London. But the road to further education ran through Dadaab, not Somalia. 'There's nothing for me there,' Kheyro said. After years of lobbying and planning, Kenyatta University in Nairobi, tired of the restrictions on refugee students who wanted to take its courses, had decided to come to them. In 2013 it opened a campus in Dadaab. A project with York University in Canada called Borderless Higher Education had also just started issuing online diplomas in the camp. When the new semester started next year, Kheyro was determined to enrol.

37

Welcome to Westgate

The Westgate shopping mall is in the leafy Westlands area of Nairobi, not far from the offices of UNHCR. It is an affluent district with expensive residential apartment blocks, gated villas, and smart nightclubs and restaurants, markedly different from the opposite, edgier side of town where the Somalis live, Eastleigh. The Israeli-owned mall epitomised the neighbourhood's luxury identity. Inside the huge butter-coloured concrete rectangle, glass lifts gently rose and fell and Nairobi's elite glided up escalators, browsed in boutiques, dined in restaurants and bought their artisanal bread from the expatriate meeting place of choice, the ground-floor ArtCaffe. Even before gunmen attacked it in the powder blue afternoon of 21 September 2013, the gleaming shopping mall announced itself as a target. The National Security and Intelligence Service had warned more than once of plans for attacks on shopping malls and, only a week before, Western agencies had issued an alert for Westgate including on the day in question.

Around noon that sunny Saturday, a Mitsubishi car pulled up outside the mall. Gunmen got out, tossed a grenade and opened fire on the diners in the open-air restaurants overlooking the road. Then four armed men walked into the mall, two up the vehicular ramp into the car park of the building and two through the pedestrian entrance, and began shooting everyone they saw. On the top floor of the multi-storey car park, a children's cookery competition was under way. Five minutes later the tarmac was covered in upturned tables and chairs and amid the spilled food and blood, dead and dying children and their parents. All around, people walking to or from their cars had thrown themselves beneath parked vehicles.

Downstairs, the gunmen walked slowly through the mall taking aim and shooting methodically. CCTV footage showed them moving through the mall as if in a video game. Terrified shoppers and staff initially ran towards the oncoming attackers and then, realizing their mistake, fled in the opposite direction. People tumbled over the terrace of the ArtCaffe onto the road, rushed out of emergency exits and crawled around corners out of the building. The hundreds still trapped inside huddled in cupboards and toilets listening to shots ringing out through the building and the occasional explosion of grenades.

Outside, ambulances had started to arrive as well as crowds of onlookers, journalists and vigilantes from an Indian rifle club. Police tried to seal off the area, including firing tear gas to disperse curious crowds even as bloodied victims emerged from the entrance. Eyewitnesses spoke of ten attackers, shouts of 'Allahu Akbar' and 'We are al-Shabaab', of automatic gunfire, of dozens of bodies scattered over floors covered in glass and blood. At some point it seemed the gunmen stopped indiscriminately shooting and began differentiating Muslims among the hostages and sparing women and children. They asked victims to recite the shahada or name the prophet's mother. Those who failed, they shot.

The people trapped inside were texting, tweeting and even videoing what was going on around them and the images had already circled the globe. In addition, there were around 150 security cameras in the building, most of them still working. This was the most videoed terrorist attack in history. Shoppers in Nakumat supermarket filmed themselves walking down aisles stocked with food as gunshots exploded ever closer. CCTV captured pictures of people running with children in their arms, of crowds pouring down the central aisle, of tear gas streaming out of air vents, of numbers of men in civilian dress holding handguns, of bodies slumped against glass displays. And there are the attackers, in hooded tops and trainers, rifles slung casually on their arms like cricket bats or fishing rods; walking down the aisle of a super-market talking on the phone, taking orders perhaps. They have baby faces, they are young. The eldest was twenty-three, the youngest just nineteen.

At 1.45 p.m., ninety minutes after the shooting began, the first police tactical team arrived. Five minutes later, the Interior Ministry sent a tweet, saying 'Keep off #WestgateMall @PoliceKE has taken charge,' but arguments about jurisdiction with the army erupted and no one entered the building. Inside, many people cowering behind the meat counter in the supermarket or under tables in the restaurants were slowly bleeding to death.

Frustrated with the police delay, vigilantes armed with hand-guns – former special forces members and the son of the former Minister of Defence, Yusuf Haji – began a rescue mission to pro-vide cover for people trapped inside to escape. No one seemed to be in control of the response. As one survivor told the *Guardian* newspaper: 'We just went slowly, feeling our way along the walls ... there were people with guns everywhere. You didn't know who were the policemen and who weren't.'

Eventually, at four p.m., the police 'Recce' unit entered the building without uniforms or badges and were soon engaged in a fierce gun battle with numerous heavily armed opponents. Only after their commander was killed did they retreat and realise the people they'd been firing at had been the Kenyan army advancing from the rear entrance. They didn't go back in. By now, the attack was all but over. Sixty-one people lay dead in the mall. Many might have been saved if the response had been swifter. Footage from the security cameras later showed the terrorists, calmly chatting in the storerooms of the supermarket, taking their time, eating chocolate bars and praying.

Outside, tanks and armoured cars arrived. Inside, all was eerily quiet. On Somali radio, al-Shabaab claimed responsibility for the attack. 'For long we have waged war against the Kenyans in our land, now it's time to shift the battleground and take the war to their land,' a Twitter account purporting to belong to al-Shabaab declared. 'The attack at #WestgateMall is just a very tiny fraction of what Muslims in Somalia experience at the hands of Kenyan invaders,' said another post, before the account was suspended. As night fell, helicopters circled overhead and occasional gunfire continued.

The next morning, President Kenyatta made a statement that bore little resemblance to the facts on the ground. Ten to fifteen 'armed terrorists' were still inside the mall, he said, and they had hostages. 'We have reports of women as well as male attackers. We cannot confirm details on this. Our multi-agency response unit has had to delicately balance the pressure to contain the criminals with the need to keep our people still held in the building safe ... They shall not get away with their despicable and beastly acts ... We will punish the masterminds swiftly and indeed very painfully.'

And so the endless circle of violent retribution was reinforced. The pictures of a multinational crowd bloodied and terrified in a place as seemingly safe and familiar as a shopping mall jarred in the world's media. For the journalists covering the siege, it was frighteningly close to home. They were lucky they weren't inside; they could have been.

The scene struck a chord around the world in the way that news of carnage on a dusty street in Hosingow in southern Somalia had not. A few months earlier, a Kenyan airstrike had destroyed several shops and at least twelve civilians, including women and children, and it barely made a headline. Although for the victims, the experience of dying abruptly among your weekly groceries was the same, killed by forces you neither knew nor understood, the world had different words for each event. One was collateral damage, the other was a terrorist attack. One could be explained away; the other provoked governments to demand brutal justice.

The second day at the Mall ended in darkness, rain and gunshots. The third began with heavy gunfire, condemnations from world leaders and a massive explosion followed by black smoke billowing into a grey, baffled morning sky. Still, piped music blared from loudspeakers echoing through the empty shops and still the automatic welcome jingle repeated itself inanely, 'Welcome to Westgate!'

At the International Criminal Court in The Hague, Kenya's Vice President William Ruto successfully petitioned to have his trial adjourned so he could return home. For the conspiracy theorists, that was the purpose behind the attack. Since taking office, the government machine had engaged every nerve in trying to get the crimes against humanity charges against the President and his deputy dropped. Ambassadors had twisted arms, petitioned the United Nations Security Council, rallied motions at the African Union – all without success. Here, now, was the perfect ruse, so the cynics said. But such deft calculation appeared well beyond the capacities of the Kenyan government. By the end of the third day, spokesmen for the military, the interior ministry, the President and the police had all variously claimed that the siege was over, that all hostages had been released, that Kenyan forces were in control of the building, while at the mall the gunfire that continued into Monday night and Tuesday morning contradicted them. The world was watching and Kenya was faltering.

Finally, on Tuesday afternoon, President Kenyatta addressed the nation. He said the siege was over and declared three days of national mourning. 'Kenya has stared down great evil and triumphed,' he said. 'We have shamed and defeated our attackers.' But in the following days, as the truth emerged about the fiasco of the response by his government; the incompetence and criminal looting of the mall by the army and the frustrating of any investigations by the police, the shame was most squarely on him. The number of terrorists would be written down, from fifteen to eight and then, finally, to four. Wild claims from the foreign minister of attackers from the US, UK and several other European countries would be proved false; only one of them would later be revealed to hold a Norwegian passport, the others hailing from Somalia. Pictures would emerge of mountains of empty beer bottles and banks and shops stripped clean by soldiers. The collapse of the parking lot claimed to have been caused by a fire started by the terrorists would turn out to be the result of a tank shell fired, allegedly, to obscure the fact that the vehicles inside had been stolen by the army. The FBI and UK Metropolitan Police would leave Nairobi in disgust having offered to help investigate only to find their efforts unwanted. The New York Police Department would release a report in which it claimed the most likely scenario was that the four terrorists escaped at the end of the first day of the siege. And, most damaging of all, having acknowledged all the errors, and promised a comprehensive investigation, the President's appointed committee would never report. For now, though, the nation was in mourning and they were giving their President the benefit of the doubt.

During the final days of the siege the President's spokespeople had been manically repeating the slogan 'WeAreOne' on Twitter and Facebook and the idea had taken off. But the 'One' nation that people rallied around did not include Somalis.

Across the city, police were already kicking down doors and

rounding up anyone they thought looked suspicious, and to them that meant anyone of Somali ethnicity. As of Tuesday evening, eleven were in custody, the President said. But that was just the beginning. The attack put the Kenyan Somalis in a difficult position. For some who felt they had to choose between their passport and their blood, it was an easy step to join the rest of the nation and shift the blame onto the refugees. A Kenyan Somali woman from Garissa who escaped from the mall summed up the national feeling to a US journalist: 'Right now, I feel like they should all be sent back. Let them go and burn each other in their homes.'

The visceral urge for vengeance exploded in several directions. In Eastleigh, the crackdown continued. The following month in Mombasa, the radical cleric and successor to the slain Aboud Rogo, Sheikh Ibrahim Amor, was gunned down with three others as they left a mosque. The government distanced itself from the assassination in a mealy-mouthed denial that fooled no one: it had a persistent habit of extrajudicial executions. The next day, after Friday prayers, riots broke out in Mombasa. And further up the coast, across the border, at two a.m. on Saturday, two speedboats carrying US commandos from Navy Seal Team Six aimed for a house near the beach in the historic Somali port of Baraawe. An hour later, after heavy gunfire, they were forced to retreat with their target – the al-Shabaab leader Mukhtar Abu Zubeyr 'Godane' – still alive. Other, less publicized operations were under way inside Somalia: more Kenyan airstrikes with their heavy, indiscriminate toll.

The head of the Kenyan parliamentary defence committee, Ndung'u Gethenji, told the media that Dadaab was being used as a 'training ground' for terrorists, and should be shut down forthwith. While the road to Somalia does indeed pass through Dadaab, there was no evidence that the attackers stayed there. Indeed, it emerged almost immediately that the attack was planned from a nearby apartment in Westlands itself. Nonetheless, other MPs soon took up the cry. And, for the refugees, that became the meaning of Westgate: the final stage in their journey in the Kenyan imagination from neighbour, to other, to suspect and, finally, to enemy. In Nairobi, the stalled negotiations between the UN, Kenya and Somalia setting the terms for the return of refugees to Somalia burst into sudden life. And the camp waited nervously for the inevitable assault, for the revenge that would surely come.

38

Westgate Two

In the days since Maryam had gone, Guled spent a lot of time watching television in the cinema in his block and that's where he was when news of the Westgate attack flashed across the screen. The boys in the MAN UNITED makeshift hall were passing the time before the game. They watched with a macabre fascination the images of explosions, people running and police aiming weapons in the unfamiliar surroundings of the shiny urban scene. When the time for the game arrived, the cinema erupted into argument. One group wanted to keep the news, the other, the football. 'Football, in this place, is supreme,' said one, as though it were a kind of temple. Most had no interest in bombs and explosions. The news from Mogadishu, Libya, Syria and Afghanistan had normalized images of violence; the attack in Nairobi held little meaning for the young inmates of the camp beyond a certain schadenfreude.

'We are used to bomb blasts and these kinds of attacks,' someone said. 'Let them also taste what it's like.'

'Yes, let Nairobi feel it too!'

Only the arrival of another television resolved the quarrel and the news hounds moved to a corner. Guled was upset at the innocent people killed. But he just wanted to watch his game. Football was his only solace these days.

Things with Maryam were bad. It was weeks since he'd sent any money. Auntie's customers owed her a lot; she was carrying bad debt and there was no profit from the khat. Maryam had called and told him to come and divorce her. But he didn't even have the money to try and reason with her on the phone. By the time Westgate happened, he had made a decision. Life in the camp was becoming too difficult; he was ready to take his chances back home. He resolved to tell Maryam, the next time she called, that he would come at the end of the year, when he had saved the money for the fare, regardless of the threat to his life. If that didn't satisfy her then he planned to switch off his phone until she changed her mind, or until he could get there in person. Then, suddenly, everything had changed. While the Westgate attack was under way, she called. She was in Jilib, on the way to the camp. He kept quiet about his concession and accepted the news warily; he didn't know what she was up to, he would have to wait and see.

Six days after Westgate, Guled met her at the bus stage in Hawa Jube. It was two p.m. She came down from the vehicle wearing the Mogadishu uniform of hijab and thick dress. Guled thought she'd changed: her skin was shining and she was fatter. The baby boy was in her arms, but the girl, Sadr, Guled was distraught to find, she had left behind with his sister. In the taxi that Guled had hired to carry them home, they greeted each other.

'How do you feel?' asked Guled.

'I am happy,' she replied. And he thought she sounded genuine.

But her mood didn't last. Although she told Guled that she had returned because she had forgiven him and decided to reconcile, they both knew that was not the whole truth. Before they were married, she had been taking a shower, outside as many wash-rooms are, in the concrete compound of her mother's house in Mogadishu. When a mortar exploded terrifyingly close her hands had instinctively shot up to cover her head and ripped an earring from her lobe. Instead of healing, the scar had grown and grown becoming a tumour that she had had removed once before in

Mogadishu. During her first stay in Dadaab it had come back and the doctors at the hospital had promised to send her to Nairobi for surgery. But when her appointed day came and she had assembled with the others at the DRA offices clutching her movement pass and patient notes, she was among those pulled out of the line and told that they would be following in a second bus. The second bus never came. She didn't know it, but it was a regular ruse: medical appointments in Nairobi were hard to come by and those with money often purchased the slots of those without. Back in Mogadishu again, the tumour continued growing, resembling now a gristly second ear grafted onto the first, and it had started throbbing. She couldn't sleep. She had come back to Dadaab now in search of health care. But although the hospital was still there, it was crowded with visitors taking advantage of the services while they verified their cards for the biometric. She couldn't get in the gate some days, an appointment was out of the question. She had come back for nothing.

Maryam's timing was unlucky. The camp was more tense than ever, braced for Kenya's retribution. Another shoot-out had rocked Hawa Jube the week after when gunmen fired on the compound of the agency Islamic Relief and the teachers who slept there were evacuated to Dadaab town. Although the rains had come, they were fitful. In a world over which they had little control, the superstitious refugees took the weather for a portent. The curse fell too upon Nisho and Billai.

Just after Westgate, Billai miscarried her baby. Neither she nor Nisho understood the reason; she had had plenty of food and milk, what Nisho could provide, but one day the neighbour called him in the market and told him to come. The hospital sent her away with painkillers and after forty-eight hours, the couple's hope for progeny slipped away into the pit latrine. Later, her aunt took her to a traditional healer who burned her with sticks – Nisho didn't know where, she didn't show him. They told each other it was God's plan. But, depressed and angry, Billai's grief found alternative targets.

Nisho still needed money to furnish the new house, to buy what he called 'equipments': a bed, cooking pots, sheets, all of which had been borrowed. The house was finished but they were still sleeping in their old rented one and the owner wanted it back. It made for a stormy time. Every night when he wanted to sleep, Billai started 'on and on' about the bed. 'Shall I cut out my organs and sell them?' he shouted at her. A wooden bed was 6,500 shillings, a month of an incentive worker's salary, nearly $80. Without one, they would be sleeping on a mattress on the sand, or trying to.

'I don't sleep,' Nisho complained. 'I am told the nagging is normal for women . . . The house was the main thing, but that is done so now it is the bed: Woo, Woo, Woo, Woo, she is like that, all night.'

With Westgate, the *baanwaqo*, literally 'God's raindrops', the season of prosperity that had miraculously appeared since Ramadan, had truly come to an end.

'Dadaab is a nursery for terrorists,' the newly appointed Cabinet Secretary for the Interior, the Honourable Minister Joseph Ole Lenku, repeated on national television. The newspapers printed every rumour with abandon: that the Westgate attackers had lived in the camps, that they had trained in Dadaab and then travelled to Nairobi via helicopter. One Dadaab policeman even claimed to have seen the helicopter although, in a crowded refugee camp with 360-degree visibility of the plain all around, it was odd that no one else had.

In his cramped office in the government compound, Mr Lukingi of the Department for Refugee Affairs laughed at the suggestion: 'A helicopter . . .? Nonsense! We would have known if Westgate had been planned here. The government should mind immigration and the customs at the airport, not refugees in Dadaab!' The former military man in the UN security office held a similar view. 'Dadaab is one of the most closely monitored places on the planet,' he said. 'In a sweaty place with a shit internet connection? It's hard to do anything sophisticated here.' And yet, both could not quite rid themselves of the habit of mistrusting the refugees, of the impulsive move towards violence in response to violence. 'What we need is a good crackdown!' Lukingi said, the whites of his eyes showing. 'If we had a good crackdown, I could sleep in the street outside my office, here,' he added, jerking a thumb towards the dusty, rubbish-strewn main street of Dadaab town. But the crackdown that everyone anticipated didn't come. The attack, when it happened, arrived from an unexpected quarter.

Sometimes, in the cinema, when there was no football, the boys would show movies instead. Hollywood things, Indian romances. On 17 October at about half past eight, Guled left three of his friends outside the cinema chatting and sending music to each other's phones through Bluetooth. Auntie had called him and told him to come back; she didn't like him being there and now that his wife had returned she thought he should be at home. He lay down on a mat outside in the fresh air of the compound, next to his sleeping son. In the hot season it is normal to sleep outside in the breeze. But he had been asleep for only twenty minutes before gunshots woke him. He gathered up the baby and ran inside the house. When the shooting stopped the screaming started: Guled recognized the voice of his friend and moved to run towards the noise, but Auntie put her hand on him.

'No.'

'The bullets have stopped,' said Guled; 'they need help!'

After a brief argument, she allowed him to leave the compound. The back door of the cinema opened directly onto the road behind Guled's house and he saw two people come crawling out, shouting for help.

Some moments to nine p.m., three men had approached his friends, one carrying a knife and two with guns. They had ordered the boys to go back inside the cinema, followed them into the packed hut and immediately started shooting. One fired from the waist, aiming at the legs of the boys watching the Indian film, the other above their heads. Everyone scrambled towards the end of the hall near the screens, fighting to get out of the back door. The police later counted seventeen spent rounds inside the building and the walls and roof resembled a collander. Several of the boys inside the hall could not walk, bullets had shattered their thighs. Two were lying on the ground on the road outside Guled's house, their trousers heavy with blood. He called the mother of one of them on the phone and she came with a donkey cart on which they took him to the hospital, the other boy Guled pushed in a wheelbarrow. Seven were injured in total, not the sixty-seven killed in the real Westgate, but the terrorizing effect was similar enough for the refugees to call the cinema attack 'Westgate Two'.

In Nairobi, people now avoided shopping malls. In the camp, no one went any more to the cinemas at night and, if they went in the day, they locked the halls from the inside and let no one in or out. There were no more Indian movies either; people said the boys had been watching porn, which was why the extremists had targeted them. Some of the boys in the cinema even confessed, 'We know them, who did this' – it was the work of al-Shabaab copycats, homegrown jihadis from the camp, but no names were spilled. 'That is the problem of Ifo,' complained Guled, 'you will tell the police, they will be arrested, then they will pay some money and walk free, and then how will you sleep at night?' He had never seen anyone he recognized from his time with the group, but that didn't stop him worrying.

For days afterwards Maryam wailed, 'Why have I come?' She felt her life was cursed. Since the cool, blessed, weather of Eid had given way to unpredictable rains and unseasonal heat, the mood in the camp turned darker. First Westgate, then the cinema attack, and then, on 1 November, the worst news of all: the World Food Programme began cutting food rations by 20 per cent. No one believed the official pronouncements that it was due to a shortage of funds; they saw it as a form of collective punishment for Westgate and as an encouragement to go back to Somalia. On 3 November there was a rare solar eclipse. Teachers showed primary school children how to construct little cardboard boxes to view it, but when the ethereal shadow passed over the plain that afternoon most people in the camp shuddered at the bad omen, taking it for yet another unlucky sign.

The following week, the bad news that the eclipse seemed to portend duly came to pass. On 10 November the governments of Kenya and Somalia and the UN Refugee Agency finally signed the 'Tripartite' agreement to support the 'voluntary and spontaneous' return of those refugees who wanted to go back to Somalia. The timing, though, clearly had nothing to do with conditions on the ground in Somalia and everything to do with Westgate.

Two weeks later, a senior representative of the government finally showed his face in Dadaab to spell out the meaning of the agreement to the refugees. On the morning of 23 November the Cabinet Secretary for the Interior, Joseph Ole Lenku, a former hotelier, and his entourage stepped out of a government jet simmering on the Dadaab airstrip into the hot whirling dust of the border country. The welcoming committee included the head of the UN operation, local elders and Albert, the corpulent District Commisioner for Dadaab, the President's representative in the town. The VIPs travelled the 500 metres to the UN compound in an armoured convoy through the chaos of Dadaab town scattering donkeys and pedestrians. Once safely inside the blast walls, in the 'Ban Ki-moon Meeting Hall' surrounded by delicate, whitewashed paths and pretty pink bougainvillaea, the Minister addressed his audience of refugee leaders, members of the host community, UN staff and journalists. Ole Lenku was a young man, tall, with fleshy cheeks and black eyes and his attire was casual: a blue-and-white-striped shirt, with no tie, and a jacket he took off before standing to speak. The UNHCR press release about the agreement had underlined the word 'voluntary' in the title. As the cameras rolled, Ole Lenku prepared to disregard it. In precise English, he told the audience that his government wanted the refugees gone.

'There is no turning back,' he said. 'It is time to say goodbye and wish you the best as you go back home. Go and help your country rebuild.' His finger pointed the way from the Ban Ki-moon hall, out across the orange scrub towards the border.

When it was their turn to speak, the refugee leaders reported the views of the four hundred thousand registered refugees. They said conditions for return were not favourable yet and that Somalia was still at war. Ole Lenku repeated the fiction that Somalia was safe for return but remained silent on the facts: no mention of the ongoing clashes between Kenyan forces and al-Shabaab in southern Somalia, of the suicide bombings that continued to rock Mogadishu, or of the food shortages caused by the fighting. The Honourable Minister, however, was no longer in the hospitality industry: he had not come to listen. 'Dadaab Camp Officially Closed' was the headline on the evening news.

39

A Lap Dance with the UN

Four months later, Albert, the District Commissioner, set down his newspaper in the shade of the Indian almond tree behind his office. Ten feet away, in the entrance, his secretary sat pretending to type and airily telling visitors, 'Mr Albert has not come into the office today.' The whole of Dadaab town was glistening and sticky, uncomfortable in the heat. Albert shifted in his chair and plucked his shirt from his shoulders where it had pasted itself like wallpaper. It was March 2014, the short Deyr rains had been poor and the Jilaal had been harsh. The long Gu rains were due any day now.

'The UN are stalling,' he said, irritably. 'Dadaab is the buttered side of their bread.'

Ever since he had accompanied the Honourable Minister to the UN, Albert had been waiting for orders to implement the return agreement. None had arrived. In hindsight, the Minister's grand speech about going home now seemed like a joke. Albert was frustrated.

At the end of the year, tens of thousands had been stripped from the food manifest for not showing up to collect their rations for two successive distributions. The official count was down from over 400,000 to 342,835. 'This biometric is really working, huh!' Hans, the tall, tanned head of the World Food Programme, had trilled. He had saved WFP $2.9m and shrunk the official size of Dadaab by nearly 20 per cent simply by cleaning up the list. But the Kenyans were not satisfied. Many of those struck off were new arrivals who had trickled back over the past two years, only finally, now, accounted for. Nobody had, officially, gone back to Somalia.

'We are having a lap dance with the UN,' Albert snapped. To an extent, he was right.

On the shores of Lake Geneva, a few blocks from the shining water, an ugly angular white building painted with odd yellow stripes houses the headquarters of the United Nations High Commissioner for Refugees. Established in 1950, with a three-year mandate to help resettle the displaced in Europe after the Second World War, UNHCR quickly became a permanent part of the UN constellation, kept in business by emerging crises ever since. Inside the ugly building, the tripartite agreement and the Minister's reckless speech had caused a storm: the UN stalled.

International refugee law and UNHCR procedures governing protection and repatriation of refugees are strict. In Somalia it is unlikely that all the criteria for the declaration of peace and thus the benchmark 'conditions conducive for return' will ever be met. The tripartite agreement was a messy, hasty compromise the details of which were far from clear.

The lawyers in UNHCR's protection department thought it was irresponsible to be talking about return to a war zone, a sentiment shared by human rights organizations who cautioned against *refoulement*. Their more pliant colleagues in Nairobi had been bounced by a forceful Kenya into a process of voluntary return that might encourage people to go back to a place where they still stood a good chance of being raped or killed. In practice, the agreement had been less about peace in Somalia than about Kenyan politics.

In Dadaab a senior official was forgiving: 'Return is always political, sometimes they need a little push, eh?' The most compelling argument, though, came from the Somali head of the Dadaab operation, Ahmed Warsame: 'Who are we to say when they should or should not go back?' The point, he said, was to help them if they desired it. But doing that in a humane and orderly way was complicated and officials in Geneva fretted about how to square Kenya's demands with their responsibilities under the UN Charter. They had to come up with a 'returns package' and a plan for the repatriation. It was a tall order.

One cynical diplomat put it like this: 'If you give someone $200 to go home are you helping him or making him a target? He has no papers, no ID, no transport, he has to travel through al-Shabaab territory even to reach Kismayo. The UN is becoming an official smuggler!' Moreover, if the UN could be seen to be supporting returns to Somalia, it would help European governments with their domestic legal battles to deport Somalis too. Precisely what the scrupulous officials in Geneva feared.

'If we wanted the refugees gone at eight a.m. tomorrow morning they would be gone!' Albert said, implying that the formalities of UN procedure were simply a matter of politesse. But things were not so simple. Reclining in the shade and running his hand reflexively over his convex middle, he acknowledged that politicians, the military and the police were all in business together in Dadaab and in Somalia, that the weak Kenyan government did not have control of its different institutions, and that there were powerful forces in favour of the status quo: keeping the camps exactly as they were. 'It makes my life difficult,' he said. 'There are warlords, whose campaigns for office are even paid for by the refugees.'

His sodden shirt stuck to the plastic chair as he leaned forward shouting orders into his mobile phone. Kosgey, a driver in a light-blue uniform, came with the news that some of the so-called warlords were waiting to see him, to complain about the decision of the National Security Agencies Committee (NSAC) the previous day not to allow any more shelters to be built or renovated in Dadaab. It was meant as an encouragement to the refugees to return but the contractors were worried about their contracts. 'They can go to hell,' said Albert, 'they've been eating for so many years!' Kosgey laughed. 'Tell them, even if it rains, we don't want to hear about it!' said Albert. Kosgey in his uniform bowed and left.

This was the trap in which Dadaab was stuck: no improvements, no investments, but no movement either. The UN had set up 'return desks' in their field offices in all the five camps, but in the past four months only 2,422 people had expressed an interest in going back. But, although history may have turned the Honourable Minister's speech into an embarrassment, it had succeeded in one respect. It had changed the tone. With the tripartite agreement, Kenya had managed to confirm Dadaab's official temporariness by assuming a direction of travel: towards a peaceful Somalia, towards full-scale repatriation. Henceforth it would be impossible to acknowledge Dadaab's de facto permanence. Kenya had set the clock ticking.

Even before the ink was dry on the agreement, donors had begun revising their programmes and NGOs rushed to draw up projects supporting returns. Budgets were cut, then cut again. Red lines on protected services were redrawn, revised downwards. The World Food Programme had switched the rations to cheaper sorghum. Resettlement quotas shrank. Core UN positions were abolished and the health budget raided; the lines at the UN field offices and the hospitals got longer.

Kenya had succeeded in constructing an official narrative about the camp, one that had an ending. And even though it was a fantasy, that narrative arc cast a cruel shadow. Daily life simply got harder.

*

There was a palpable shift in the mood outside the camp too, as blame for the violence erupting onto the streets of Kenya's cities was placed squarely at the refugees' door. As Albert sweated in the shade that day, two terror suspects were shot dead by police in Mombasa. They were said to be behind the attack the previous Sunday, 23 March, on the 'Joy in Jesus' church in Likoni, Mombasa, in which six worshippers had been gunned down and twenty wounded, including several children. Although the two dead suspects were neither Somalis nor refugees, the government was happy to blame the Somali refugees. Angered perhaps by the delay in repatriation, or maybe moved by some darker motive, flailing officials reached for what they could control, in the only terms that they understood: force.

The Monday after the church shooting, 24 March, ignoring the High Court decision that had ruled it illegal the previous year, the Minister Ole Lenku reissued the government's relocation order for urban refugees. It was as if since Westgate a circuit had been established and the Kenyan security apparatus hard wired. Like a switch, when a bomb went off or a shooting happened, a radical cleric was invariably sacrificed and refugees hunted.

The following week, three bombs ripped through Eastleigh killing six and injuring twenty-five. The next day, 1 April, another controversial preacher, Abubakar Sherrif, was shot dead by government assassins, his bullet-riddled face all over the newspapers. His nickname had been *makaburi*, 'graveyard', in Swahili; he had foreseen the manner of his own death and told anyone that would listen, including Al-Jazeera, that he was a dead man walking. Indeed, the government had made a habit of eliminating troublesome clerics. Predictably, riots followed his killing and the government announced another crackdown against illegal aliens in the cities, this time called 'Operation Usalama Watch'. 'Usalama' means security in Swahili.

*

Fish had gone back to Nairobi at the beginning of the year to enrol for the new semester. Although Nairobi carried risks, at least it offered a glimmer of progress, a future, while the view from Dadaab led nowhere. With Usalama Watch, though, the risk:reward ratio of staying in the city was rapidly diminishing.

A police truck appeared on the corner of 11th street in Eastleigh, next to the Nomad Hotel, where, daily, officers stopped those passing and demanded papers and money. Fish was forced to turn again to tapping his friends in the diaspora for caution money but the costs were becoming unsustainable. And not having money was unthinkable: those who couldn't afford the petty bribes were taken to Kasarani football stadium in the city. Four thousand were rounded up and detained there in the first weeks of April. At least two people died: a pregnant woman who was beaten up, and a six-month-old who starved to death after being left in an apartment when her mother was suddenly taken, just one of the three hundred children separated from their parents in the operation. In the stadium that activists had christened 'Kasarani Concentration Camp', the detainees were supposed to be 'screened', whatever that meant. In theory perhaps an interrogation about one's Kenyan ancestry, in practice most likely simply a question of cash. Journalists and human rights workers were forbidden from entering. A smuggled photo showed hundreds of men incarcerated in enormous cages in the stadium like battery chickens.

Public support for the pogrom against Somalis was high; the atmosphere in the capital was vicious. In the tall *Nation* media building in downtown Nairobi, the managing editor admitted his shock: 'I've never seen a public mood like it,' he said.

One day when Fish had only 2,000 shillings for the police instead of the usual 3,000, they shouted at him '*Panda Gari!*' – get in the van! But after some special pleading they took his money and let him go. Soon after, one day in May, the apartment block was raided again at three a.m. He listened as officers rattled through the building thumping on doors with truncheons. 'You have to believe that God will protect you,' he said. 'It's so frightening.' He fled to Dadaab again.

Back in Hagadera he hung out with Tawane and dozens of other friends who had disappeared for years into the urban sprawl and now suddenly reappeared at home to escape the punitive taxation and the beating in Eastleigh. 'If someone doesn't pick [up] the phone twice, you know they are in Kasarani,' said Tawane. The '92 group started a self-help fund to bail out people they knew.

Any supposed terrorist with 3,000 shillings could buy his freedom. The fact that it was all about a show of force – and extorting money – seemed apparent from the shambolic nature of the screening process that was unable to identify even Kenyan citizens, some of whom were mistakenly deported to Mogadishu and Dadaab. In the end, only several hundred, mostly Congolese who had never been to Dadaab, were deported to the camp. And those, after being installed in a tent on a scorching square of sand, didn't stay long. Within two months they had all melted away, back to the city once more.

If the actual implementation of the round-ups was a sorry, and brutal, failure, the diplomatic consequence was a stunning success. When they were sworn in a year before, President Uhuru Kenyatta and Vice President William Ruto had been awaiting trial at the International Criminal Court. Western governments had warned of 'consequences' for Kenya if it elected the two leaders suspected of inciting the previous violence in 2007 and claimed to be preparing for a diplomatic relationship limited to 'essential contacts'. A year on, the front page of the weekend *Nation* carried a photo of a smiling Kenyatta relaxing in State House receiving the envoys of the United States, the United Kingdom, Canada and Australia in a joint visit to pledge moral and material support for Kenya's war on terrorism. It was a fantastic turnaround.

The final irony was that Usalama Watch, although responsible for a temporary exodus from Eastleigh, had little effect on the size of Dadaab. AMISOM's dry season surge complicated the plans for returns as southern Somalia was instead gripped by fierce fighting. Trade routes were disrupted, aid remained warehoused in Mogadishu and food prices spiked again. Across the south people struggled towards the roads to raise weak hands to passing convoys that roared by, spitting gravel into a cloudless sky. One hundred thousand were freshly displaced within Somalia in 2014, some of whom made their way across the militarized border to Dadaab. To the Kenyan government's chagrin, instead of shrinking, Dadaab was growing once again.

40

A Better Place

On Monday 8 December 2014, with great fanfare and after several false starts, a light-blue bus with the words 'Sabrin Bus Service' painted on the side above yellow, green and red waves, departed Dadaab camp for Kismayo in Somalia with ninety-one people on board. They were no longer refugees. They were, over a year since the signing of the agreement, the first convoy of 'spontaneous, voluntary returns': they were going home.

The 450-kilometre journey through the barren border country would be completed in two phases with Kenyan and Somali police providing security escorts. Although the Kenyan army was in control of Kismayo, al-Shabaab moved as it liked in the surrounding countryside and inside Kenya too. The previous week, in two shocking attacks, al-Shabaab had massacred twenty-eight bus passengers and then thirty-six miners, all Kenyan Christians, near the border town of Mandera. The refugees' return was not due to the fact that war was over; on the contrary, war was everywhere. 'Peace' had been redefined. Heavily armed peacekeepers still feared to venture outside their bases, while civilians were expected to carry on with daily life. And, bravely, they did.

The return package that had taken nearly a year to approve was as follows: when they left Kenya they would be given a jerrycan, a mosquito net, a sleeping mat, one blanket, one solar lantern and phone charger, and sanitary kits for the women. Upon arrival in Kismayo they would receive plastic sheeting, nails and fifty metres of rope, a kitchen set, three months of food rations and $150 per person up to a maximum of $600. All of which, the UN hoped, would be enough to get the returnees established in their new life.

It was a hard time to be starting over. On the same day as the convoy made its way towards the border, in a press conference in Mogadishu the UN Humanitarian Coordinator appealed for $863 million to meet urgent needs in Somalia in 2015: 'Over 3 million Somalis are in urgent need of humanitarian assistance,' he warned. 'Of these, an estimated 1 million are unable to meet their minimum food requirements – a 20 per cent increase compared to the same time last year.'

And this time the camps offered no relief. There was hunger on both sides of the border. Dadaab was stricken with another, more severe, cut in rations. It was becoming an annual event. WFP was facing a global funding crisis and in November 2014, while they launched a glossy campaign to raise money for their Syrian operation, the organization slashed rations in Kenya again, this time by an unprecedented 50 per cent. They hoped to resume full feeding in the new year, but for the mothers in Ifo 2 that laid their children at the gate of the WFP food warehouses in protest, the prospect of several more weeks without food was impossible. 'What do you want us to do?' they asked.

'We are preparing for deaths,' a UN health worker confessed. Not among the healthy adults – an adult could get by on two months of starvation rations – but newborns, sick children and the elderly. It was the vulnerable that would pay the price for the world's indifference. There was a crime here on an industrial scale: confining people to a camp, forbidding them to work, and then starving them; people who had come to Dadaab fleeing famine in the first place.

The weak and hungry mothers of Ifo 2 saw the ration cut as a deliberate attempt to starve them into returning. Whatever the

WFP asserted, it began to have that effect. In Isha's block, M2, populated by many of the poorer refugees, she claimed that 'Not 20 out of 180 families in the block want to stay.' When the rains stopped and the roads north cleared, they'd be gone. 'A person who has eaten sorghum porridge for breakfast only, it cannot sustain him the whole day, and after nine days he has not even that? Such people cannot stay here. There is no point even waiting for the UN,' she said.

It was the poorer newcomers who would become the poster children for the UN's return programme. Those who had failed to establish themselves in Dadaab, for whom leaving the camp was a gamble worth taking. Food was the only thing keeping them here and when that ended, so did the reason for staying. As the biometric proved, many had already left. People like Hawo, Isha's neighbour and fellow would-be solar engineer, who had given up waiting for the Indians. But, where Kenya wanted to see a flood of returnees, there was only a trickle, and at less than a thousand a month it would not outstrip the birth rate.

Ranged against the Kenyan desire to see Dadaab levelled was not just the law, but all the forces of human ingenuity and determination that had raised a city in this most hostile desert. Dadaab worked. It served a need, for the miracle of schools and hospitals and a safety net of food, and for respite from the exhaustion of the war. It had become a fact. Through the accumulated energy of the generations that had lived there it had acquired the weight and drama of place. It was a landmark around which hundreds of thousands oriented their lives. In the imagination of Somalis, even if not on the official cartography, Dadaab was now on the map.

The food manifest was only one measure of population, there was no official census. The nearest approximation of a head count was a polio vaccination campaign concluded the previous year. The result was an explosive, closely guarded secret. Marking each person's thumb with indelible ink so as not to treat them twice, the health workers had immunized over 600,000 people, aid workers, the host community, as well as refugees. It raised the possibility that Dadaab was in fact bigger than anyone knew, attracting migrants from across the region with its industry of aid, commerce and services; an urban mecca on the arid red plain, the biggest city for 500 miles around. The city made of thorns now had a life of its own, beyond the refugees: it would not be so easily destroyed.

Despite Isha's struggles, she was not planning on going anywhere for the time being. The dream of India had died a slow death. It was well over a year since she had filled in the forms for the UN passport in the UN compound with Sam, and she had heard nothing. Having placed her faith in Bunker and the Barefoot College, resigned her position at the school and abandoned her business, she had been forced to take credit from the neighbours to supplement their diet until her husband, Gab, found work washing dishes in the school where she had once been a governor. 'I had never dreamed of working in such a dirty place,' he said, but if he stopped the family would go hungry. He looked old, his hair had gone white in the camp, but he took his descent in status with forbearance. Isha vowed to sue the Indians and the UN for compensation whenever they showed their face again: 'I will fight them!' she said. In fact, after Westgate, the government had fired the head of immigration and fifteen other officials for selling passports and visas to Somalis and suspended the issuing of all passports, refugee travel documents included. But no one had told Isha and Hawo, or even Bunker himself.

She and Gab still dreamed of their old life in Rebay, and they planned to return there eventually. For now, though, Isha's commitment to her children's education was such that she was ready for her family to endure the hunger of the ration cut in exchange for school. This was the prize for which Isha had marched her children across the baking desert three years before. They knew it, and they would not let their mother down. With their newly minted English, the boys had written all over the tin door to their hut the proud declaration: 'PEOPLE WHO LIVE THIS HOUSE HAVE EDUCATION.' In case, even for a moment, they ever doubted that the journey had been worth it.

'It has made me to think a lot. It is worrying me. How to feed my family,' said Nisho of the drop in food. In the last days of Ramadan, Billai had successfully given birth. They called the boy Abdishafee. He was a plump, light-skinned child with Billai's delicate features. But the price of his health was Nisho's hunger: he made sure Billai had enough to eat, but for himself, he could not remember the last time he had been full. He was thinner, malnourished. The tables had turned. Billai was settled now, she had stopped her nagging and looked after the baby. It was Nisho's turn to worry: 'Fatherhood has changed me,' he said. 'It has made me more frightened.'

When he went to work in the market, he worried about Abdishafee falling off the bed, or crawling into the fire. And he worried about his own strength; he could not work as hard. There had been a huge fire in Bosnia; among the victims was his wheelbarrow. The impact on the market in general and on his business in particular was big. 'If I get 100 shillings in the market, I must decide, shall I give it to Billai and the baby or shall I eat lunch?'

The middle class with incentive jobs, or the wealthy with their businesses, were insulated against the ration cut. For the lower classes, it was simply another Kenyan tryanny that they were forced to endure. But Kenya was a familiar tyrant. After twenty-five years, Somalia was a foreign country.

'If I go back, what will happen to me there – I don't know

anyone, I don't know the market, how will I survive? If you leave your home, where you grew up, you will become a nomad!' said Nisho. And he did not use the word in a good way. 'If they say "go" I will think about it then, if I must.' As long as there was Ifo camp, in the little mud house in block B, there would be Nisho.

He thought instead about trying to find work on the trucks again, driving to Mogadishu. It was the only real alternative to lifting sacks. When he and Mahat talked about it, Mahat, in his lackadaisical way, wanted to come too. 'Maybe I'll get a job in Mogadishu,' he wondered, vaguely.

'Yes, sure,' said Nisho, preoccupied. Mahat was young, he was aimless, the world that was available to him held little promise and he was content to go with the flow. Nisho though, had responsibilities. And so the next morning, after a thin breakfast of sorghum porridge, he rubbed his red eyes and itched the skin around his mouth that had begun to crack and go white from a lack of vitamins and dragged his heavy limbs to the market to begin once more the long day's hustle for a precious dollar, or, if he was lucky, maybe two.

Not everyone's luck was poor. Tawane had navigated the tangled politics of return with skill. One day in November, he went with several other members of his NGO United Youth for Peace and Development (UNYPAD) for a meeting in a mock-castle amid tall hardwood trees on James Gichuru road in Nairobi. Built as some colonial folly by a white man with a sense of humour, the castle now housed the Department for Refugee Affairs, and the new commissioner, Mr Komon. Tawane had an appointment to discuss modalities for cooperation between the Kenyan government and UNYPAD. He stood ready to assist with the returns, eager to take the Kenyan government's money, and help out other members of the '92 group where he could.

Fish was one of UNYPAD's first employees. He was back in Nairobi now, building relationships with aid agencies at their head-quarters, while he tried to complete his studies. He had also found a job on the quiet. It required him to sneak around though, and he still hoped for bigger things. UNYPAD carried a weighty cargo of dreams. It was the last chance for a generation who felt they had been left behind: 'No resettlement, no integration in Kenya, no life in the camp, no nothing . . . it's disturbing you know,' said Fish. 'If UNYPAD fails, I think the earth doesn't want to hold us any more.'

Fish had to skip the meeting with Mr Komon to go to work, but Tawane and the others waited in the reception area, dressed up for the occasion. Immaculately groomed as ever, Tawane was proud and he was hopeful. He looked tired – running up and down fundraising was exhausting and expensive – but determined. He was a fighter, a striver, he would make the best of whatever straits he encountered and he would pull up those around him, inject them with confidence and set them to work. His tragic flaw, if he had one, was the breadth of his own horizons: 'What if I had had the chance? What could I have achieved?' he said wistfully. 'If I was free of the camp, outside, in the world . . . I could have accomplished so much more.'

But UNYPAD had already had some success. The small print of the funding applications for USAID, the UN and Oxfam had been a trial, but after writing up policies on corporate accounta-bility, health and safety, gender balance and so on, they had won their first contract as an implementing partner. It was a project just over the border in Dhobley, promoting reconciliation between two warring clans there and equipping the primary schools with footballs and stationery. When Tawane arrived with the money and the supplies, the little border town received him like a prodi-gal son. The mayor, the teachers, the children lined up singing songs. He was shocked at the peace and relative prosperity he saw. 'One could live here freely,' he thought.

It was his first trip back to Somalia since he had fled on his father's back, aged seven, in 1992. The bus had taken him out onto the plain and, at the border, after he presented his documents and was assured of his right to come back again, he walked across the shadow of the roadblock on the sand, kneeled down and kissed the white dust of his homeland.

'Long time!' he murmured to himself. 'Long time.'

The female members of the '92 group were less sentimental about their homeland. For them, a future in Somalia was a nastier prospect. 'If al-Shabaab see me walking around without a man, me, an educated woman,' Kheyro said, 'they can slaughter me.' She preferred the Dadaab that she knew. 'I grew up here, it is home, I trust it,' she said.

Her incentive work had kept the family insulated from the ration cut, even though she had recently had to resign from teaching because she had been doing another job at the same time: working as a rape counsellor at the Danish Refugee Council. The UN had made an announcement threatening anyone working two incentive jobs with blacklisting and Kheyro had been afraid. The school was sorry to see her go, she was the only teacher who had finished high school, but they understood. The counselling paid 9,000 shillings ($110) a month. And she preferred it. Talking for an hour at a time to clients instead of the consuming work of teaching, although 'I see a lot of distress,' Kheyro said of her new job. 'The men of Dadaab are very traumatized. They want to be violent towards women.'

But Kheyro needed the money more than ever. Her mother was sick and her younger sister had dropped out of school to get married. For several months now, Rukia had been complaining of pains in her back and in her chest and she spent most days at home lying down in block A2. The years of wood gathering had exacted a toll.

With her savings, Kheyro had acquired a second-hand laptop. She wistfully browsed the webpages of universities abroad but her plans for higher education were on hold. 'I would love to study,' she said. 'The dilemma is, who will look after my mum?'

In the neighbouring block, A6, White Eyes' new wife, Fatuma, was enjoying her confinement after giving birth, well supplied with food by her doting husband, unaffected by the ration cut. White Eyes had escaped the ill omens of the season – *Nasib* smiled for him once again. His nose for gossip and his loquacity had landed him a coveted job as one of two refugee reporters for the local radio station, Dadaab FM, at about the same time that Fatuma got pregnant. He had, he said, 'done a lot of work', so that 'she become fully charged', and had taken her urine to the clinic at the earliest sign.

The radio station gave White Eyes a room in a converted container parked among the scrub next to a tall steel antenna on the outskirts of Dadaab town. On the wall was the station's motto: 'seek truth and report it, minimize harm, act independently'. The station managers were Somali Kenyans and they flouted the rules governing incentive workers and paid everyone the same. White Eyes had a computer which he used 'to enter Google to do my research', although without glasses, he suffered from what he called 'screen friction'.

He roamed the camp collecting stories: about malnutrition from the ration cut, and its other effects, a couple who claimed they were too weak to have sex and wanted to sue WFP for their impending divorce. And he had a talk show every afternoon called *Xogwaran*, which meant, literally, many stories. He had found the perfect job. 'Now, in the camps, people respect me, they greet me.' Professor White Eyes had been transformed into DJ White Eyes; he had become famous overnight: 'All my dreams are coming true at the same time,' he said.

In mid-November, the day after his wife Fatuma had given birth to a healthy baby boy, White Eyes got a call from the US Immigration and Naturalization Service. His case had been called: they told him to prepare to go for a resettlement interview. Dadaab is deemed too dangerous for officials to visit, so the US government built a centre at Kenya's other refugee camp Kakuma, the one near the Sudanese border, far from al-Shabaab.

White Eyes was euphoric. 'Back in Action in Africa!' he exclaimed to a bemused Fatuma lying on a plastic mat in the shade of her mud house, tenderly stroking their mewling day-old child. Beside her was a cup of orange juice – her husband was insistent about the benefits of fruit. She worried about missing him, but in reality, even once called to prepare for Kakuma, it can take years for the US to send a bus to come and collect you, and in the meantime you must wait in Dadaab. There are over 15,000 refugees in the pipeline for resettlement to the US. At the current rate, it will take over fifteen years before all of them make their way there.

For now, though, that thought didn't spoil White Eyes' excitement or his sense of vindication. He had chosen well, at last. 'This wife is a lucky person,' he said. Not like the other one. She had borne him the son that he had longed for, and for whom he now had, by God's grace, the means to provide. He bent to pick up the little bundle wrapped in several cloths and held him gingerly in one hand. 'Although I have seen a lot of life, this is new for me,' he said. 'His name is Moulid' – it meant 'the prophet's birthday' – 'and he is the one who will save us.'

*

A few weeks later, another baby arrived in Dadaab. It should not have been born there at all. Muna and Monday's case for urgent resettlement to Australia should have been completed years ago but by December 2014 they were still waiting. They had waited so long in fact, that they had got back together and were expecting another Christian-Muslim child.

The reconciliation had come during the hot season. Muna had left the sinful corner of *Grufor* and moved back to Monday's compound in the Sudanese block. Monday believed she had come back to him because of his sweet words and the promise of money. She, on the other hand, claimed it was because of rising harassment in block E1. Other kids had kicked Christine and knocked her unconscious for over an hour. Their reunion was a question of safety. Monday beamed at her return but Muna looked downcast: the fighting and grief of the last three years had wasted her.

At first, Monday was upbeat about the delay in the Australian bureaucracy: 'They say now it is the time of Syria, and then they will come back to us.' But since they had been promised an imminent departure, an election had returned a new Australian government with a very hard line on immigration that was going slow on all resettlement cases. This they didn't know.

When Monday learned of Muna's pregnancy, he became more impatient. The scandal spread fast. Fearing the shock would kill their mother, Muna's brothers had evacuated her to Somalia before she found out. Muna's sister in Nairobi went too, out of shame. Again, the blocks were on fire with gossip and Monday moved his family back to Transit for their safety. That June, Christine had her third birthday in a plastic UNHCR tent.

As the months wore on, their enquiries to the UN about their case became more and more frantic and less and less polite. By early December, the impending birth brought matters to a head. Last time, the mob had threatened to infiltrate the hospital and

Muna's extremist relatives still worked there. Monday was insistent his wife give birth away from the camp, in Nairobi or in Dadaab town. But Monday was so angry with UNHCR he could not speak to them without exploding so Muna went to the office instead. In a stroke of luck, the head of protection at UNHCR, the fierce but fair Leonard Zulu, came to hear about the case and demanded to know the cause of the delay. Finally, seventeen months since the medical had cleared them to go, a UNHCR official sent an email to the Australian embassy asking what had happened. The Australians had forgotten about the case: there had been a change of government, a rotation of personnel, they were full of apologies. For want of an email, Muna and Monday's life had slipped through the cracks.

Sweetee had gone to America earlier in the year in a much faster process. But she worked as a cleaner in the UN compound. When she started coming late to work or broke down crying on the job, a kind supervisor asked her what the matter was. Instantly, the staff who had refused to believe her stories of harassment and attempted rape by the police and G4S security guards, were ordered to spring into action and she was whisked away from the camp. Muna was not so well connected.

By the time Leonard Zulu intervened it was too late to move the heavily pregnant Muna to Nairobi and on Sunday 7 December she bore another girl in the health centre in Dadaab. After a week, the family were promised, once the new addition was registered with the UN field office, they could be relocated to Nairobi and then onwards, at last, to Australia: to a new life far away, alien, but safe.

'I don't trust them, these people ... they're just trying to confuse me!' said Monday. Paranoia had overtaken him. He smoked even in the mornings now, in the tent, in front of the kids. He went to work with yellow eyes, stumbling like a madman. He was convinced the UN was trying to sell his only, hard-won, slot of freedom. It was Muna instead who cooled him down, serene with motherly hormones. 'We have no option,' she told him, gently. 'We just have to be patient.' She felt calm, believing that her wait was nearly at an end.

'You'll miss Dadaab when you go there,' her friend said. 'They all do.'

'Really?' Muna smiled. 'I don't think so.'

Guled's mind, too, was racing away from him, over the globe. Looking out from the little shop made of wooden spars on the corner of the main street in Hawa Jube where they had moved the khat business after Auntie had returned to Mogadishu, he watched the rain coming down. A puddle slowly threatened at the door. The 50 per cent ration cut and the rains had arrived at the same time. Beside him, on sacks on the floor, sat Maryam wrapped in folds of black polyester. Behind, the children stood playing with the damp cloth that covered the little bundles of green khat wrapped with strips of banana leaf. Maryam had proved an adept saleswoman and, for a while, life in the camp had looked up; they had even managed to send for their daughter Sadr from Mogadishu. But even Maryam could not magic a profit from khat in the rainy season; the market was flooded. The roads too – so that often the ordered stock arrived too late, and spoiled. An 8,000 shilling ($90) debt had crushed them.

For several weeks now they had eaten only sorghum. Tasteless porridge for breakfast and the same for dinner. They rarely had the money for the oil and sugar to make it palatable. Maryam was angry, hungry and pregnant. She was close to quitting the camp again.

Her mother had heard about the ration cut on the BBC and phoned Maryam: 'What are you doing there? There's no food! Do you want to deliver there? We know your husband is broke, do you want to die of malnutrition?' Now she sat in the shop, quiet except to talk of going back to Mogadishu. Guled had abandoned trying to reason with her.

He was thin. His stomach ached. Every day he gave his share of the food to Maryam and the kids. Malnourishment showed in his face which was even more gaunt than usual, and in his eyes, which bulged, looming white. The anxiety made him thinner still. And on his head, right in the middle of his twenty-three-year-old crown was a single snow-white hair. He was soon to be a father of three. In a matter of years, he had passed from childhood to middle age and it seemed as if his body had suffered through all the years in between. Two phrases played in a frantic loop in his mind, 'If I had money . . .' and '*Tahrib*'.

Tahrib is the Somali word for 'migration' but it has come to mean more than that. It is the term for the long journey and illegal entry into Europe, usually overland, via the Mediterranean sea. At a loss for how to generate money in Dadaab, with neither capital nor connections, his brain kept returning, like a moth flying in ellipses around a flame, to *tahrib*.

Mogadishu was not an option. 'Never,' he said to himself. 'The security situation is bad, government officials are being killed every day, what about a normal person like me?' And even if Maryam returned, he could not stay in Ifo camp. He would need to provide. 'I will go to a better place and work,' he decided. Even though, rationally, the odds of surviving and finding work were probably better in Mogadishu, the traumatic past, the perilous future, and the present humiliation of being unable to provide for his family were too much.

But even *tahrib* needed money. It was mostly the well-off youth who made the trip. 'I can do it step by step,' Guled thought. He knew drivers who drove trucks from the port at Mombasa bringing the food for the World Food Programme to Dadaab. They had promised him a lift to Mombasa. From there, he could find a ride to Nairobi and then on up to Sudan. After that? He knew the journey was hard, but it was better than this.

As he stared ahead, out the door, at the rain, and at his children playing quietly on the floor of the shop, the tears came then in a rush. For the first time since he had come to the camp, since he could remember, he cried. He covered his face with his Manchester United T-shirt and pushed the red cloth into his sockets and walked away, his body shuddering with great heaving sobs through which he struggled to breathe.

He talked to his friends, he went through his options, he asked around for work. And as the days ticked by, he got thinner. The pressure from Maryam increased. Every day she started and didn't stop. It was three months to go before she gave birth to their third child. Guled wanted her to deliver in the camp – the hospital was better than those in Mogadishu – but she was determined to return. It was a tragedy. They had come through so much. Only to be torn apart at the last. 'Any day now, I can go,' Maryam warned. 'Anytime! As soon as the rains slow and the road clears ...'

Tahrib. The word repeated in his head like the throb of blood in his temple. It was a risky and expensive thing to do but it at least had the virtue of action; it was something, a decision, an honourable effort, even if he died trying: a kind of kamikaze mission, a noble suicide. 'The life we are in today, it is better for me to die in the Sahara or in the sea,' he said. On the day the UN return convoy departed for Kismayo, Maryam gave him a look. It meant the roads were drying. Soon, it meant. Soon she would go back to Somalia. And when she did, Guled resolved, he would begin another journey: the first step on that harsh lonely trek, the treacherous road to Africa's northern shore.

Epilogue

May 2015

I was on my final research trip to the camps. On successive days I invited Nisho and Mahat, Kheyro and Guled for a meal in the best restaurant in Dadaab town, a pink concrete structure with a pretty garden in a courtyard called the Hanshi Palace. I wanted to read to them what I had written, to show them what I had done with the stories they had shared with me. For various reasons, the others I met elsewhere. Meeting in Dadaab was difficult for the refugees: they had to take a taxi or a bus. But it gave us more time. The kidnap risk for foreigners remained elevated throughout my time researching in the camp and the UN security office kept reducing the recommended period of time for staying in one place: from two hours to one and, by the end, to thirty minutes. Plus it allowed me to avoid the annoyance of travelling with police escorts. No one appreciated me turning up at their house with a police pick-up truck loaded with the four heavily armed men that the UN security office required.

Nisho and Mahat came first. At the gate to the restaurant, the security guard wouldn't let them in and the owner demanded to know what business had these two dusty refugee boys in his establishment. I was called to the entrance to vouch for them. After some hurt pride and a few barbed comments from Nisho, the owner apologized and soon the boys were watching the television on the wall and sipping juice.

It was a struggle to turn their attention from the TV to the sound of my reading voice but once we got going they were hooked. They hooted at my descriptions of them and punctuated each sentence with 'Sa!' to indicate that what I had written was accurate. They had, strangely, no anxiety about whether something was flattering or no: their only concern was with the truth.

At the buffet, they piled their plates high with as much chicken, rice and vegetables as they could carry and polished off the lot. Catching sight of the bill, Nisho was horrified. He was shocked that someone could pay 500 shillings ($6) for a meal. 'It can bring conflict!' he said. 'In Ifo a plate is 80 shillings [$1], everyone the same.' Poverty is a powerful social leveller.

When it was Kheyro's turn, she arrived in a gold dress with a full niqab veil covering her face. 'People talk!' she said, in explanation. As we spoke, she looked around suspiciously at the other men in the restaurant; they were all watching us. She wouldn't eat. 'I only eat at home,' she said; a demure woman eats in private. Kheyro read her own story on the computer screen in concentrated silence as I watched with rising apprehension.

'Okay,' she said finally. 'It is all right.'

Often, talking to me was uncomfortable for people, their mind forced to go to places they would rather avoid. Eating in the restaurant, I hoped, would be a kind of treat, a more relaxed setting outside the camp, without the clamour of families and neighbours and the dangers of gossip. But the experience of a modicum of plenty caused only contradiction and confusion and showed how much, even after four years, I still had to learn.

Guled, too, refused to eat. 'My family has not eaten today, how can I eat without them?' He sat and listened distractedly to me reading to him aloud. But without food, malnourished as he was, he struggled to stay awake and called a halt before the end. 'I need to get back,' he said. The last I saw of him, he was walking down the dusty road of Dadaab, the watchtowers of the UN compound looming behind barbed wire, a plastic bag with two roast chicken legs clutched in one hand.

Until the end of my research I had been reluctant to intervene in the lives of the refugees. Now, finally, I asked what I could do to help. For the ones who were settled, like Nisho and Isha, there was little an outsider had to offer apart from money. This too was Kheyro's need, so her mother could be looked after while she went in search of education, although her options are more limited after the gruesome al-Shabaab massacre of the students at Garissa University College at the beginning of April. White Eyes had his good job now and his resettlement hope, Tawane and Fish had their organization. But for Monday and Muna, and for Guled, a more urgent, bureaucratic solution was needed.

Monday and Muna's case I followed up with UNHCR and that was how it came to the attention of the head of Protection, Leonard Zulu. He made enquiries and demanded to know how many other so-called 'emergency' resettlement cases were pending and Monday and Muna's file was rapidly reactivated. And six months later, in June 2015, the family finally boarded a flight to Melbourne, Australia.

When I sat with Guled and debated over and over the relative merits of *tahrib* and the other options available to him, it emerged that when he had originally arrived in the camp, he had told no one in the UN of his past with al-Shabaab. If he had, he would likely have been prioritized for child protection and possible resettlement abroad, but he hadn't known at the time. Despite his mistrust of the UN and his cynicism that anything would come of it, he humoured me and returned to the UN to explain to them his whole story.

He is no longer a child, but he is at risk in the camp if his story becomes known and, as such, he should be a priority for the UN to try and find him a resettlement slot in another country. However, six months after I left him in floods of tears vowing to walk to the Mediterranean, he is still in Ifo, waiting to hear about the chance of being transferred to Europe or the United States. If this UN effort failed, he warned me repeatedly, he would still be going north. I said I understood.

Postscript

In March 2016, the European Union and Turkey struck a deal: Turkey would build camps to house refugees refused entry to Europe and the European Union would pay for them – 3 billion euros in the first instance with another 3 billion euros to follow. Kenya was watching closely.

In May, the Kenyan government announced once more that Dadaab would close and the refugees be returned to Somalia. Funding for the camps was at an all time low of 44 per cent of needs. But this was not about the needs of the refugees, it was a demand for ransom. In a vulgar attempt to buy itself out of its international obligations, the European Union had started a bidding war. The refugees had become bargaining chips.

To prove its seriousness, the Department of Refugee Affairs stopped registering new arrivals – many of whom were among those who had taken the voluntary return package over the last two years, forced back to Dadaab because of a resurgent al-Shabaab in Somalia. It also cancelled all movement passes: critical patients referred to hospitals in Nairobi died.

In Istanbul, the Deputy President William Ruto said Dadaabians should be resettled elsewhere – to Europe and North America, that Kenya had done more than its fair share. This was true of course. But the European Union could not agree to share out the refugees already arrived in Europe, let alone welcome more. This is what the word crisis means: no solutions.

'Where will we go?' The refugees asked themselves and visiting journalists, suddenly interested again in Dadaab. Who would move them? Did the government even have enough buses and bulldozers? Would Kenya send in the army? Turn off the bore-holes? Stop the food distribution and starve people back to war-torn Somalia? Would the international community stump up enough money to encourage Kenya to do the right thing and let them stay?

Monday and Muna had made it, at last, to Australia. But all the others were still there in the camp. The 30 per cent ration cut had become permanent. With his share of the advance from this book, Guled had purchased a motorbike to use as a taxi and shelved his plans for *tahrib* to Europe, for now.

The fear was not that Kenya would actually close the camp. Everyone believed such an idea to be impossible. It was the fact that with each fresh demonisation of the place and tightening of restrictions, funding would fall, movement would become more and more circumscribed, and earning a living would get tougher. 'You always think things can't get any worse,' said Fish, ruefully. 'And then they do.'

As world leaders argued over numbers – of people and dollars – life in the camp ground daily on. Nisho, Fish, Tawane, Kheyro and Guled kept going to work and collecting their rations, supporting their families and trying to stay out of trouble. They argued and discussed and considered their options back in Somalia and, always, despite themselves and the evidence, hoped for a chink of light, for something to change. But mostly they did what they had done their whole lives: they tried not to think too hard about the past, the present or the future and they set their minds to wait.

Ben Rawlence, May 2016

Notes

I first went to Dadaab in 2010 as a researcher for Human Rights Watch. In 2011, I returned for the first of what would become a series of seven extended visits to the camp to document the lives recounted here. In total I spent around five months in the camp for the project and interviewed hundreds of residents. In addition, the intensive interviews of thousands of people I conducted for Human Rights Watch between 2006 and 2012 in Kenya, Somalia, South Sudan, Uganda and Ethiopia educated me in the intricate politics of the Horn of Africa and the tough situations facing those forced to flee their homes across the region.

The material for this book was collected in several ways. In some cases, I witnessed the events described first hand. In others, I have reconstructed what happened through interviews with the subjects themselves and attempted to cross-check the accounts with witnesses or with reports in the public domain. Interviews were conducted in Swahili and English where possible, or in Somali with the aid of translators where necessary. Two of the characters' names have been changed where security concerns made it impossible to use real ones; all the other names are real. I also drew on photographs, videos, personal interviews with, and reports from, the media, NGOs, the UN and national governments. A selection of other sources is listed in the 'Further Reading' section. Where there are sources referred to in the text I have added a note below.

PART ONE

1. The Horn of Africa

There has not been a census in Somalia since 1975. Estimates since put the population at anywhere from 7 to 9 million. A new population estimation survey for Somalia is under way by the UN Population Fund: see www.unfpa.org/somalia

2. Guled

Al-Shabaab's Swahili language newsletter *Gaidi Mtaani* is available online. The quotes from it appear in issue 2. All issues are available at: http://jihadology.net/category/gaidi-mtaani/

The recruitment of children by al-Shabaab is described in detail in Human Rights Watch, *No Place for Children: Child Recruitment, Forced Marriage and Attacks on Schools in Somalia* (2012). 'A whole generation,' a teacher lamented, 'join the armed groups because of hunger,' is a quote from that report (p. 23). So is the story of the boy whose head was left on the step as a warning (p. 25), and the account of the bodies of the fathers who refused to sign the agreement allowing al-Shabaab to recruit in Shabelle primary school (p. 26).

Casualty figures for the Battle of Mogadishu are from an organization in the city called 'Lifeline Africa Ambulance Service', and reported in the UN news wire: 'SOMALIA: Accusations Traded over Casualties at Mogadishu Market,' Integrated Regional Information Network (IRIN), 2 December 2010.

The number of 870,000 displaced in the city since the Ethiopian invasion of 2006 is according to 'Statement of 52 NGOs on the rapidly deteriorating humanitarian crisis in Somalia', 6 October. See also BBC Online, 'Somali "Ghost City" Wracked by War', 6 October 2008.

The data for primary school enrolment is taken from UNICEF quoted in *No Place for Children*. The figure of 2,000 children kidnapped during 2010 comes from UN General Assembly, 'Report of the Secretary-General on Children and Armed Conflict', 23 April 2011.

3. Maryam

That 45 per cent of girls are married before 18 is according to UNICEF. See www.data.unicef.org

Guled was one of 2,000 sneaking across the closed border in November 2010. The exploding numbers, and all other UNHCR figures cited in later chapters, are recorded in UNHCR arrivals and population statistics: see www.data.unhcr.org/

4. Ifo

The story of the founding of Dadaab in 1954 by the British was told to me by one of the elders of the town and matches the account of the British Army Engineers' drilling operations in Northern Kenya recorded in a 1977 USAID report, 'The Geohydrology of Northeastern Kenya'.

The idea that al-Shabaab was dormant in the camp prior to 2011 is derived from conversations with refugees living there at the time and with security analysts in the region. Divining the motives of a secretive militant group is difficult but despite several years of threats against Kenya, before 2011 al-Shabaab had not attacked the country and their public pronouncements suggested that they finally attacked only in retaliation against Kenyan support for Ethiopian forces and other militias inside Somalia.

5. Nisho

The economy of Dadaab is hard to measure but a 2010 study suggested that the camps contributed at least $14 million to the regional economy and turned over at least $25 million annually. See 'In Search of Protection and Livelihoods', Danish, Kenyan and Norwegian governments, September 2010.

6. Isha

Statistics on rainfall and crop prices come from the Famine Early Warning Systems Network. There is an archive of assessments and warnings at www.fews.net. The 80 per cent jump in the prices of staples in southern Somalia was reported in the Food Security and Nutrition Analysis Unit, Somalia 'Special Brief: Post Deyr 2010/11 Analysis', 15 February 2011.

The allegations of collusion between WFP staff and food traders with links to al-Shabaab diverting over 50 per cent of food aid in 2009/10 caused a major scandal and prompted an internal probe as well as a US suspension of funding. See Channel 4 News, 'UN Probe after Aid Stolen from Somalia Refugees', 15 June 2009 and the UN response: 'Report of the External Auditor on WFP Operations in Somalia', 14 February 2011.

7. Hawa Jube

The situation in N Zero and Bulo Bacte and the numbers living there was reported by Médecins Sans Frontières in several updates in early 2011. See www.somalia.msf.org and Médecins Sans Frontières, 'Dadaab, Back to Square One', February 2012.

The information about WFP's operations: the shipping of 8,000 tonnes of food to the camp of which one fifth is locally sourced comes from an interview with Hans Vikoler, then head of WFP in Dadaab, August 2013.

8. A Friday in Nairobi

It was the 15 March alert from FEWS which said: 'substantial assistance programs should be implemented'.

The quotes from aid workers, 'The map of Somalia turns red every year', and 'all we can do is hope for the best', as well as the response from the donor official that the warning 'was not useful to unlock resources', are taken from Rob Bailey, 'Famine Early Warning and Early Action: The Cost of Delay', Chatham House, July 2012. The later quotes: 'It's because of the US Patriot Act and the OFAC sanctions that criminalize us for paying fees to al-Shabaab', 'It's because of Haiti – the world can't cope with more than one disaster at a time'; and 'It's because the industry is geared around disasters, a famine averted doesn't generate profile' are my attempt to paraphrase conversations I had with aid officials in Nairobi at the time.

Aid workers in Nairobi told me that some agencies were fundraising in the UK while aware that they could not spend the money with confidence inside Somalia.

9. Maiden Voyage

The land on which the camps sit has never been officially gazetted by the government. It is still, technically, what in Kenya is called 'trust land' held by the government on behalf of the community, and customary land tenure in Kenya is a source of bitter political struggle. What is described here is the picture that has emerged after three years of conversations with business owners and residents. I was told that the local ethnic Somali chiefs have been known to issue 'title deeds' handwritten, for a fee; that these then change hands to signify ownership and that Kenyan government tax collectors extract tolls from shop owners on this basis.

The descriptions of Mogadishu are from a visit I made a year after Nisho in October 2012. The 2011 market rates for weapons and the sources of resold weapons is reported in Hamza Mohamed, 'Illicit Gun Trade Barrels Ahead in Mogadishu', Al-Jazeera, 12 February 2013.

10. The Silent March

The estimates of the numbers of children dying per month were arrived at after the famine was over and are contained in the UN's Food Security and Nutrition Analysis Unit technical report: 'Study Suggests 258,000 Somalis died due to severe food insecurity and famine: Half of deaths were children under 5', FSNAU, 2 May 2013. In total 10 per cent of the population of children under five in southern Somalia died during the famine.

11. Muna and Monday

Several different refugee incentive staff who worked at the registration centre during the famine told me of alleged bribes being paid to G4S guards for access and the system of recycling old refugees for a fee.

13. Billai

The figure of 70,000 outside the bounds of the camps is based on MSF's estimates for Dagahaley camp in July of 25,000 in 'Humanitarian Crisis in the Outskirts of the Overcrowded Dadaab Camp', and extrapolated from the numbers being relocated from the outskirts to the new camp of Ifo 2: 63,000 in the first instance, according to the UNHCR data archive and news reports.

The information about the real reasons behind the delay in the opening of Ifo 2 camp emerged from discussions with UN officials, journalists and Kenyan officials and politicians at the time.

The account of the Interlocking Stabilized Soil Blocks (ISSBs) and the Kenyans calling a halt to the building programme came from an interview with the former head of shelter at UNHCR Dadaab, Ahmed Elgoni, in November 2013.

The results of the August 2011 UN malnutrition survey are summarized in FEWS, 'Rapid Assessment, Garissa district /Dadaab refugee camps', 12 October 2011.

PART TWO

15. The Jubaland Initiative

The revelation from WikiLeaks that the US and UK had urged Kenya not to invade Somalia was reported by Alan Boswell, 'WikiLeaks: US warned Kenya against invading Somalia', McClatchydc.com, 18 November 2011. The cables include the admission that this was the third time Kenya had asked the US for support.

Human Rights Watch first reported the recruitment of young men by Kenya to fight in Somalia in 2009, see HRW 'Kenya: Stop Recruitment of Somalis in Refugee Camps', 22 October 2009.

18. Kheyro

The figures on enrolment of trained and untrained teachers in 2011 come from, 'Kenya-Somalia: Hungry for Learning in Dadaab Camps', IRIN, 22 March 2011.

The exam results for the 2011 KCSE and an analysis of them, including the allegations of bribery, are available at: http://blog.theonlinekenyan.com/kcse-2011-results-analysis

19. Police! Police!

The tweets from Major ChirChir warning residents of ten towns across Somalia to expect airstrikes, and that 'large movements of donkeys would be considered al-Shabaab activity', have been deleted. They were, however, reported in the media. See Mariya Karimjee, 'Kenya's military tweets: don't sell donkeys to militants', GlobalPost.com, 3 November 2011.

The number of 100 people arrested following the 5 December explosion was reported on the Kenyan radio station Capital FM, by Bernard Momanyi, '100 suspects arrested after Dadaab attack', 6 December 2011.

The story of the rape of Fartuun and the estimates of people injured and money looted is taken from the report by Human Rights Watch,

Criminal Reprisals: Kenya Police and Military Abuses Against Ethnic Somalis, 4 May 2012.

On the airstrike on Hosingow see 'Kenya Jets Kill 10 in South Somalia Air Raid', Agence-France Press, 21 December 2011. See also Human Rights Watch, 'Kenya: Investigate Bombing of Somali Village', 21 December 2011.

20. Nomads in the City

The new reliance on refugees was presented as an innovation in a UNHCR news story, 'UNHCR employs alternative strategies in managing Dadaab camps', UNHCR, 27 January 2012. That report gives a sense of the sheer scale of work being tackled by Tawane and his volunteers:

> The new measures include stronger and deeper involvement of the refugee communities in the day-to-day running of the camps, by reaching out to different groups within the refugee population, such as elders, the business community, and youth ... Refugees have always had a role in making camps work. However at Dadaab that role is being expanded ... health posts are managed by refugee staff who have been trained over the years to provide basic medical services and refer more serious cases to the camp hospitals. Refugee staff are also getting refresher courses on management of sensitive cases of sexual or gender based violence ... In addition, refugee leaders and refugees working for partner agencies are being trained to identify individuals and families who require immediate protection or life-saving assistance ... In the area of water and sanitation, refugees are building new latrines on sandy and rocky ground and are collecting and transporting solid waste by donkey carts to allocated waste disposal sites ... More than 30 camp schools remain open and are run by refugee teachers. Despite insecurity, the Kenyan National Exams took place in the camps at the end of last year ... The exams were made possible because the community patrolled the schools and guarded the gates.

The figures of 30 per cent of Nairobi's tax revenue and 100,000 shoppers a day come from Hamza Mohamed, 'Somali Businesses Feel the Heat in Nairobi', Al-Jazeera, 18 May 2014. The $100m estimated drug money laundered through Kenya each year comes from Peter Gastrow,

Termites at Work: A Report on Transnational Organized Crime and State Erosion in Kenya (International Peace Institute, 2011).

21. We Are not Here to Impose Solutions from Afar

The private admission that Ethiopia and Kenya were pursuing their own agenda in Somalia, and the associated quote, was made to me in a meeting with officials from the UK Foreign Office in London, December 2011.

The two wars referred to are the 1963 so-called 'Shifta War' when Somalia declared war against Kenya and the 1977 'Ogaden War' in which Somalia fought Ethiopia for control of the land ceded by the British.

The Report of the UN Monitoring Group on Somalia and Eritrea, July 2013, alleged that 80 per cent of withdrawals from the Somali central bank were for private purposes. It is available at: http://www.un.org/sc/committees/751/mongroup.shtml

On the UK admission of the diversion of its aid to al-Shabaab, see Andrew Gilligan, 'Britain's foreign aid has fallen into the hands of al-Qaeda, DfID admits', *Telegraph*, 10 August 2013.

The US officials speaking about the drone strike the day after the London conference were quoted in 'US Drone Strike Kills 4 in Somalia', Associated Press, 24 February 2012. The later revelations about the British identity of the 'international' militant were reported by the Bureau of Investigative Journalism, 'Parents of British Man Killed by US Drone Blame UK Government', thebureauinvestigates.com, 15 March 2013.

22. Y = al-Shabaab

The feelings of men being emasculated in the camp and unable to perform their traditional roles were the subject of a round table I attended, organized by the Rift Valley Institute in Nairobi. See the report of the meeting: 'A War on Men?', RVI, Nairobi, 26 July 2013.

23. Buufis

The quote 'Real men are those who go to the USA', is from a book by Cindy Horst, *Transnational Nomads: How Somalis cope with refugee life in the Dadaab camps of Kenya* (Berghahn Books, 2005).

The resettlement corruption scandal of 2001 was the subject of an investigation by the UN Office of Internal Oversight Services. See OIOS,

Investigation Into Allegations Of Refugee Smuggling At The Nairobi Branch Office Of The Office Of The United Nations High Commissioner For Refugees, UN Doc A/56/733, 21 December 2001.

25. In Bed with the Enemy

A former diplomat serving in a European embassy in Nairobi confirmed to me that a French warship was also involved in the September 2012 shelling of Kismayo.

The picture of the 'pax commercial' was reported by the UN Monitoring Group on Somalia in its July 2011 report. The UN Monitoring Group report of 24 October 2014 said, 'Al-Shabaab continues to benefit from revenue generated, on a scale greater than when it controlled Kismayo, at charcoal production sites, from checkpoints along trucking routes and from exports, in particular at Kismayo and Barawe, all of which to date have been uninterrupted by the military offensive against the group' (p. 44). The percentages of the cut taken by each armed group are from the same report. The estimate of 60–70 per cent of illegal sugar coming from Kismayo came from an interview with a European intelligence agency official interviewed in Nairobi in November 2014.

The name 'Selma' is a pseudonym.

The dire, 'untenable' situation in the camps at the end of 2012 was highlighted in the unprecedented appeal from the NGO coalition, entitled, 'The Human Costs of the Funding Shortfalls for the Dadaab Refugee Camps', and released in November 2012. It was signed by CARE, Catholic Relief Services, Danish Refugee Council, International Rescue Committee, Lutheran World Federation, Norwegian Refugee Council, Oxfam and Terre des Hommes.

The $100m shortfall was reported by UNHCR in early 2013. See Refugees International, 'Kenya: Government Directive Leads to Severe Abuses and Forced Returns', 26 February 2013.

PART THREE

26. Crackdown!

The Department for Refugee Affairs' relocation order of 13 December 2012 is hosted on the Human Rights Watch website: see 'Kenya: Don't

Force 55,000 Refugees Into Camps', 21 January 2013. The estimate of 100,000 illegal aliens in the country is not based on any evidence but is a figure regularly offered by Kenyan officials from the DRA in interviews, including several with me in Nairobi and Dadaab in 2011, 2012, and 2013.

The crackdown is covered in detail in Human Rights Watch, *You Are All Terrorists: Kenya Police Abuse of Refugees in Nairobi* (2013). The quotes: 'This is Kenya, we can rape you if we want to,' and 'You are all al-Shabaab and you are all terrorists,' are taken from the report.

27. The Stain of Sugar

The farce of the press conference announcing the election results is from a description by Michela Wrong, 'To be prudent is to be partial', *New York Times*, 14 March 2013.

John Githongo, 'Moving On: Welcome to Kenya Inc,' Africanarguments.org, 22 May 2013, includes his claim that the election was 'stolen well'.

The findings of the unpublished newspaper report about sugar racketeering were shared with me by a source within the publishing house who does not wish to be named.

29. Too Much Football

What Guled called the 'Tabliq' are a Muslim missionary group whose proper name is Tabligh Jama'at. The Tabligh are a transnational, non-violent evangelical group with origins in India in the nineteenth century. In recent years they have won many converts in eastern Africa.

30. The Night Watchmen

UNHCR reported the killings as follows: 'On May 23 three refugees working as watchmen in the market were killed and one injured in a bandit attack ... the motive behind the killing is unknown.' UNHCR Dadaab Update 7/13, 16 May–15 June 2013.

The allegations of Ethiopian intelligence assassinating ONLF leaders inside Kenya were made by Kenyan local government officials. See Boniface Bosire, 'Authorities Concerned Spillover Conflict in Ethiopia', Tesfa News, 1 August 2014.

31. Sugar Daddy

The allegations about Sharif's involvement in sugar smuggling and the sums involved were mentioned to me by several different police officers and confirmed by refugee journalists working in the camp, by businessmen working in Dadaab town as well as the admissions of UN officials mentioned in the text.

On Michael Adebolajo's detention in Kenya see 'London terror suspect had been detained in Kenya', *Daily Nation*, 25 May 2013. The UK Parliament's Intelligence and Security Committee found that MI6 did not investigate Adebolajo's claims of torture: 'This is surprising: if Adebolajo's allegations of mistreatment did refer to his interview by [Arctic] then HMG could be said to have had some involvement – whether or not UK personnel were present in the room.' Arctic is a code name for the Kenya Police Anti-Terrorism Police Unit which is funded in large part by the UK and US governments. The possible complicity of MI6 in the torture was, at the time of writing, the subject of another inquiry. See Lucy Fisher, 'MI6 faces inquiry into "torture" of Woolwich killer Michael Adebolajo', *The Times*, 28 November 2014.

32. Italy, or Die Trying

The routes from the Horn of Africa via Yemen, Sudan and Egypt and Libya are monitored by an organization called the Regional Mixed Migration Secretariat. The data on refugee flows in this chapter comes from there. The accounts of the migrants drinking benzene, dying in the desert and paying ransoms on the way to Libya and the amounts of money paid for passage on the boats is from an RMMS report, 'Going West: Contemporary mixed migration trends from the Horn of Africa to Libya and Europe', RMMS, June 2014.

Stemming the flow of migrants was part of the deal struck with President Gaddafi for the rapprochement with the EU: see Human Rights Watch, *Stemming the Flow: Abuses Against Migrants, Asylum Seekers and Refugees* (2006).

The quote 'You are paying $1,000 to purchase death . . .' comes from the UNHCR film about the Mediterranean sea crossings, *Rescue at Sea* available at: http://tracks.unhcr.org/2014/07/rescue-at-sea/

Italy launched an investigation into the video of migrants forced to strip in Lampedusa: see 'Italy probes treatment of Lampedusa migrants "forced to strip"', BBC, 18 December, 2013.

The information about Italy's attitude to the migrants and the descriptions of overflowing hostels in Sicily was from a research trip I made in 2008.

33. Waiting for the Moon

The statistics about the biometric food distribution system are taken from a WFP update, 'Biometrics', dated 1 February 2014, provided to me by staff in Dadaab. The figures for those removed from the food manifest in Hagadera come from the UNHCR Dadaab Update 9/13, 1–31 July 2013.

36. Knowledge Never Expires

The heartbreaking letter to the media written by Fish and other members of the '92 group describing the injustices of the incentive worker system is one of the few testimonies available in English where the refugees speak in their own voice and in telling detail about the iniquity and humiliation of life in the camp. It was published in 2010 on a private blog and is available at: https://dodona777.wordpress.com/2010/03/09/a-voice-from-the-voiceless-dadaab-refugee-camps-kenya/

They write:

> We talk, but our voices are never heard. We move, but only inside a cage. We have many skills and talents, but we are denied our chance to maximize our potential ... The incentive system is often claimed to be necessary because of limited budgetary resources and because refugee staff members are not allowed to officially work under Kenyan law. However, in actuality, these supposed justifications serve only as mere excuses for the agencies to hide behind so that they can continue to exploit refugee labor ...

The standard bribe of 5,000 shillings for a movement pass is common knowledge in the camp and was repeated to me by numerous interlocutors. When I raised the matter with Department for Refugee Affairs officials they denied knowing the amount, but smiled.

37. Welcome to Westgate

The description of the Westgate attack draws on the wealth of material in the public domain as well as conversations with diplomats and journalists who were there or who had access to privileged information about what was happening. Along with the documentary film by Dan Reed called *Terror at the Mall* screened on HBO and BBC on the one-year anniversary of the attacks, among the many accounts I read, the ones cited are: James Verini, 'Letter From Kenya: Surviving Westgate', *NewYorker.com*, 27 September 2013, for the comment from the Kenyan-Somali woman about 'they should all be sent back . . .'; and Guy Alexander: 'Kenyan Mall Shooting: they threw grenades like maize to chickens', *Observer*, 22 September 2013 for the quote 'we went slowly'.

The information about specific warnings prior to the attack was provided by two intelligence officials working in different European embassies in Nairobi.

The catalogue of blunders during the attack emerged later, most comprehensively reported by Daniel Howden, 'Terror in Westgate mall: the full story of the attacks that devastated Kenya', *Guardian*, 4 October 2013. Howden mentions the looting and empty beer bottles, images of which are online.

According to the *Sunday Nation* newspaper, the President's Commission of Inquiry was shelved, 'after he was advised it could expose sensitive details and lead to the passing of a no-confidence vote in security chiefs in the middle of an anti-terror war'. See Andrew Teyie, 'Commission of Inquiry that never was,' *Sunday Nation*, 20 September 2014.

Human rights groups have long accused the state of a string of extrajudicial executions, especially of terror suspects in Mombasa. See 'We Are Tired of Taking You to the Court', Muslims for Human Rights and Open Society Justice Initiative, 2013.

The less publicized airstrikes inside Somalia that followed Westgate I heard about from refugees in Dadaab and from former Kenyan military personnel working in Dadaab.

39. A Lap Dance with the UN

The numbers of those stripped from the food manifest as a result of the new biometric procedures are from the WFP 'Biometrics' Briefing paper on file with me. The $2.9m figure came from an interview with Hans Vikoler, then head of WFP in Dadaab, in November 2013.

The information about budgets and posts being cut and NGOs initiating programmes to facilitate returns is from a range of interviews with UN officials and NGO staff in Dadaab in March and November

2014. See also the MSF appeal, 'Dadaab: Agreement on refugee repatriation should not affect aid delivery', 28 November 2013 which reported an MSF survey that four out of five refugees did not want to return given current conditions and also that 'Policies by donors to reduce funds are having concrete effects on the refugees in Dadaab.'

Al-Jazeera made a documentary about the killing of Abubakr Sherrif in which serving Kenyan policemen confess to a wide-ranging programme of extrajudicial executions: 'Inside Kenya's Death Squads', Al-Jazeera, September 2014.

UNHCR spoke out about the large numbers of children separated from their parents in the Usalama Watch crackdown. In its own report on the operation UNHCR said over 600 refugees were shipped to Dadaab, many without their children: UNHCR Dadaab Update 09/14, 16–31 May 2014.

The impression of the media at that time and the comments of Joe Odindo, then managing editor of the Nation media group, come from an interview with him and a visit to the Nation offices in Nairobi in April 2014 and a round table for journalists organized by Journalists for Justice, Stanley Hotel, Nairobi, 14 April 2014.

The fate of the Congolese refugees deported to Dadaab, housed in Kambi Os camp, who then absconded I learned from UNHCR staff in November 2014.

I wrote about the political benefits of the crackdown for the President and his deputy in 'Kenya's Anti-Terror Strategy Begins to Emerge', africanarguments.org, 9 April 2014. That piece attributes the 'consequences' comment to Johnnie Carson, the US Assistant Secretary of State at the time and the 'essential contacts' quote to the UK High Commissioner Christian Turner.

On the dry season surge of AMISOM and fighting in the areas targeted for returns, see the 'OCHA Flash Update 4: Humanitarian Impact of Military Operation', April 2014 which said 40–44,000 people had been displaced by the offensive. In September 2014 UNHCR Somalia reported that 100,000 had been displaced so far that year in the country as a whole: 'Over 100,000 people displaced in Somalia so far this year as IDPs bear brunt of food insecurity crisis', UNHCR Briefing Notes, September 2014.

40. A Better Place

The substance of the returns package offered to the refugees that volunteer to go home is listed in a UNHCR document entitled, 'Repatriation

Assistance for Spontaneous Returns to Somalia' provided to me by UNHCR staff in Dadaab in November 2014.

Details about the WFP ration cut were informed by a conversation with the WFP press office in Nairobi in December 2014.

The anomaly of the number of people immunized in the polio campaign of 2013 was widely discussed among agency staff in Dadaab at the time although not reported in the media.

Further Reading

Amnesty International, 'No Place Like Home: Returns and Relocations of Somalia's Displaced', (2014)

David Anderson and Jacob McKnight, 'Kenya at War: Al-Shabaab and its enemies in East Africa', *African Affairs*, Volume 114, Number 1, January 2015

Tarak Barkawi, 'On the Pedagogy of Small Wars', *International Affairs*, Volume 80, Issue 1, January 2004

Cedric Barnes and Harun Maruf, 'The Rise and Fall of Mogadishu's Islamic Courts', Chatham House, Briefing Paper, April 2007

Laurence Binet, *Somalia 1991–1993: Civil War, Famine Alert and UN 'Military-humanitarian' Intervention* (MSF Speaks Out Series, 2013)

Anneli Botha, 'Radicalisation in Kenya' and 'Radicalisation and al-Shabaab Recruitment in Somalia', Institute for Security Studies (South Africa), September 2014

Mark Bowden, *Black Hawk Down* (New York: Atlantic Monthly Press, 1999)

Walter Clarke and Jeffrey Herbst (eds.), *Learning from Somalia: The Lessons of Armed Humanitarian Intervention* (Perseus, 1997)

Mohammed Diriye, *Culture and Customs of Somalia* (Westport, CT: Greenwood, 2001)

Dave Eggers, *What is the What? The Autobiography of Valentino Achak Deng* (London: Penguin, 2006)

Nuruddin Farah, *Maps* (London: Pan, 1986)

Nurrudin Farah, *Gifts* (London: Penguin, 1993)

Nurrudin Farah, *Secrets* (London: Penguin, 1996)

Nurrudin Farah, *Crossbones* (London: Granta, 2012)

Jonathan Fisher and David Anderson, 'Authoritarianism and the Securitization of Development in Africa', *International Affairs*, Volume 91, Issue 1, January 2015

Debi Goodwin, *Citizens of Nowhere* (Toronto: Doubleday, 2010)

Gerald Hanley, *Warriors and Strangers* (London: Hamish Hamilton, 1971)

Mary Harper, *Getting Somalia Wrong* (London: Zed/African Arguments, 2012)

Barbara Harrell-Bond, *Imposing Aid: Emergency Assistance to Refugees* (Oxford: OUP, 1986)

Cindy Horst, *Transnational Nomads: How Somalis cope with refugee life in the Dadaab camps of Kenya* (Berghahn Books, 2005)

Human Rights Watch, *Screening Ethnic Somalis: The Cruel Consequences of Kenya's Passbook System* (1990)

Human Rights Watch, *Shell Shocked: Civilians Under Siege in Mogadishu* (2007)

Human Rights Watch, *Ballots to Bullets: Organized Political Violence and Kenya's Crisis of Governance* (2008)

Human Rights Watch *Collective Punishment: War Crimes and Crimes Against Humanity in the Ogaden area of Ethiopia's Somali Region* (2008)

Human Rights Watch, *So Much to Fear: War Crimes and the Devastation of Somalia* (2008)

Human Rights Watch, *From Horror to Hopelessness: Kenya's Forgotten Somali Refugee Crisis* (2009)

Human Rights Watch, *Welcome to Kenya: Police Abuse of Somali Refugees* (2010)

Human Rights Watch, *You Don't Know Who to Blame: War Crimes in Somalia* (2011)

Human Rights Watch, *Criminal Reprisals: Kenya Police and Military Abuses Against Ethnic Somalis* (2012)

Human Rights Watch, *No Place for Children: Child Recruitment, Forced Marriage and Attacks on Schools in Somalia* (2012)

Human Rights Watch, *High Stakes: Political Violence and the 2013 Elections in Kenya* (2013)

Human Rights Watch, *Hostages of the Gatekeepers: Abuses Against Internally Displaced People in Mogadishu* (2013)

Human Rights Watch, *You Are All Terrorists: Kenya Police Abuse of Refugees in Nairobi* (2013)

Human Rights Watch, *I Wanted to Lie Down and Die: Trafficking and Torture of Eritreans in Sudan and Egypt* (2014)

Human Rights Watch, *The Power These Men Have Over Us: Sexual Exploitation and Abuse by African Union Forces in Somalia* (2014)

Human Rights Watch, *Yemen's Torture Camps: Abuse of Migrants by Human Traffickers in a Climate of Impunity* (2014)

International Crisis Group, 'Somalia's Divided islamists', Africa Briefing No.74, Nairobi, 18 May 2010

International Crisis Group, 'The Kenyan Military Intervention in Somalia', Africa Report No.184, 15 February 2012

Stig Jarle Hansen, *Al-Shabaab in Somalia: The History and Ideology of a Militant Islamic Group, 2005–2012* (New York: Oxford University Press, 2013)

Lidwien Kapteijns, *Clan Cleansing in Somalia: the Ruinous Legacy of 1991* (Philadelphia: University of Pennsylvania Press, 2012)

Parselelo Kantai, 'The Rise of a Somali Capital', *The Chimurenga Chronic*, March 2013

I. M. Lewis, *A Modern History of the Somali* (Woodbridge: James Currey, 4th edn, 2002)

Emma Lochery, 'Rendering Difference Visible: The Kenyan State and its Somali Citizens', *African Affairs*, Issue 111/415, September 2012

Michael Maren, *The Road to Hell: The Ravaging Effects of Foreign Aid and International Charity* (New York: Free Press, 1997)

Nene Mburu, *Bandits on the Border: The Last Frontier in the Search for Somali Unity* (Trenton, NJ: Red Sea Press, 2005)

Nadifa Mohamed, *The Orchard of Lost Souls* (London: Simon and Schuster, 2014)

Solar Mamas (2012), a film by Jehane Noujaim

Reports of the UN Monitoring Group on Somalia and Eritrea, UN Security Council Committee Pursuant to Resolution 751: http://www.un.org/sc/committees/751/

Alex de Waal, *Famine Crimes: Politics and the Disaster Relief Industry in Africa* (Woodbridge: James Currey, 1997)

Michela Wrong, *Our Turn to Eat: The Story of a Kenyan Whistleblower* (London: Fourth Estate, 2010)

Acknowledgements

The greatest debt is to the individuals who bravely shared their time, their homes and their stories with me in the hope that doing so might help bring a solution to Dadaab's protracted crisis a small step closer. Secondly, the project would have remained a fantasy without the generous support of a fellowship from the Open Society Foundations and the assistance of the Open Society Initiative for East Africa, in particular Rachel Reid, Bipasha Ray, Christine Seisun, Adam Radwan, Steve Hubbell, Binaifer Nowrojee, Mugambi Kiai and Mary Gathegu. Thirdly, the Dadaab sub-office of the United High Commissioner of Refugees was for a time a home from home; to everyone there: thank you. Ahmed Warsame was an enthusiastic and generous supporter of the project and Osman Tulicha, Leonard Zulu, Mans Nyberg, Silja Osterman, Mackentric Shigali and many others made the work of research much easier (and more fun) than it might have been.

I worked with several translators at different points, all of whom brought a unique contribution to the work: Ahmed Noor, Abdir Izak, Abdi Noor, Mohammed Omar and, above all, the tireless and imaginative Aden Hassan Tarah. Daud Yusuf and Khader Abdi provided much needed context and advice. I have given the Kenya Police a lot of bad press over the years but the officers in Dadaab were welcoming, helpful and lots of fun: thanks for looking after me.

My Human Rights Watch colleagues: especially Leslie Lefkow, Chris Albin-Lackey, Neela Ghoshal, Laetitia Bader, Felix Horne, Otsieno Namwaya, Gerry Simpson, Bill Frelick and Jamie Vernaelde, alongside whom I learned about the region, shaped the understandings that in turn have shaped this book. Emilio Manfredi,

Tristan McConnell and Tiggy Ridley gave me food, shelter and conversation in Nairobi. Simon Rawlence was at the end of the phone and Patrick Hogan built the inspirational writing shed.

Credit for the original idea goes to my literary agent extraordinaire, Sophie Lambert at Conville and Walsh: a steadfast guide, reader, editor and friend. The script also benefited from early readings by Zanna Jeffries and Emily Hogan Turner and from the expert advice of Leslie Lefkow and K'naan. I have been blessed by the editorial triumvirate of Amanda Betts, Stephen Morrison and especially Laura Barber, whose sensitive and rigorous engagement shaped the final drafts to a considerable extent.

While I was researching and writing, my wife Louise endured long periods of pregnancy and early motherhood alone. This book is for her and for the residents of Dadaab whose confinement knows no end.